LEAVES NOT DIVIDED INTO LEAFLETS—I.E. SIMPLE

LEAF SHAPES

LINEAR
e.g., ASTER

HEART
e.g., ASPEN

LEAVES ENTIRE

OVAL
e.g., MANZANITA

OVAL-SERRATED
e.g., ALDER

LOBED & SERRATED
e.g., MT. MAPLE

DEEP CLEFT
e.g., WOODLAND STAR

LEAVES DIVIDED INTO LEAFLETS—I.E. COMPOUND

e.g., MT. ASH

e.g., PTERYXIA

PALMATELY COMPOUND
e.g., LUPINE

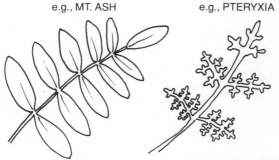

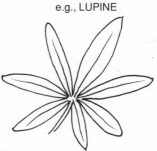

LEAF ATTACHMENTS

BASAL ROSETTE
e.g., PUSSY PAW

ALTERNATE
e.g., ASTER

CLASPING
e.g., STREPTANTHUS

OPPOSITE
e.g., ARNICA

WHORLED
e.g., LILY

Wildflower Walking
in Lakes Basin
of the Northern Sierra

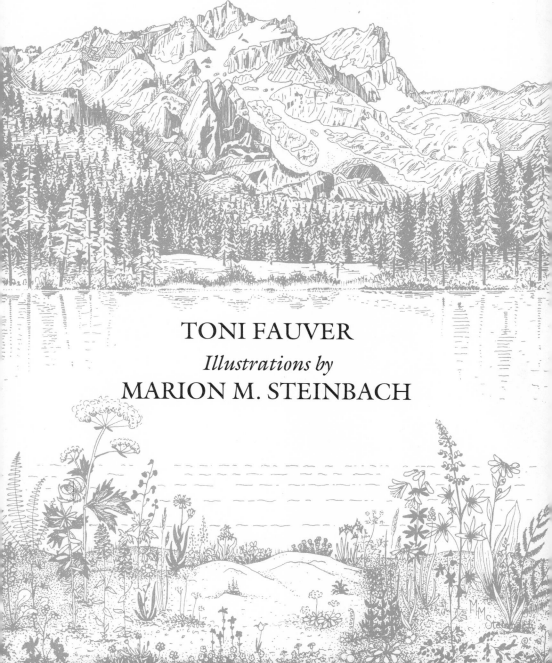

TONI FAUVER

Illustrations by
MARION M. STEINBACH

Published by Comstock Bonanza Press
18919 William Quirk Drive, Grass Valley, CA 95945-8611
530-273-6220
T. Fauver, P.O. Box 2322, Orinda, CA 94563

Designed and produced by Dave Comstock
Printed and bound by Thomson-Shore, Inc. on acid-free recycled paper
Library of Congress Catalog Card Number 92-70906

ISBN 0-933994-19-2

Third Printing

*To the memory of my friend, Marion Steinbach, the
talented artist who drew all the illustrations.
We had many beautiful wildflower hours together
backpacking in the high Sierra and strolling in the Swiss
Alps. I have happy memories of collecting plants in
Lakes Basin together.
As Marion's strength gave out, I brought her plants to
draw, and she got much pleasure out of unwrapping each
flower and discussing where it grew, where she had seen it
and what special characteristics of it should be illustrated.
I miss Marion's friendship and her organizational
abilities, and I wish with all my heart that she could be
here to share in the praise for her drawings
in the finished product.*

ACKNOWLEDGMENTS

SPECIAL THANKS to Susan D'Alcamo for the many plants she contributed when we started this project together; thanks to Patricia Paddock for helping compile the historical data. We appreciate the help with willow identification from Alice Tulloch Echols. A thank-you to Lawrence Heckard, James Hickman, and Elizabeth Neese of Jepson Herbarium for generous help with difficult genera. Gladys Smith, botanist, author, and my mentor and botany teacher, has given help and encouragement throughout the project. The Plumas National Forest Service, especially Linnea Hanson, the forest botanist, and Bob Rowand, at Mohawk Ranger Station, have been very helpful. The enthusiasm of the lodge owners, particularly Sugie Barker, has enhanced the book with their wonderful stories. Thanks also to my students and "flower friends," especially Cindy Shaw and Sandra Beyaert, who have given constructive criticism and kept me company on my hikes of the Lakes Basin trails. Karen Wetherell, a computer consultant and flower friend, has been invaluable and so has my sister-in-law, Catherine Fauver, a professional copy editor.

Very special thanks to David Comstock, our book designer, whose fast work made it possible for Marion to see what her art would look like when it was printed.

Finally, Marion and I could not have produced this book without the encouragement of our understanding and supportive husbands, Henry Steinbach and Richard Fauver.

TONI FAUVER

CONTENTS

PREFACE

THIS BOOK IS A RESULT of my love for the mountains and my need to find a reason for spending time there. I have been lecturing to garden clubs and teaching wildflower identification classes in northern California for fifteen years, and more recently expanded my horizon to the Swiss Alps. It has taken six summers to do the research for this book.

Marion Steinbach, the illustrator, painted and drew all her life and was very knowledgeable about Indian art and crafts. Some miniature Indian baskets she made are part of a display in the Gatekeeper's Cabin Museum at Tahoe City. We met through garden club activities and hiked and backpacked together for thirteen years. I profoundly regret that she did not live to see our work in its final printed form.

The pressed plants collected from Lakes Basin have been donated to the University of Nevada, Reno, Herbarium.

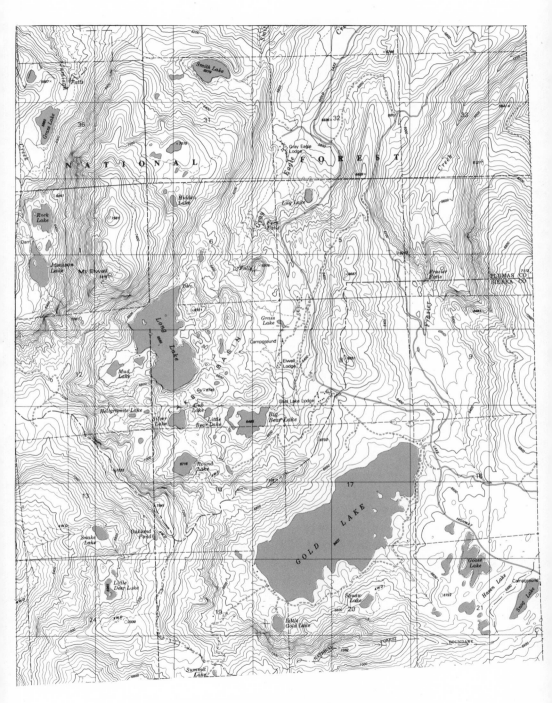

Northern Section of Gold Lake Road

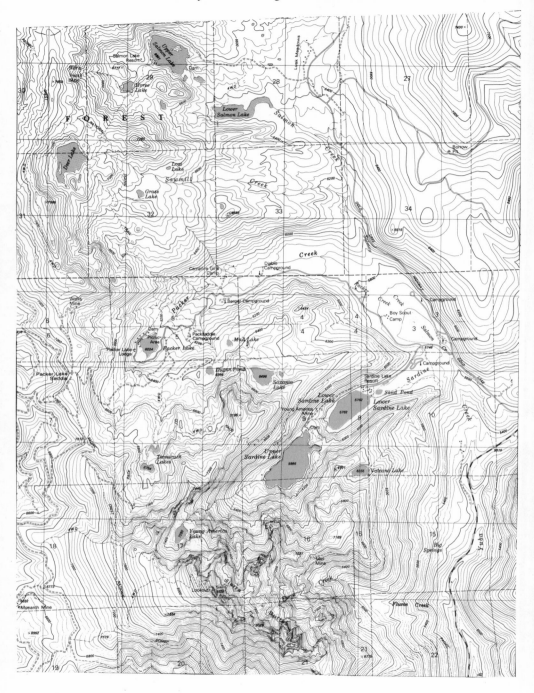

Southern Section of Gold Lake Road

INTRODUCTION

IT IS OUR HOPE that this book will kindle in you new interests in the outdoors. Its primary purpose is to help you identify wildflowers and increase your knowledge of plants. As you search for new flowers, you will become aware of beauty and of flowers that you had never noticed before. Roads and paths that had been boring will become interesting.

Lakes Basin's many glaciated lakes, craggy Sierra Buttes, numerous trails, and abundance of wildflowers make it a delightful place to study nature. A pleasurable method of learning the plants is to photograph them or to use watercolors or colored pencils to fill in the colors of the illustrations in the book. Or you can make the book a personal journal of your hikes in the mountains by noting beside each illustration where you located the plant, who you were hiking with, what the weather was like, and any other bit of information that will help you recall the plant.

Wildflowers bloom in Lakes Basin from late May to mid-August, although the peak time is mid-June to mid-July. The great diversity of the plants in this part of the northern Sierra is due partly to the migration of plants from northern California and Oregon mixed with the Sierran flora from the south, partly to the variations in elevation from 5,800 feet at Gray Eagle Lodge to 8,500 feet at the Sierra Buttes lookout—and, finally, to the volcanic terrain that was re-formed by the action of glaciers. The experienced flower follower will enjoy adding more flowers to his or her plant list, while the beginner will learn new flowers easily because the same flowers recur on many Lakes Basin trails. The book also includes brief mentions of Indian rock art, pre-World War II lodges, and beaver ponds, as well as a list of birds and mammals of the Lakes Basin area.

Location

Lakes Basin is an off-the-beaten-track corner of northern California about an hour's drive north of Truckee and Lake Tahoe on Gold Lake Road. It is forty minutes up Highway 49 from Downieville, a historic gold rush town. The former logging center of Graeagle on Highway 89, twenty minutes away, is now a popular village for golfers and a good place to pick up a secondhand paperback to read when you are tired of hiking. Historic Bassetts at the junction

1

of Highway 49 and Gold Lake Road is a good place to buy snacks, a flashlight, or anything else you might have forgotten to pack.

Terrain and Land Use

The beautiful scenery of Lakes Basin, as well as the diversity of plants, is due in part to the region's volcanic origin and glaciation. The glaciers scooped out lakes, dammed the valleys, and created ridges with their debris, dividing the country into five separate lake basins. The basins are bounded on the east by Gold Lake Road and on the west by the Pacific Crest Trail, or PCT. These basins differ in appearance, type of recreational use, and flora. Each area has a colorful old lodge that attracts returning guests year after year.

Since 1850 gold mining has altered the landscape just west of the PCT and continues to do so to the present day. Mine entrances and tailing piles are visible in a few places, such as at the Round Lake overlook, although in general the vegetation conceals past mining activity. Dr. Tom Stoddard's "gold lake" supposedly initiated the gold rush in this area. In the fall of 1849, while lost with a companion, Stoddard came upon a creek lined with gold. The two men filled a canvas bag with gold, shouting hysterically, and observing there was a whole fan of gold at the place where the creek emptied into the lake. On the way to Downieville, Stoddard's friend was killed by Indians, but he, with winter setting in and carrying thirty-four pounds of gold, eventually made his way alone to Downieville. People there called him "Crazy Stoddard" and refused to believe his tale about a lake of gold. Nevertheless, the following summer brought an epidemic of men with "gold fever" trying to find Gold Lake. Stoddard was never able to locate it again and finally had to flee from the misled angry miners. The Kentucky Mine, Sierra City, and Eureka State Park Museum have additional historical information available.

For greatest enjoyment of the area, visit each one of the lake basins along Gold Lake Road, since there are different recreational uses in each basin. The northernmost area, from Gray Eagle Lodge to Gold Lake Lodge, has delightful loop trails, many lakes, creeks, and springs, and few people, because motorized vehicles are not allowed in the area. Gold Lake, the largest lake in the area, has stables, a boat ramp, and jeep access to Tahoe National Forest. The Salmon Lake area has a small lake about a mile off the main road with a peaceful lodge and a boat ride away from civilization. The hiking country between Salmon Lake and Packer Lake has beautiful views, pretty Deer Lake, and very few people. Packer Lake, Sardine Lake and the Sierra Buttes have heavier use because of the striking alpine beauty of the buttes, excellent fishing in the lakes, and good swimming in Sand Pond. Sardine Lake campground has interesting evening programs and a wonderful beaver ecology walk. There is also jeep access to Tahoe National Forest near the trailhead to the buttes.

Lakes Basin can provide everything from the simple pleasures of hiking, swimming, fishing, camping, or relaxing with a book in a sunny meadow to very fine dinners in some of the lodges. Enjoy it all.

Prehistoric Indian Rock Art

Petroglyphs, or designs pecked into stone, have been observed on massive smooth rocks in the Lakes Basin area. All the petroglyphs found in Nevada and eastern California have been sited in association with big-game trails where you might also find obsidian chips, tools, and arrowheads. The Maidu Indians, though not year-round residents of Lakes Basin, were the principal tribe of the area and probably obtained the obsidian from the Washoe or Paiute tribes. The illustrator of this book, a collector and student of Indian art and crafts for fifty years, enjoyed drawing and researching the petroglyphs found in Lakes Basin. The designs may represent weather, animals, or people. The Forest Service has requested that the actual locations not be included because of potential vandalism. A Forest Service article says: "Native Americans seasonally occupied the entire Lakes Basin Area during prehistoric times. There is reasonable probability that the area was inhabited on a seasonal basis at least 3,000 years ago . . . the generalized hunting-gathering activities that were conducted in the area have left characteristic site types as evidence of their passage. Hunting blinds, surface flake scatters, bedrock mortars, long term (reoccupied) seasonal campsites, surficial quarry areas and rock art panels all attest to the presence of the Native Americans."[1]

1. *Environmental Assessment of the Gold Lake Composite*, USDA Forest Service, Plumas and Tahoe National Forests (Beckwourth and Downieville Districts, 1980), p. 3.

HOW TO USE THIS BOOK

ALL THE PLANTS ILLUSTRATED here have been drawn from live material collected in Lakes Basin. Each illustration shows several views of the flower and includes the key characteristics like glands, hairs, or seeds that are necessary to identify the plant. Beside each drawing a scale (measured in inches) shows relative size, but some flower closeups have been enlarged.

The plants are arranged by flower color: (1) WHITE to cream, (2) YELLOW to orange, (3) PINK to rose, (4) RED, magenta and maroon, (5) BLUE to lavender, and (6) plants with GREEN or brown flowers such as those trees and shrubs with discreet catkins and miniature flowers, conifers with cones, and grasslike plants. Within color groups plants are arranged by family to show similarities between related groups. Each illustration is accompanied by the following information: **common name, botanical name, plant family, height, growth habit** (perennial, shrub, tree, and the like), **color, habitat, blooming time**, and **trail** on which to find the plant. There are also a few interesting facts to help you remember the plant, such as the derivation of the botanical name, whether the plant is poisonous or edible, and sometimes its landscape potential.

The **botanical name,** or scientific name, usually consists of two Latin or Greek words, the first being the **genus,** or general name, and the second the **species,** or specific name. Some plants will have a third name, a varietal or subspecies (ssp.) name for additional differentiation. The scientific names are used worldwide. In a flower book on the Swiss Alps written in German, you can identify the plants by their scientific names. The botanical name is always italicized and the genus name is capitalized. Often the genus name is descriptive—for example, *Chrysothamnus* means gold shrub. Some genera are commemorative, such as *Castilleja* (paintbrush), which is named after a Spanish botanist. Others might refer to medicinal uses. Old common names have sometimes been Latinized, and some names are derived from mythology. The specific names, or species, are often descriptive, such as *albidus*, referring to white—think of albino. Interesting stories or "handles" that will help you remember the botanical names are often included. You must know the botanical name if you are buying a native plant for your garden or are investigating the edibility or medicinal use of a plant.

Common names are easy to remember because they are often descriptive. However, when common names are used, it is sometimes hard to know what plant is being discussed without pictures. The more common a plant the more "folk names" it will have. Columbine, for example, on page 169 has several common names because of its wide distribution and attractiveness.

4

A family is a large group of plants with similar characteristics that are usually recognizable. An example is the pea family, whose members have a distinctive flower and seed pod that most of us are familiar with. Lupine is a typical member of the pea family.

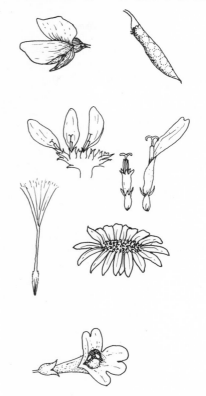

The composite, or sunflower, family is a very large plant family in California. Its members usually have flowers in heads such as a dandelion or daisy, and seeds that look like mini-sunflower seeds with thistledown attached. Aster is a typical composite. (See the illustration inside the front cover.)

The figwort, or snapdragon, family includes a number of showy mountain plants. This family has irregular flowers and might be confused with the mint family except that mints are aromatic. The *Penstemon* and Monkey-flower are typical members of the figwort family.

The **height** given for each plant is only a general guideline, since heights vary depending on available moisture, light, surrounding plants, and soil nutrients. For example, in a drought year the plants may be dwarfed. The **growth habit** of the plant, such as annual, perennial, shrub, or tree, is noted next, along with the **color** of the flower, the **habitat,** and its **blooming time.** According to alpine botanist Carl Sharsmith, the general bloom time of a plant can vary by as much as two weeks depending on the snowpack.

A further aid to identification is the **habitat** in which the plant is generally found. The Lakes Basin Recreation Area has many different habitats. There are moist areas, such as lake edges, creek banks, meadows (which can become dry in late summer), and bogs. The dry habitats include meadow edges, dry woods, dry slopes and montane chaparral, which is shrubby and almost impenetrable, and is typified by the presence of manzanita. Gravel flats are rich in flowers, which tend to bloom earlier here, from late May to mid-July, since they get their water from the snowmelt. Rock habitats consist of large rocks with nooks and crannies where plants can grow. Many plants thrive in the microclimate created at the base of rocks; moisture runs off a rock and collects under it, creating a reservoir for plants. Also, some plants choose the sunny side of rocks for the reflected heat, and others choose the north side for its cool shade. A scree habitat runs along much of the western boundary of Lakes Basin; it differs from the gravel flats in that it has very little soil or organic material.

The **trail** name and a fairly exact location for each plant allows you to set out on a treasure hunt for one particular flower if you wish.

A plant list by habitat follows the section on the individual plants.

To help you identify the plants more quickly, you might attach a colored index tab at the beginning of each new color section in the book. If there is one page you use often, such as the glossary or the plant index, turn the corner down or put a tab on that page so you can find it quickly. If you are vacationing in the area and have the time to sit down and fill in the illustrations with colored pencils or watercolors (mini-watercolor sets are available in art supply stores) or make notes beside the illustrations, the plants and their names will be more memorable to you.

Happy hunting. Remember: "Take only pictures, leave only footprints."

TRAILS AND LODGES

Our FAVORITE TRAILS combine an abundant and diverse flora with the best views and the prettiest lakes. We will first describe some trails of the Lakes Basin Recreation Area near the Lakes Basin Campground, in Plumas County, toward the northern end of Gold Lake Road, and then will move south along the eight-mile Gold Lake Road, ending at the Sardine Lake Campground area, in Sierra County. (Jeffrey Schaffer's *The Tahoe Sierra* gives detailed descriptions of all trails.) Hiking distances are not great; you will rarely be more than three hours from a trailhead. However, there is an elevation gain of up to 3,000 feet on some of the trails, so you should wear layered clothing and carry rain gear, food, water, and a map in a day pack. You will often be lured over one more ridge, and your exploring is likely to keep you on the trail longer than you expected.

There is a topographic map on page ix for the northern section of Gold Lake Road and on page x for the southern section, and a more general map inside the back cover. The many places in Lakes Basin where the flowers are reliably beautiful are noted on the latter map. These are usually where there are springs; the larger springs not only support beautiful wildflower gardens but often have lodges nearby. Highlights about the old lodges in the area, most of them near trailheads, are mentioned with the trail descriptions.

LAKES BASIN CAMPGROUND, on the southern edge of Grass Lake, has several creeks that flow into Grass Lake and provide lots of flowers throughout the summer. The campground is scheduled to be moved to higher ground in order to preserve this riparian zone and incorporate it into the trail system. When that happens, you will be able to photograph the beautiful Leopard Lilies and Cow Parsnip without dust on their leaves and a camper in the background.

ELWELL LODGE, situated near but not visible from the campground, was built in 1920 by William Frank Drew, grandfather of Miriam "Sugie" Barker; she and her husband, John, are the present owners. The lodge consists of a large dining hall perched high in the rocks, with a view of Mt. Elwell and the Sierra crest, a colony of cabins and a fabulous recreation hall furnished with an unusual square grand piano, antique furniture, a beautiful fireplace, and a Ping-Pong table. These sturdy buildings have withstood seventy winters, suffering only some cracked rafters from the winter of 1983. Sugie Barker recalls her mother, Miriam Childs, telling about gangsters who spent a winter at the lodge sometime in the 1930s and about an official throwing a slot machine out of Mr. Drew's office around the same time. Mrs. Childs also remembered having to ski from the lodge out to Graeagle one winter when she was a little girl. Sugie's husband, John, used to summer in the area, at his family's cabin on the west shore of Long Lake.

Elwell Lakes Lodge does not serve meals to the general public. Special arrangements can be made to see the lodge by phoning 916-836-2347. There are lovely wildflowers in the vicinity of the creek near the old dam, in the meadow to the north of the lodge toward the Bear Lake trail and on the trail to Long Lake near the spring that supplies the lodge. A flower list is available from Sugie. She also keeps a photo album on the piano showing most of the flowers.

Lakes Basin Campground Trails

LONG LAKE TRAILHEAD. *Easy, 0.7 mile from the campground trailhead, by the old organizational camp, to Long Lake.* After the second crossing of the creek feeding Grass Lake, the right side of the road/trail is wet and therefore is particularly rich with Sierra Laurel (*Leucothoe davisiae*), Labrador Tea (*Ledum glandulosum var. californicum*), Shooting Stars (*Dodecatheon alpinum*), two species of orchids, Rein Orchid (*Habenaria dilatata*) and Bog Orchid (*H. sparsiflora*), Monkshood (*Aconitum columbianum*), little white Macloskey Violet (*Viola macloskeyi*), and many other plants. This is the shortest trail to Long Lake, through Aspens, dappled shade, and past huge boulders on which rock climbers sometimes practice. The trail is prettiest in late June, when the Bitter Cherry (*Prunus emarginata*) is in bloom. You can use this trail as part of a shortcut loop return on a hike starting from the Bear Lake trailhead, at the same parking lot; or from Round Lake, Silver Lake, or Helgramite Lakes and the PCT.

BEAR LAKE TRAILHEAD TO LONG LAKE, SILVER LAKE, ROUND LAKE, AND HELGRAMITE LAKES. *Moderate hike of about 2.5 miles from the campground to Silver Lake, with an elevation gain of about 700 feet.* The trailhead is located just south of the Long Lake trail, also at the end of the campground road near the organizational camp. It has nice flowers near the spring that supplies Elwell Lakes Lodge with its water. In early June, keep your eyes glued to the rocks alongside the trail as you emerge from the forest into rocky open terrain and you might be rewarded with the tiny Steer's Head (*Dicentra uniflora*). Later in the month and in July you will find Leopard Lilies (*Lilium pardalinum*) and carpets of the white Yampah (*Perideridia bolanderi*) in the almost dry creekbed. At the Bear Lake marker sign you can choose to go either to **Round Lake Trail** or to **Long Lake** and **Silver Lake.** To get to the Round Lake trail, cross the outlet of Bear Lake and follow the creek a short way, and you will be treated to the blue Camas Lily (*Camassia quamash ssp. breviflora*), in bloom in June. The trail that crosses the outlet will take you to the Round Lake trail not far from Gold Lake Lodge. For a shortcut to the Round Lake trail heading toward Round Lake and the PCT, cross the Bear Lake outlet. Just where the trail leaves the lake, you will find a small trail heading southwest (keep Bear Lake in view) which climbs a fairly steep hill. Take a last look at Bear Lake, and just over the knoll, through the pale yellow Buckwheat (*Eriogonum marifolium*) and Purple Fritillary (*Fritillaria atropurpurea*), you will come to the Round Lake trail.

Returning to the Bear Lake marker on the northeast corner of Bear Lake, continue on to Long Lake and Silver Lake. This part of the trail runs along a hot exposed south-facing slope of typical montane chaparral plants, including Silktassel Bush (*Garrya fremontii*), Greenleaf Manzanita (*Arctostaphylos patula*), and Prostrate Manzanita (*A. nevadensis*). On the ridge

there are a few sentinels of *Pinus jeffreyi* and *Pinus monticola*, the Western White pine. Can you tell the difference between them? See pages 230 and 233. Close to Bear Lake you will find Dwarf Huckleberry (*Vaccinium arbuscula*) and Mountain Ash (*Sorbus californica*) along with some young Red Firs (*Abies magnifica*). There is a string of small lakes and then, over the hill, you come upon the beautiful **Long Lake overlook**, with Mt. Elwell in the background. Don't stop here! Continue on uphill another twenty to thirty minutes to Silver Lake, our favorite lake in all of Lakes Basin.

Just as you leave the Long Lake view, see if you can spot the Dwarf Juniper (*Juniperus communis*), a wonderful landscape plant, climbing over the rocks. A little way beyond, you come to a small tarn. Depending on how much water is left from the snow, you will find yellow, blue, or rosy-pink flowers. If there is still a puddle, then the tarn may be yellow with Water-plantain Buttercup (*Ranunculus alismaefolius*). If the water has evaporated, Bilberry (*Vaccinium nivictum*) may be in bloom. If the tarn is completely dry, you will find *Spiraea densiflora*, the showy pink shrub worthy of garden use. In August you can often taste the tiny blue Bilberries while admiring the Asters.

Beyond the depression of the tarn and over one more small rise is lovely **Silver Lake**. Sierra Laurel (*Leucothoe davisiae*) and Labrador Tea (*Ledum glandulosum*) are thick along the edge of the lake at this trail junction. Round Lake is just over the ridge to the south, and the Helgramite Lakes are up the steep hot trail to the west, about forty minutes away. Silver Lake is a good destination for children. The water is pleasant for swimming and there are rocks to sunbathe on afterward. White Mountain Heather (*Cassiope mertensiana*) and Mountain Hemlock (*Tsuga mertensiana*) both grow at Silver and Round Lakes— low elevations for these two plants.

You can make another loop trip from here by crossing the Silver Lake outlet, going over the ridge (where we have heard grouse) and down to **Round Lake**, where you cross the outlet, go uphill to the mine, and return by Round Lake trail and then cut back to Bear Lake. The trip from Silver Lake to the mine on Round Lake trail takes about an hour. There are no special flower gardens in this area, and if you are tired or have young children along, this route can get very long, since there is still an hour's walk from Round Lake Mine back down to Bear Lake. (See the Round Lake trail description on page 14.)

Helgramite Lakes and the cirque behind, carved out by a glacier, are about a forty-minute steep uphill hike from Silver Lake. It is worth the climb for flower followers and explorers. For the flowers of this area, see page 18 in the Round Lake trail description.

GRASS LAKE TO LONG LAKE OR GRAY EAGLE LODGE. *A moderate hike to Long Lake of 1.5 miles and return to Gray Eagle Lodge of about 3 miles, with an elevation at Grass Lake of about 6,300 feet, at Long Lake 6,555 feet, and Gray Eagle Lodge about 5,800 feet.*

Grass Lake, just north of the campground, behind the screen of Aspen, has many interesting plants growing in or adjacent to the water, the showiest being Buckbean (*Menyanthes trifoliata*), which usually blooms in early July.

Just downstream from the Grass Lake outlet is a swimming hole at the site of the former Lakes Center Lodge, which was removed because improvements did not meet the standards of Plumas National Forest authorities. The stone foundations and a nice swimming hole are all that remain of this lodge, which was built in 1912. The trail to Long Lake has lots of creeks and springs that create beautiful wildflower gardens, but it is fairly long for children, about two or two and a half hours. You can hike directly downhill to Gray Eagle Lodge instead and arrange a shuttle by leaving a car at the lodge or having someone pick you up there, so you don't have to hike back uphill over the same trail.

The trail from the Grass Lake bridge, across the Grass Lake outlet, starts in a sunny area that has Paintbrush (*Castilleja applegatei*) and Lupine (*Lupinus latifolius*) growing together. Few photographers can pass this red and blue color combination without a picture. Soon you are in a Red Fir forest. Watch for Coral Root *(Corallorhiza maculata)* and Snowplant (*Sarcodes sanguinea*) in the shade. In several places where springs cross the trail there will be orchids and lilies and perhaps Monkeyflowers and the Bird's Foot Trefoil (*Lotus oblongifolius*). This trail is a good place to observe these plants without damaging a meadow to get to them. There is one tricky creek crossing that can be managed more easily if you have a stick to hang onto while balancing on the rocks. While waiting your turn to cross the creek, look at the Mountain Ash (*Sorbus californica*) and peek under the shrubs to find ferns in the shade. The trail junction for Long Lake and Gray Eagle Lodge is just after this crossing. In early June, near the sign, you might be lucky enough to find Fawn Lilies *(Erythronium purpurascens)* still in bloom (see page 74).

At this point you can choose to hike down to Gray Eagle Lodge, about forty-five minutes away (for trail description see the Gray Eagle to Long Lake hike, page 13), or to Long Lake, about an hour and a half uphill. Even if your destination is Long Lake, pause to walk out on the rocks where the creek you have just crossed cascades into a canyon. This moist waterfall habitat and the waterfall at Gray Eagle Lodge are the only two locations where we have seen Five Finger Fern (*Adiantum pedatum*, page 225). We often stop for a snack here, and take off our boots and soak our feet for a few minutes.

Before getting back on the trail, look for some of the treasure plants that grow in this rock garden. We have marked this spot on the inside back cover map as one of the special flower gardens of the Lakes Basin region. Some of the plants you will find growing in the rocks are Bear Buckwheat (*Eriogonum ursinum*), Hot-Rock Penstemon (*Penstemon deustus*), Brewer's Rock Cress (*Arabis breweri)*, Jewel Flower (*Streptanthus tortuosus*), and Mariposa Lily (*Calochortus leichtlinii*).

Leaving the rock garden and returning to the Long Lake trail, you will soon come to a moist slope. Try to step on rocks in this wet fragile area. There are orchids (*Habenaria dilatata* and *H. sparsiflora*) in this sunny wet meadow, tiny white *Viola macloskeyi*, and a plant not often found, Bog Asphodel (*Narthecium californicum*). Its bright yellow lilylike flowers are out in mid-July. Even if you miss the bloom, you can note its profusion from the seed pods of the previous year. The shade of the Red Fir forest is welcome as you make your way uphill. Beyond a small pond the trail climbs through a rock outcrop that has two species of Saxifrage, Granite Gilia or Prickly Phlox (*Leptodactylon pungens ssp. pulchriflorum*), the late-blooming California Fuchsia (*Zauschneria californica*), and possibly in the wet cracks some Monkeyflowers. Stop at the top of the rock steps and see if you can find **"King Jeffrey,"** a magnificent example of *Pinus jeffreyi* that

has split a boulder with its massive roots. It is just across the little valley, to the southeast from where you are standing.

The rest of the way to Long Lake offers lots of interesting plants, and the many springs bubbling out of the southern flank of Mt. Elwell provide flowers well into August. This is another of the garden spots we have marked on the inside back cover map. The orchid called Ladies Tresses (*Spiranthes romanzoffiana*) grows in the flat, wet, rocky areas, along with Bilberry (*Vaccinium nivictum*), Wandering Daisy (*Erigeron peregrinus*), and some scattered willows. In some places you might spot a groundcover of small white leaves; this is Pussy Toes (*Antennaria rosea*), a close relative of the Swiss Edelweiss.

If you see the pink Flat-Stemmed Onion (*Allium platycaule*), rock-hop up the mossy slope to the source of the spring. It is icy cold and bubbles out of the mountain right under the willows. In mid-August, Grass of Parnassus (*Parnassia palustris var. californica*) can be found in this wet area just below Long Lake.

At **Long Lake**, not far from the outlet and before you pass the huge boulder, there are some nice flat rocks where you have a choice of sun or shade while you eat lunch. Beyond the large boulder is a tiny rock beach, from which we like to swim out to a rock in the lake. You probably will prefer to hike back on the trail to Gray Eagle Lodge or Grass Lake, unless you love a long and tough cross-country hike the length of the lake. At the south end of the lake is a small boathouse where the Elwell Lakes Lodge boat is stored along with the boat John Barker's parents still use to get to their cabin across Long Lake. It is a short walk from the boathouse back to the campground.

For the really hardy who want to climb **Mt. Elwell**, the trail continues beyond Long Lake. There are some nice dry meadows with Lupine (*Lupinus andersonii*), Jewel Flower (*Streptanthus tortuosus*), and Yampah (*Perideridia bolanderi*), and closer to the summit there are *Angelica breweri* and *Arnica cordifolia*. The Mt. Elwell trail is not particularly rewarding for botanists, but it is a good workout for a hiker who enjoys a good view and wants to get to Gray Eagle Lodge by a different trail. Plan the hike so that you have lunch on top of Mt. Elwell.

The trail from the top of Mt. Elwell to Smith Lake is obscure. Don't lose sight of the Gold Lake Road or you may end up in Eureka State Park. Remember to have a car at the Smith Lake trailhead near Gray Eagle Lodge; otherwise you will have a long uphill walk to Lakes Basin Campground at the end of the day. It is enjoyable to stop at Gray Eagle Lodge for a refreshing drink at the end of the hike.

GRAY EAGLE LODGE TO GRASS LAKE JUNCTION. *Uphill about 2.5 to 3 miles from Gray Eagle Lodge, at 5,800 feet, to Grass Lake, at 6,300 feet.* There is trailhead parking at the Smith Lake trailhead and the Long Lake trailhead, which is just before the gates to Gray Eagle Lodge. The trail to Long Lake is fifty yards or so up the Smith Lake fire road through a fir forest and out onto a rocky area kept moist by the same springs that supply Gray Eagle Lodge. There is a garden of moisture-loving plants here, including Columbine (*Aquilegia formosa*), Bog Asphodel (*Narthecium californicum*), Death Camas (*Zigadenus venenosus*), and Bigelow's Sneezeweed (*Helenium bigelovii*).

GRAY EAGLE LODGE, along Gray Eagle Creek, has fifteen cabins, some of them dating back to the 1930s. The original lodge collapsed under a heavy snow load in the early 1980s and has been reconstructed by the new owners, Sam and Grace Smith. Gray Eagle Lodge serves wonderful dinners (reservations required; phone 916-836-2511), or is a welcome stop for a cold drink at the end of the day. The most original structure on the grounds is the hydroelectric powerhouse with an intact generator, pelton wheel, and electrical appliances, all in working order, but abandoned in the late 1960s or early '70s. The powerhouse is up the creek from the lodge, at the site of the swimming hole and waterfall. At the waterfall, your patience may be rewarded by the sight of a **Water Ouzel**, or Dipper bird. The bird nests on the ledges of rock behind the waterfall.

A trail from the lodge merges with the Long Lake trail near a huge rock outcrop. There is great plant diversity in this area because of the proximity of large rocks, an usually dry creekbed, and underground moisture from the springs. A professional botanist and a beginning enthusiast who only wants to sketch could both spend all day here enjoying the variety of plants. Birders are also pleased if they spot a

13

Green-tailed Towhee. The trail to Long Lake passes through montane chaparral consisting of Greenleaf Manzanita *(Arctostaphylos patula)*, Silktassle Bush *(Garrya fremontii)*, Huckleberry Oak *(Quercus vaccinifolia)*, and Bitter Cherry *(Prunus emarginata)*.

Near the Lily Lake junction sign watch for the small Sierra Onion *(Allium obtusum)*, which you are likely to smell before you see it. The Lily Lake area, because it is so close to the Gold Lake Road, is less interesting than other parts of Lakes Basin, however, there are a few plants that have been found only at this lower elevation along the trail to Lily Lake. Wild Rose, Sugar Pine, and White Brodiaea, besides some beautiful Douglas Firs that have an unusual weeping form, are found growing here.

Past Lily Lake junction on the way to Long Lake, you will come upon a large open gravel area bounded on the southeast by an Alder thicket along the creek. This dry gravelly meadow is another of our special gardens marked on the inside back cover map. We have not come across another habitat quite like it in the Lakes Basin area, though we have seen the same plant grouping closer to Lake Tahoe. The plants here usually bloom in early July while there is still moisture in the soil from melting snow. There are lots of showy perennial plants in this gravel meadow, the most noticeable being the Scarlet Gilia *(Ipomopsis aggregata)*, Blue Delphinium *(Delphinium nuttallianum)*, and the Mountain Sunflower *(Helianthella californica var. nevadensis)*. Some of the ethereal annuals in this area are *Gilia leptalea*, which is lavender-pink, the pink *Linanthus ciliatus*, or Whisker Brush, and pink *Collomia linearis*. These "belly flowers" are all in the phlox family (see pages 150-151). The gravel meadow soon dries and looks like a dusty path, in which you can find only seeds remaining of the beautiful wildflowers.

A mixed evergreen forest begins at the end of the gravel meadow, and you will see such plants of the shaded woods as Mountain Snowberry *(Symphoricarpos acutus)*, Sweet Cicely *(Osmorhiza chilense)*, False Solomon Seal *(Smilacina racemosa)*, Sierra Currant *(Ribes nevadense)*, Bracken Fern *(Pteridium aquilinum)*, and Service-Berry *(Amelanchier pumila)* growing most of the way up the hill. You emerge onto a rock outcropping near the Grass Lake-Long Lake Junction. Here you will want to take a break at the rock garden by the cascading creek before continuing uphill. This pretty rock garden is described in the Grass Lake trail (page 10), with the Long Lake trail description following.

ROUND LAKE TRAIL FROM GOLD LAKE LODGE TO ROUND LAKE, THE PACIFIC CREST TRAIL (PCT), HELGRAMITE LAKES, AND SILVER LAKE. *A strenuous hike of about 2.5 miles from the trailhead to the PCT, almost 1 mile along the PCT, and about 3 miles back past Silver Lake with an elevation gain of about 1,000 feet. Allow seven hours for chasing flowers, lunch break, and a swim at*

Silver Lake. The trailhead for the Round Lake hike starts near Gold Lake Lodge, just off the Gold Lake Road. This is a high point between Gold Lake and the Lakes Basin Campground area; you start the hike at 6,600 feet instead of the 6,300 feet of the Lakes Basin Campground.

GOLD LAKE LODGE, just downhill from the Round Lake trailhead, was opened in 1912 by Mac and Mava Machovich, with some help from their friends. Guests would arrive at Blairsden by train and be brought up to the lodge by horse and buggy, and later by motor car. The original lodge burned down in 1925, but by 1926 the current dining hall was being built. Take a look at the southwest cornerstone of the building. Ann and Pete Thill, the present owners, tell many stories about this old lodge, which has been nominated for the National Register of Historic Places (for reservations phone 916-836-2350). The cozy dining hall is a wonderful spot to have breakfast before taking off on an all-day hike to the Sierra crest and back.

Spring comes later on this trail because of the northern exposure and the slightly higher altitude. If you see snow on the distant ridge, it is a sign that you will not be able to complete the loop on the PCT and should consider the alternate route of returning from the PCT to Round Lake and then on to Silver Lake. It is only about two and a half miles to the prominent white rock outcrop on the western ridge, which is usually our lunch destination. But it takes about four hours to get there, what with all the flowers and birds, the Round Lake Mine remains, and photography to slow the pace. The white rock outcrop is the halfway point of the hike. The remainder of it does not take as long—it goes downhill, and presumably you have already identified most of the flowers. Try to get to Silver Lake by mid-afternoon for a swim.

Flowers abound from your first footstep on the trail. The springs above Gold Lake Lodge provide perfect conditions for a multitude of moisture-loving plants such as Corn Lily (*Veratrum californicum*), Giant Paintbrush (*Castilleja miniata*), Bog Lupine (*Lupinus latifolius*), Groundsel (*Senecio triangularis*), and willows.

Red Fir (*Abies magnifica*) and giant Jeffrey Pine (*Pinus jeffreyi*) form the gateway to a dry meadow that almost always has lots of butterflies hovering over the white Yampah (*Perideridia bolanderi*) and Pennyroyal (*Monardella odoratissima*). Some of the more colorful flowers in the meadow are three species of blue penstemon (all three of the blue species are illustrated in the book), Pink Sidalcea (*Sidalcea oregana ssp. spicata*), and the Woolly Mule Ears (*Wyethia mollis*). As you walk through the Red Fir forest, keep your eyes open for the Coral Root Orchid (*Corallorhiza maculata*) and Snowplants (*Sarcodes sanguinea*). Notice the level at which the **Staghorn Lichen** (*Letharia columbiana*) starts growing on the Red

Firs. This chartreuse lichen indicates the snow depth in this area. Also watch for shy Blue-eyed Mary (*Collinsia torreyi*).

When you emerge from the forest, the gravel and the slight southern exposure present a new set of plants, such as Phlox, Buckwheats, Pussy Paws and the hard-to-see Fritillary Lily. You will soon reach the ridge that overlooks Bear Lake. Farther to the north is Mt. Elwell, with Long Lake at its base. The trail drops a little here, and several springs come off the hill to the south. There are treasures to be found near the springs. Pink Pyrola (*Pyrola asarifolia*), Rein Orchid (*Habenaria dilatata*), and *Viola macloskeyi* grow in the moist areas near alders. Early in the summer, if there are still some snow patches, watch for Steer's Head (*Dicentra uniflora*) in the drier stretches along this part of the road. Mountain Hemlock (*Tsuga mertensiana*) and Thimbleberry (*Rubus parviflorus*) welcome you into a rocky habitat. Bitter Cherry (*Prunus emarginata*) is the predominant shrub in this area. Now you have a climb up to the **Round Lake** overlook at Round Lake Mine. Magenta Pride of the Mountain Penstemon (*Penstemon newberryi*) and Bridge's Fern (*Pellaea bridgesii*) grow in the rocks beside the trail.

The mine was active into the 1920s, when flooding from Round Lake closed it. Sugie Barker, the third-generation owner of Elwell Lakes Lodge, can relate stories from her mother about the mine. The view from the overlook here reveals the Bear Lakes, Long Lake, Round Lake, and Mt. Elwell. Notice the white rock outcrop and decide whether you can wait about an hour to reach it before you stop for lunch. You still have about forty minutes of climbing to get to the PCT, and you will not enjoy that walk uphill after lunch. This is also a good place to check for snow on the ridge, which would mean you cannot make a loop trip. The alternate route takes off at the mine, past Round Lake outlet and over the ridge to Silver Lake, and will cut about two and a half hours off the trip. Let the Phlox help you make up your mind. The fragrant white flower is an early bloomer and very showy on the way up to the PCT. If it is just beginning to bloom you may be a little early for flowers on top of the ridge; on the other hand, the views of the Sierra Buttes are enhanced when there is snow on the north-facing slopes. If the Phlox is just finishing its bloom, the PCT should have good flowers.

There are many other flowers to distract you from the climb to the PCT.

You might want to detour into the Round Lake cirque near the Mountain Hemlocks (*Tsuga mertensiana*) to see the cascades of Red Heather (*Phyllodoce breweri*) and *Arnica diversifolia*. Along the trail in the gravel you will find Phlox (*Phlox diffusa*), Woolly Mule Ears (*Wyethia mollis*), Wild Onion (*Allium campanulatum*), and shrubs of Cream Bush (*Holodiscus microphyllus*). Soon Gold Lake is below you.

The prominent ridge that separates Gold Lake basin from the Lakes Basin Recreation Area and campground is the Plumas-Sierra county line. The ridge has several interesting features that would be worth exploring another day. According to Bob Rowdan, a longtime ranger at Mohawk Ranger Station, there is a rock structure at its summit with the date 1873 inscribed on it. Indian fireplaces and ancient volcanic vents are also to be found on the ridge and somewhere, nestled in a hollow between Gold Lake, the PCT, and the ridge, Joe Vowells, who owned Gold Beach Lake Resort for twenty years, found a gold mine complete with mine cart and rails.

Once you enter the Red Fir forest, it is not far to the PCT. Heading north at the junction soon brings you to an entirely new plant habitat. The plants of this sterile scree habitat are not found at lower elevations. Meander along the crest to the highest point, being careful not to step on the *Lewisia kelloggii*, Pincushion Flowers (*Chaenactis nevadense*), or Ball-headed Gilias (*Ipomopsis congesta*), and look north to Mt. Lassen and south to the Buttes. The bright Sulphur Buckwheat (*Eriogonum umbellatum ssp. polyanthum*) and cheery sunflower of Balsamroot (*Balsamorhiza sagittata*) are beautiful against the blue sky. There are a few dwarfed Jeffrey Pines and several species of small shrubs, a prostrate form of Bitterbrush (*Purshia tridentata*) and White-stem Rabbitbrush (*Chrysothamnus nauseosus ssp. albicaulis*). As you step carefully through the delicate plants, you may see obsidian chips, a reminder that Indians also took advantage of the view while working on their tools in this area of plentiful game.

Going north along the ridge to the white rocks you may encounter snow on the steep northeast-facing slope. If the snow has melted, you will find some of the real treasures of Lakes Basin: Sierra Primrose (*Primula suffrutescens*) cascading like a waterfall down the steep northeast-facing slope, the rosy-pink Rock Fringe (*Epilobium obcordatum*) with its blue-gray leaves, Gray's Bedstraw (*Galium grayanum*), two species of *Raillar-della*, *Lewisia kelloggii*, and the pretty Wood Rush (*Luzula divaricata*), abundant Columbine (*Aquilegia formosa*), *Angelica breweri*, and Paint-brush (*Castilleja applegatei*).

It is a beautiful place to stop for LUNCH. We generally climb up into the rocks and stay a while to enjoy the beautiful views. Cordell Durrell's *Geologic History of the Feather River Country, California*, discusses the rock formations of this area in great detail and would enhance a geologist's enjoyment. What Mr. Durrell refers to as the "nearly white silicic volcanic breccia of the Sierra Buttes Formation" is our lunch area.

The white rock outcropping and the impenetrable thicket of montane chaparral, composed of Bitter Cherry (*Prunus emarginata*), Tobacco Brush (*Ceanothus velutinus*), Buckbrush or Snow Bush (*Ceanothus cordulatus*), and Mountain Snowberry (*Symphoricarpos vaccinoides*) cause the trail to dip down on the western slope into the forest for about forty-five minutes. Then the trail returns almost to the ridge, and for plants and views it is worth making little detours up to the crest to peek over into Lakes Basin. We have tried to hike cross-country along the ridge, and it is nearly impossible because of the jumble of rocks. Soon the trail joins an old jeep road and passes a former campsite where there are some delightful springs with the pink Lewis's Monkey Flower (*Mimulus lewisii*) along the edge. As the forest thins you are once again on the western ridge of the Lakes Basin Wilderness Area, looking toward Long Lake, with small Mud Lake directly below you. If you look carefully you might even spot the cabin belonging to John Barker's family nestled in the forest at the edge of Long Lake.

At this junction, you will walk downhill, following the signs to Silver Lake, through some of the most beautiful gardens in the northern Sierra. Shrubs of Sierra Laurel (*Leucothoe davisiae*) and Labrador Tea (*Ledum glandulosum*), along with Mountain Bluebell (*Mertensia ciliata*), Bog Lupine (*Lupinus latifolius*), yellow Arnica (*Arnica diversifolia*), and Giant Red Paintbrush (*Castilleja miniata*) stop you in your tracks to admire the riot of colors. These gardens are the result of the springs you passed up on the PCT. Check the moist rocky areas for **White Mountain Heather**

 (*Cassiope mertensiana*). This is quite a treasure to find at such a low altitude. Your senses have a rest now while you climb another small ridge into the **Helgramite Lakes**.

Upper Helgramite Lake is on its way to becoming a meadow. There are Shooting Stars (*Dodecatheon alpinum*), two species of Elephant Heads (*Pedicularis attolens* and *P. groenlandica*) and the wonderful Bog Laurel (read the note about *Kalmia polifolia* on page 163). Due to the springs in this area, the flowers last well into summer. Explore the cirque above Upper Helgramite Lake and you will find lots of treasure plants. In late August the bright red California Fuchsia (page 144) blooms in the rocky walls of the cirque.

Continuing around the south side of these small lakes, you drop over into the **Silver Lake** Basin, where you get a good view of your destination beyond Silver Lake to the Bear Lakes. In the distance you might be able to spot Grass Lake near the campground, and to the south the mine tailing pile at the edge of Round Lake is visible. As you walk down the steep, hot, south-facing slope through Manzanita and Huckleberry Oak, consider taking a swim in Silver Lake; you rarely have to share the lake with anyone else, and it is large enough for you to find your own private cove. There is still about an hour of walking, whether to the campground or to the Round Lake trailhead, but the flowers the rest of the way down should not delay you much, since you have already seen most of them. However, John Muir's favorite plant, White Mountain Heather (*Cassiope mertensiana*), may lure you to the southwest rocky corner of Silver Lake if you missed it in the rocks above the PCT spring gardens. The flowers for the rest of the walk back to Gold Lake Lodge are after Bear Lake outlet. If you are going back to the Gold Lake Lodge area, don't miss the Camassia in the creek just after the Bear Lake outlet.

GOLD LAKE is the next lake basin south on Gold Lake Road. It is separated from the Lakes Basin Campground area and Round Lake by a prominent ridge 7,100 feet in elevation. Gold Lake Pack Station and Stables, located just off Gold Lake Road at the southeast corner of the lake, is operated by Russell Reid. The stables have guided trail rides, can customize a trip for you, or can pack you into the wilderness. There is a public boat launch near the stables where the boat taxi from Gold Lake Beach Resort picks up guests. A rough jeep road on the south side of Gold Lake eventually leads over the Sierra crest into Tahoe National Forest.

GOLD LAKE BEACH RESORT, on the western shore of Gold Lake, was developed in 1921. Patty Twist, a descendent of the Haven family, said that her great-great-uncle, Philo Haven, was the first gold miner to find gold here. This fact is mentioned in a local history book by Major Downie. Her

grandfather, James Haven, had a quartz mill and lumber mill near the outlet of Gold Lake. Patty still enjoys visiting the family property here.

Joe Vowells, who lives in Graeagle, owned and operated the lodge for about twenty years. He obviously loves the country. He tells of taking his guests four-wheeling to see various mines tucked up in the ridge and to meet a sort of pioneer couple, a former Bechtel engineer turned gold miner and his wife. Asked about the fishing, Joe remembers one day when seventy fish were caught. During his time at the resort Joe equipped one of his boats with a fire pump and hose and used it to put out five forest fires. Also because of his land phone, his four-wheel-drive vehicles, and his boats, he brought out three heart-attack victims over the years. He recalls that in the winter of 1954 there were forty-two feet of snow at the resort

19

and the ridgepole was "popped" by the weight. Janie and Greg Spitz own Gold Lake Beach Resort and now serve lunch at the lodge.

The best wildflowers in the Gold Lake basin are in the meadows on the southwestern and western edge of the lake and along the springs that supply the resort. The habitat list (pages 244–247) for moist plants includes most of the plants you will see here.

Opposite the road into Gold Lake is the Old Gold Lake Road, which goes to **Frazier Falls.** It is about a ten-minute drive and then a twenty-minute walk through pretty flower gardens to get to the waterfall.

UPPER SALMON LAKE TO HORSE LAKE, DEER LAKE, AND PACKER LAKE. *Moderate hike of about 2.5 miles one way with about a 500-foot elevation gain.* The Salmon Lake area is reached by turning west off Gold Lake Road and driving about three-fourths of a mile to Upper Salmon Lake, where there is a trailhead that will take you past the Salmon Lake Lodge to Horse Lake and on to Deer Lake and Packer Lake.

SALMON LAKE LODGE. The lodge was built by George and Ann McGee in the late 1920s on old mine tailings, and supported itself at first from both mining and tourism. Winslow Christian acquired the lodge in 1958. The ruins of an old stamp mill can be seen near the lodge, and most of the cabins are tucked in a little valley behind the main lodge.

The elevation gain on the hike from Salmon Lake, at 6,500 feet, to Deer Lake at 7,100 feet, is hardly noticeable because of the beauty of the trail. Between Salmon Lake Lodge and Horse Lake there are beautiful gravel gardens consisting of Sierra Onion (*Allium campanulatum*), Jewel Flower (*Streptanthus tortuosus*), Mountain Spiraea (*Spiraea densiflora*), Sandwort (*Arenaria congesta*), Catchfly (*Silene douglasii*), Cinquefoil (*Potentilla glandulosa*), Buckwheats (*Eriogonum marifolium* and *E. latifolium*), Scarlet Gilia (*Ipomopsis aggregata*), and blue *Delphinium nuttallianum*. There are also some nice rock gardens on the trail between Horse Lake and Deer Lake where you will find Dogbane (*Apocynum pumilum*), Mountain Pennyroyal (*Monardella odoratissima*), California Sunflower (*Helianthella californica*), Bitter Cherry (*Prunus emarginata*), and Scruffy Mountain Asters (*Aster integrifolius*). **Deer Lake** is a good lunch stop, whether you are hiking from Packer Lake to Salmon Lake or the reverse. The flowers between Packer Lake and Deer Lake are not spectacular, as is often the case on dry south-facing slopes.

SARDINE LAKE BASIN is the most popular stretch of Gold Lake Road because of its accessibility by car, the pleasant campground, the relatively warm and clean water for swimming in Sand Pond, and the spectacular backdrop of the Sierra Buttes. There is an interesting nature walk in the vicinity of the Sardine Lake Campground and Sand Pond. Beavers are altering the ecology of the area, flooding the campground and causing many of the Lodgepole Pines (*Pinus murrayana*) to die. Western Azalea (*Rhododendron occidentale*) and *Spiraea douglasii*, two plants I found nowhere else in Lakes Basin, are endangered by the flooding. The network of beaver dams is amazing. At dawn you can see the beavers swimming across Sand Pond.

SARDINE LAKE RESORT was completed in 1941 by George Browning, his family, and friends. Dorothy Browning Hunt and her husband, Chandler, operate the lodge now, with the help of their two children, Janis and Thomas. Some of their guests have been coming to the resort for over forty-five years and have watched the children grow up. The resort has been in the same family for fifty years, and the Hunt children are likely to continue the tradition.

Dorothy Hunt recalls her parents helping fight a fire on the north ridge of the lake in the 1940s. A more recent incident was the time a bear tore the door off the freezer to get at a New York strip, twelve pounds of sirloin steaks, a couple of very intense chocolate tortes, five pounds of chocolate chips, and numerous other goodies. Chan Hunt decided the freezer needed more protection and enclosed the porch with 1″ × 12″ boards, which the bear ripped off. Fortunately, this was at the end of the season, so no one was disturbed when Chan took a couple of shots over the bear's head. The marauder did not test Chan's patience again that year.

Dorothy tells a fish story about the largest German Brown taken out of the lake. One of her guests was fishing and saw a large fish float belly-up to the surface, apparently dead of old age. The Hunts towed it in to the dock, and found it weighed sixteen pounds and was twenty-eight inches long. They kept it frozen for a while to show to guests.

Sardine Lake Resort has a spectacular alpine view of the rocky crags behind the lake, and it serves wonderful dinners. (Be sure to phone 916-862-1196 for reservations.) The best flowers here are in the campground and in the meadows below and just south of the beaver ponds.

For spectacular views and flowers go up to the Sierra Buttes lookout. You can hike there from Sardine Lake if you are in great shape: otherwise drive up past Packer Lake to the ridge and start your hike from there. The Packer Lake and Sierra Buttes road is between the Sardine Lake Campground and Gold Lake Road. Just past the intersection on the Packer Lake Road, on the north side of the road, look for lots of dead trees. This is another result of the flooding from the beaver dams. Continuing on up the road, you may want to turn off at Packer Lake Lodge to pick up something to drink or some film. Actually, we really enjoy sitting on the porch with something cool to drink after the hike.

PACKER LAKE LODGE, built in 1926 by a family named Hallock, is a rustic log lodge. The Raidar Winther family, who bought the lodge in the 1950s, tell about how Eric and Alec Ostrom went out in the woods and cut the Tamarack or Lodgepole Pine (*Pinus murrayana*), stripped the bark, stacked the logs for the walls, let them dry, then chinked the spaces with plaster. John Winther, a teenager at the time, recalls putting lots of nails between the logs to help snug the plaster.

Raidar Winther used to take his guests down to Sierra City occasionally for a night on the town—making sure the guests agreed with the local custom that they would not disclose the secret of the wonderful fishing to the tourists in town. During mining days Packer Lake was a stopping place for the pack trains on their way to the mines on the west slope of the Sierra Buttes. Perhaps the packers wanted to have some good fishing along the way.

Bill McQuattie is the present owner of Packer Lake Lodge, which is open to the public for meals and snacks and has a little store that stocks film, maps, and candy bars behind the counter, in case you forgot something for your hike. (For dinner reservations call 916-862-1221.)

The best flowers are near the rocks and waterfall on the west side of the road just as you enter the lodge grounds. A trail leads around the north side of the rocks, uphill, to a superb flowery meadow where a photographer or artist could spend hours. By the picnic ground, on the south side of the lake, there are some treasures, like Ginger-leaf Wintergreen (*Pyrola asarifolia*) and Orchids, under the Alders.

SIERRA BUTTES LOOKOUT TRAIL. *A strenuous walk on a hot afternoon, but not bad in the morning; a steep, almost 1,500 feet elevation gain over 1.5 miles from the trailhead to the lookout tower.* The Sierra

Buttes Lookout trail, located above the Sardine Lake area, has lots of flowers on the exposed rocky ridges and east facing scree, some of them not seen elsewhere in Lakes Basin. The height of bloom usually occurs in mid-July.

Park your car on the ridge above Packer Lake Lodge at the trailhead for the lookout. This is also part of the PCT. Plan on about six hours for the hike to the top and back. Bring a snack and plenty of water, since this exposed area can be very hot, as you climb from the trailhead at 7,000 feet to the lookout at 8,500 feet. Montane chaparral and pretty yellow *Arnica sororia* are seen along much of the trail. You will welcome the occasional Red Fir forest for the shade, and then it is nice to return to the open and enjoy the views and rock gardens.

In the forest watch for the seed pods of the May- or June-blooming Fawn Lily (*Erythronium purpurascens*). White *Angelica Breweri*, shoulder high, accented by magenta *Penstemon newberryi* and Sulphur Buckwheat (*Eriogonum umbellatum var. polyanthum*), is found on the ridge. Pink puffs of Lobb's Buckwheat (*Eriogonum lobbii*), a pink form of *Lewisia kelloggii*, Gray's Bedstraw (*Galium grayanum*), beautiful blue Polemonium (*Polemonium pulcherrimum*), which only grows at an elevation of over 8,000 feet, and Mountain Primrose (*Primula suffrutescens*), which used to be at the foot of the lookout stairway, are some of the treasures to be found in this alpine garden.

Be sure to climb the stairs to the top of the rocky pinnacles. The friendly couple who man the lookout are happy to point out the various landmarks that can be seen all the way to Lake Tahoe and north to Mt. Lassen.

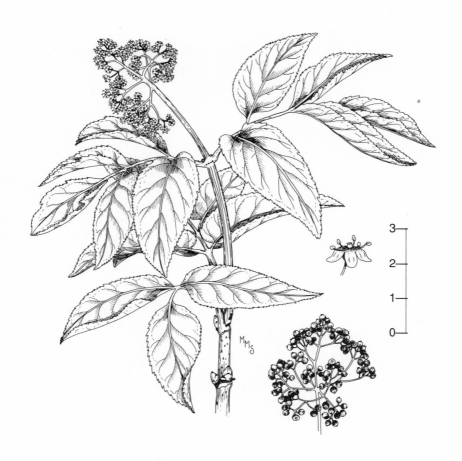

MOUNTAIN RED ELDERBERRY   HONEYSUCKLE
Sambucus microbotrys

Height: 4 ft.   Shrub   ❀ **WHITE FLOWERS, RED FRUIT** ❀
Habitat: WOODS, MOIST, OPEN   JULY
Trail: ROUND LAKE 🐾 SEEPS IN ROUND LAKE CIRQUE

Micro in the species name means small, and *botrys* refers to the grapelike cluster of flowers. Weeden (1975) in *A Sierra Nevada Flora* states that Red Elderberry is poisonous in many locations. The owners of Elwell Lodge have been serving Red Elderberry jelly for at least two generations. Perhaps the Red Elderberry that is poisonous is the coastal species, *S. callicarpa*. To be safe use only the Blue Elderberry.

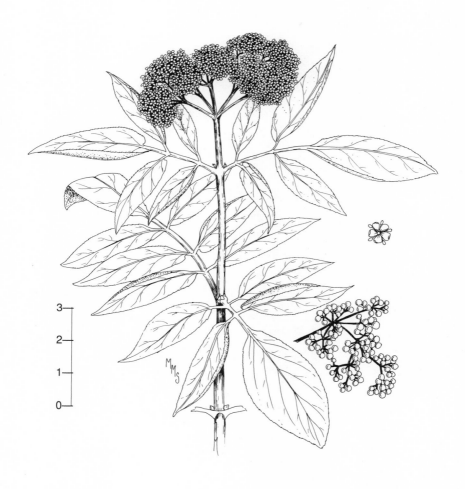

BLUE ELDERBERRY *Sambucus caerulea* HONEYSUCKLE

Height: To 15 ft. Shrub ❀ **WHITE FLOWER, BLUE FRUIT** ❀
Habitat: WOODS, OPEN JUNE LATE
Trail: ABOVE ELWELL LODGE DAM

The species name, *caerulea*, refers to the blue fruits, which make good jelly and wine. Some German friends have told me they dip the flat-topped flowers in pancake batter and make fritters. Blue Elderberry is a good landscape plant that attracts birds to the garden. This is a larger plant than Red Elderberry and grows in a drier situation.

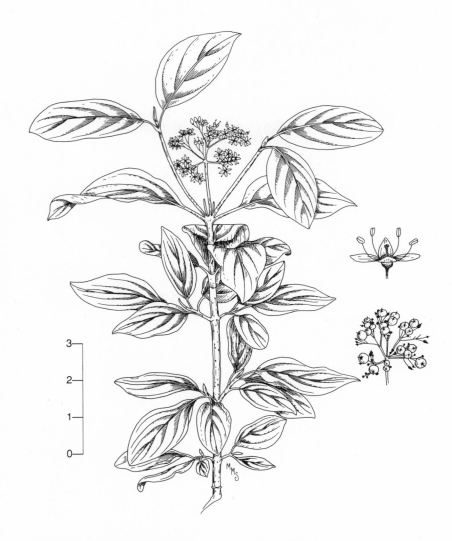

AMERICAN DOGWOOD   *Cornus stolonifera*   DOGWOOD

Height: 5 to 6 ft.   Shrub   ❀ **WHITE** ❀
Habitat: MOIST   JULY
Trail: ROUND LAKE 🍂 WHERE STREAMS CROSS THE TRAIL

Dogwood and Honeysuckle look a lot alike. To make sure you have a
Dogwood, tear the leaf. The Dogwood leaf will tear straight across leaving
weblike strands at the site of the veins. The twigs are burgundy red, and
there are green-white fruit clusters in early autumn. Dogwood was used by
the Indians as basket material, and the inner bark has some of the
properties of quinine and was used as a tea.

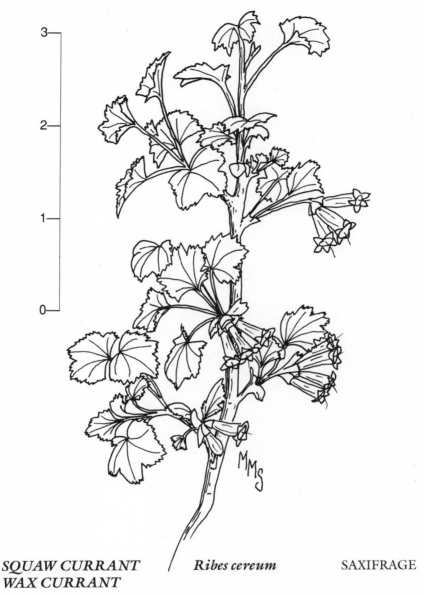

SQUAW CURRANT	*Ribes cereum*	SAXIFRAGE
WAX CURRANT		

Height: 3 to 5 ft.   Shrub   ❀ **CREAM TO PALE PINK** ❀
Habitat: DRY, ROCKY   MAY/JUNE
Trail: OPEN AREAS ALONG LAKES BASIN CAMPGROUND ENTRY ROAD
The species name, *cereum*, is from the word *cereus*, meaning waxy, which must refer to the texture of the flowers. Squaw Currant is not as attractive a shrub for landscape use as the showy pink-flowered Sierra Currant. Using a hand lens, observe the glands on the leaves. This species, like most of the *Ribes* genus, is an early bloomer.

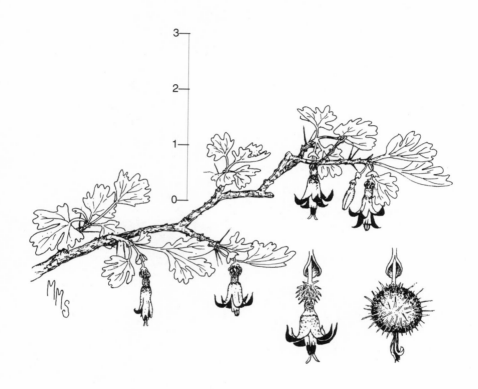

SIERRA GOOSEBERRY   *Ribes roezlii*   SAXIFRAGE

Height: To 5 ft.   Shrub   ❀ **WHITE** ❀

Habitat: DRY SLOPES   JUNE

Trail: BEAR LAKE TRAILHEAD 🐾 LAKES BASIN CAMPGROUND ENTRY ROAD

The hanging flowers of the Sierra Gooseberry have white petals and red sepals. The fruit is rosy-colored when ripe, usually in September, and makes a delicious jelly, but harvesting is difficult because of the spines. Lay a sheet on the ground under the shrub and hit the plant gently with a stick, or wear heavy ski gloves to pick, or scrape the pendant berries off the branches with a fork.

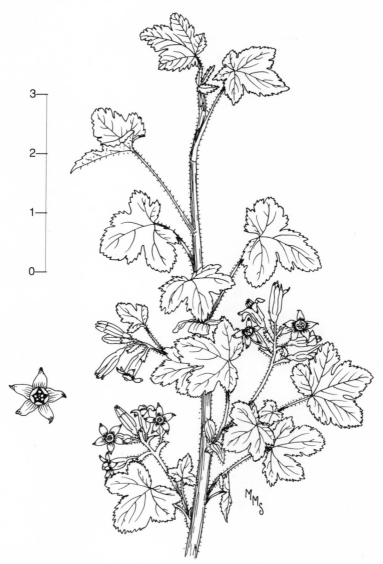

STICKY CURRANT   *Ribes viscosissimum*   SAXIFRAGE

Height: To 3 ft.   Shrub   ❀ **WHITISH-PINK** ❀
Habitat: WOODS   JUNE/JULY
Trail: LAKES BASIN CAMPGROUND

Ribes is an ancient Arabic name. This currant has bitter, spineless, black fruit. The *Ribes* genus and the pines with five needles are co-hosts to the White Pine Blister rust, a fungus originally from Europe that kills the pines. The fungus is controlled by eradicating the gooseberries and currants. For many years these plants were not available in the nursery trade.

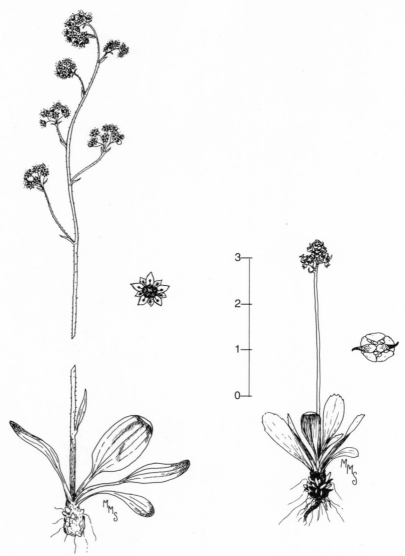

BOG SAXIFRAGE   SAXIFRAGE   *SIERRA SAXIFRAGE*
Saxifraga oregana   *Saxifraga aprica*

JULY   ❀ **WHITE** ❀   JULY
Height: 18 in.   Perennial   10 in.
Habitat: MOIST   MOIST

Trail: LONG LAKE TRAIL 🐾 IN ROCKY SEEPS BELOW LAKE OUTLET
The origin of the botanical name is Latin, from *saxum* for rock and *frango*,
to break. *Saxifraga oregana* has glandular pubescent stems and is a larger
plant than *Saxifraga aprica*, Sierra Saxifrage. Both species are found in the
same locale.

30

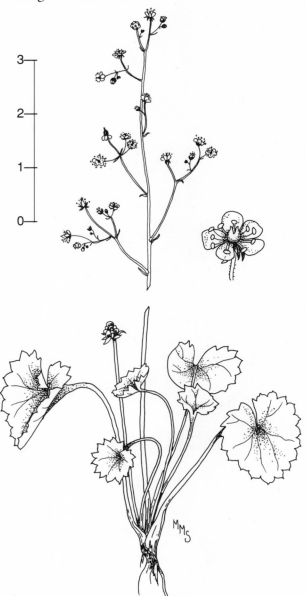

BROOK SAXIFRAGE   *Saxifraga punctata*   SAXIFRAGE
                       ssp. arguta

Height: 8 in.   Perennial   ❀ **WHITE** ❀
Habitat: MOIST STREAMSIDE   JULY
Trail: LONG LAKE TRAIL ❧ ALONG STREAM FROM ELWELL LODGE SPRING
The species name, *punctata*, meaning spots, refers to the yellow dots at the
base of the petals. You will probably get wet knees observing Brook
Saxifrage since it is always found beside a stream.

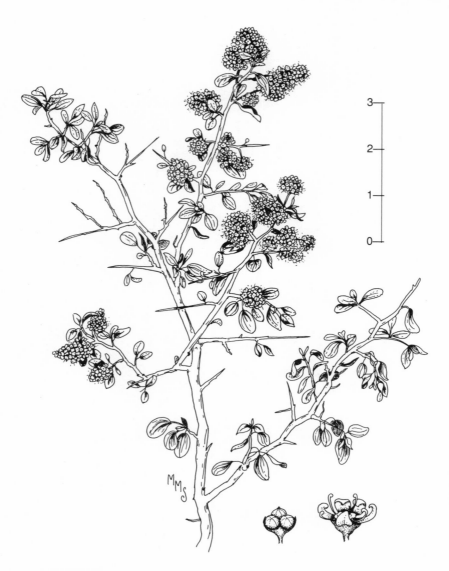

SNOW BUSH   *Ceanothus cordulatus*   BUCKTHORN

Height: To 4 ft.   Shrub   ❀ **WHITE** ❀
Habitat: MONTANE CHAPARRAL   JUNE
Trail: BEAR LAKE 🌿 ON SOUTH-FACING SLOPES ON HILL ABOVE LAKE
Ceanothus is derived from the Greek *Keanothus,* a name used by Dios-
corides for some spiny plants. It is impossible to hike cross-country
through Snow Bush because of the stout spines. Many *Ceanothus* species
are very fragrant, and a soapy lather can be made from the blossoms. The
leaves of Snow Bush have a gray-blue cast.

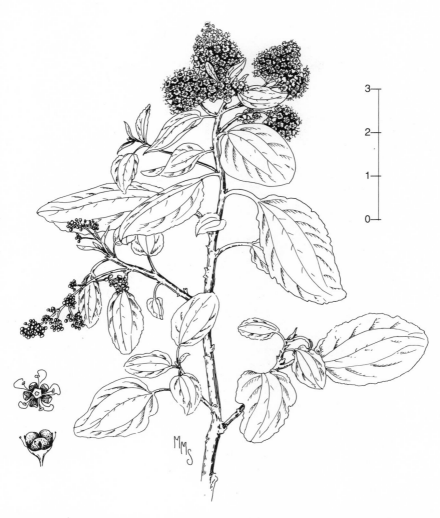

TOBACCO BRUSH   *Ceanothus velutinus*   BUCKTHORN
MOUNTAIN BALM
SNOW-BRUSH

Height: To 5 ft.   Shrub   ❀ **WHITE** ❀
Habitat: MONTANE CHAPARRAL   JULY
Trail: SILVER LAKE 🥾 JUST AFTER BEAR LAKE

The underside of the bright green leaves is covered with very fine white hairs—thus the species name, *velutinus,* meaning velvetlike. All the shrubs of this genus have a sweet fragrance. The leaves make a good tea and the Indians used the rolled leaves as tobacco. A soapy lather can be developed when the blossoms are rubbed between wet hands.

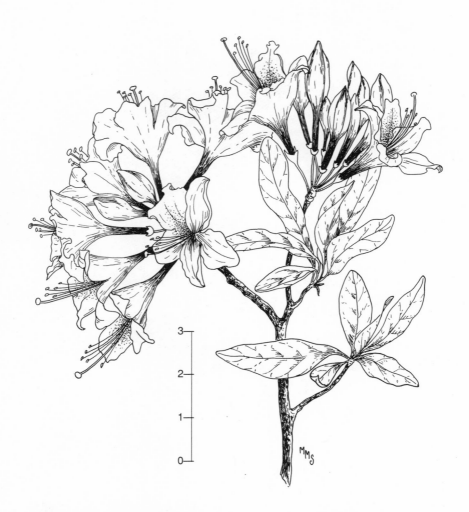

WESTERN AZALEA   ***Rhododendron occidentale***   HEATH

Height: To 10 ft.   Shrub   ❀ **WHITE** ❀
Habitat: MOIST   JULY
Trail: SARDINE LAKE CAMPGROUND TO SAND POND

The name is of Greek origin, from *rhodos*, meaning rose, and *dendron*, meaning tree. This beautiful, fragrant Azalea seems to grow only in the Sardine Lake basin, near the campground and Sand Pond, where it is threatened by flooding from the beaver dams. The white flowers are sometimes slightly yellow or pink in the throat. Azalea is a beautiful garden plant that will grow at lower elevations and is available in nurseries.

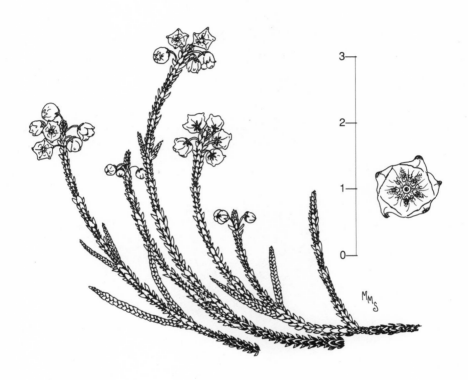

MMS

MOUNTAIN WHITE HEATHER   HEATH
Cassiope mertensiana

Height: 2 to 12 in.   Shrub   ❀ **WHITE** ❀
Habitat: ROCKY LEDGES   JUNE/JULY
Trail: SILVER LAKE NEAR THE LAKE; PCT SPRING GARDEN

These beautiful little white bells with their red sepals are named after
Cassiope, the mother of Andromeda, in Greek mythology. Alpine Heather,
another common name, was one of John Muir's favorite flowers. As this
common name suggests, you see this plant only at higher elevations so it
was a pleasant surprise to find it growing at 6,700 feet at Silver Lake.

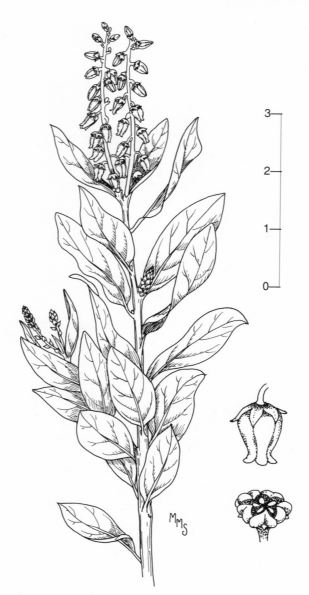

SIERRA-LAUREL   *Leucothoe davisiae*   HEATH

Height: 2 to 5 ft.   Shrub   ❀ **WHITE** ❀

Habitat: MOIST

Trail: SILVER LAKE 🌿 NORTHEAST CORNER, NEAR SIGN

This should be a garden plant. It would need the same treatment as azaleas. Sierra-Laurel resembles the garden plant *Pieris*, or Lily of the Valley shrub. The illustrator pointed out to me the way the flowers hang down, but when in fruit they turn up. This is a toxic plant.

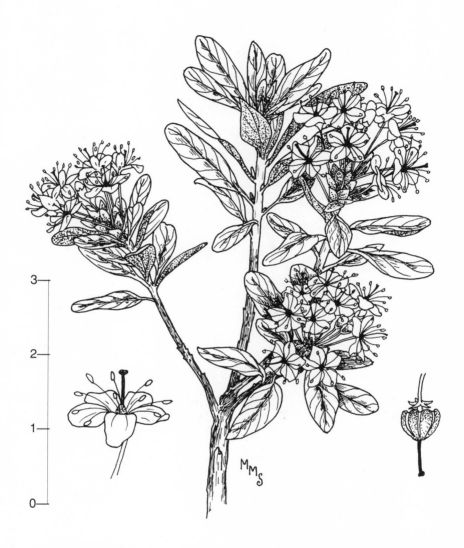

LABRADOR TEA   *Ledum glandulosum*   HEATH
var. californicum

Height: 2 to 5 ft.   Shrub   ❀ **WHITE** ❀
Habitat: MOIST   JUNE/JULY
Trail: SILVER LAKE 🐾 NORTHEAST CORNER, NEAR SIGN

Ledon is the ancient name for cistus, which also had an aromatic resin. You are at once reminded of Azalea, which is in the same plant family. For years we made tea out of this plant when we were backpacking. Lucky for us, our tea must have been weak. Labrador Tea is considered poisonous.

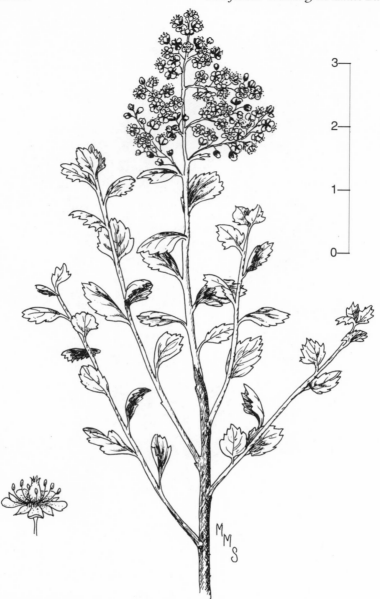

CREAM BUSH   *Holodiscus microphyllus*   ROSE

Height: To 5 ft.   Shrub   ✿ **WHITE** ✿
Habitat: ROCKS, DRY   JULY
Trail: ROUND LAKE TRAIL 🌿 ABOVE MINE AT ROUND LAKE OVERLOOK
The species name, *microphyllus*, means small leaf. A similar shrub, Ocean
Spray (*Holodiscus discolor*), is common in the Coast Range. The low-eleva-
tion Ocean Spray is a useful landscape plant because it can grow in the dry
shade of oak trees.

MOUNTAIN ASH   *Sorbus californica*   ROSE

Height: To 9 ft.   Shrub   ❀ **WHITE** ❀
Habitat: MOIST   JULY
Trail: GRASS LAKE TO LONG LAKE 🍃 WHERE SPRINGS CROSS THE TRAIL

The bright red berries of Mountain Ash are edible raw or cooked, but they taste better after frost. In early October we often drive to Ebbetts Pass on Highway 4 to see the red of the Ash and the gold of the Aspen, and then to Grover Hot Springs Campground to enjoy a hot soak in the mineral springs. Mountain Ash is a good landscape plant because of the white flowers in summer and the red berries and foliage in the fall.

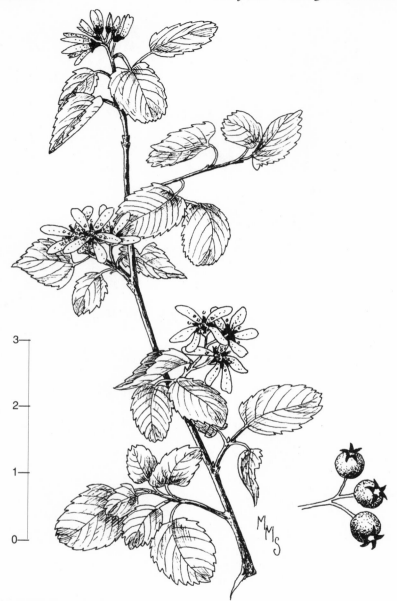

SERVICE-BERRY **Amelanchier pumila** ROSE

Height: To 4 ft. Shrub ❀ **WHITE** ❀

Habitat: WOODS, DRY JUNE

Trail: LAKES BASIN CAMPGROUND

The species name, *pumila*, means dwarf. This shrub is an eye-catcher because the white flowers show up so well blooming in the shade. The dark fruits are edible. Service-berry is an attractive plant for landscape use and attracts birds.

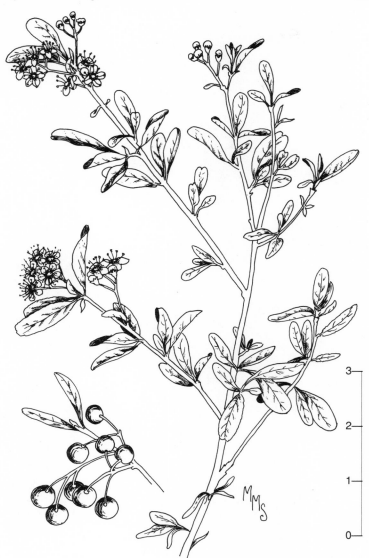

BITTER CHERRY   *Prunus emarginata*   ROSE

Height: To 8 ft.   Shrub   ❀ **WHITE** ❀
Habitat: MONTANE CHAPARRAL   JUNE
Trail: LAKES BASIN CAMPGROUND TO LONG LAKE

The common name is a warning about the taste of the Bitter Cherry. Gladys Smith was once made ill from tasting a small amount of the fruit. To identify this plant, look for Pyracanthalike flowers and lines on the silvery bark similar to those on the Cherry tree. Bitter Cherry is particularly pretty in the vicinity of Round Lake Mine and on Long Lake trail near Grass Lake.

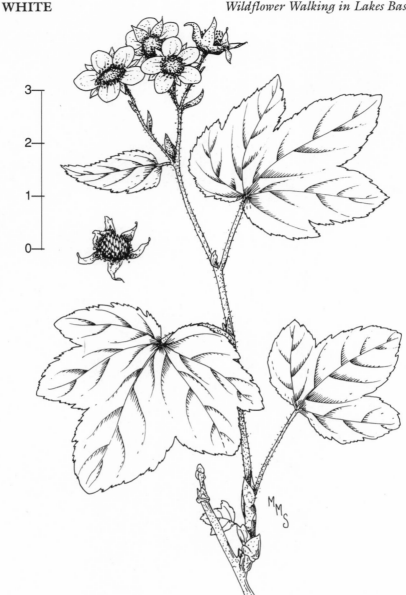

THIMBLEBERRY *Rubus parviflorus* ROSE

Height: To 6 ft. Shrub ❀ **WHITE** ❀
Habitat: WOODS, OPEN JUNE/JULY
Trail: ROUND LAKE TRAIL ❧ IN MOIST AREAS

Parviflorus means small-flowered, but this is a misnomer because the plant has a showy large white flower. It is a nice garden plant with good fall color. Delicious raspberrylike berries ripen in August. Children like to load their fingers with Thimbleberries and suck them off one by one.

WILD STRAWBERRY   ***Fragaria platypetala***   ROSE

Height: 5 in.   Perennial   ❀ **WHITE** ❀
Habitat: MOIST   JUNE
Trail: GRAY EAGLE LODGE 🍂 ALONG CREEK AFTER LILY LAKE JUNCTION
This delicious little strawberry's name is derived from the Latin *fragum,*
meaning fragrant, and *platypetala,* broad-petaled. Wild Strawberry is a
useful landscape plant for a wooded area.

43

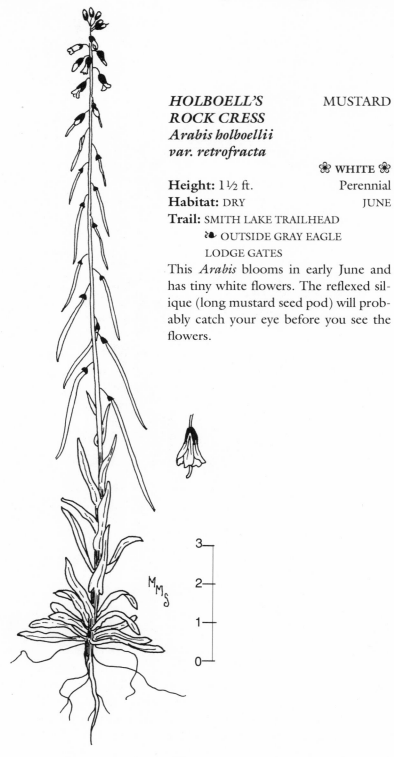

HOLBOELL'S ROCK CRESS
Arabis holboellii var. retrofracta

MUSTARD

❀ WHITE ❀

Height: 1 ½ ft.   Perennial
Habitat: DRY   JUNE
Trail: SMITH LAKE TRAILHEAD
          ❧ OUTSIDE GRAY EAGLE
          LODGE GATES

This *Arabis* blooms in early June and has tiny white flowers. The reflexed silique (long mustard seed pod) will probably catch your eye before you see the flowers.

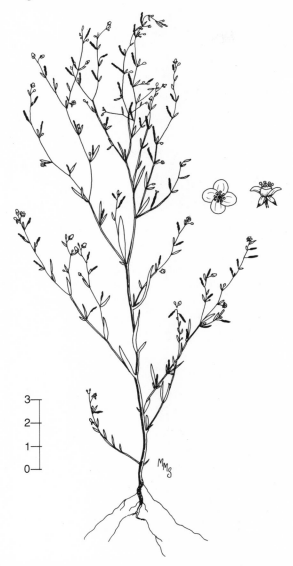

DIFFUSE GAYOPHYTUM

Gayophytum diffusum

EVENING PRIMROSE

Height: To 2 ft. Annual ❀ **WHITE-PINK** ❀

Habitat: GRAVEL FLATS JULY/AUGUST

Trail: LONG LAKE TRAIL 🐾 NEAR LILY LAKE JUNCTION

Gayophytum is a delicate plant that doesn't look as if it could survive in the hot gravel where it grows along with sandworts (*Arenaria*) and *Phlox diffusa*. Look for the long inferior ovary located beneath the calyx, typical of this plant family. Another member of the Evening Primrose family, Fireweed (*Epilobium angustifolium*), has a much more noticeable inferior ovary.

45

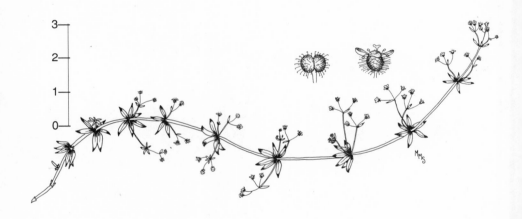

BEDSTRAW, CLEAVERS   *Galium aparine*   MADDER

Height: To 2 ft.   Annual   ❀ **WHITE** ❀
Habitat: WOODS   JUNE
Trail: LONG LAKE TRAIL ❧ BETWEEN GRAY EAGLE LODGE AND
        GRASS LAKE JUNCTION

This weak-stemmed European annual climbs on other plants for support.
It has small spines that help it to cling. It is fun to put a small piece on a
child's sweater as an aid to remembering the plant. The flowers are small
and greenish-white, a good hand-lens flower. The little twin seeds have
barbs that allow them to catch a ride and colonize a new area.

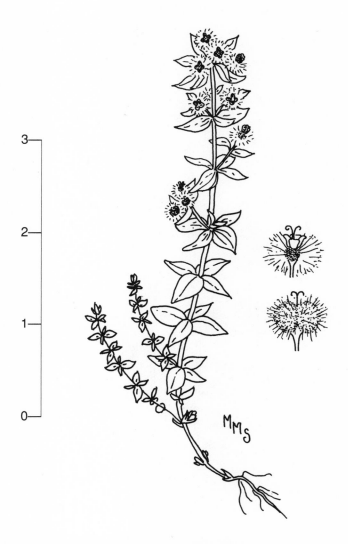

GRAY'S BEDSTRAW   *Galium grayanum*   MADDER

Height: 7 in.   Perennial   ❀ **GREEN-WHITE** ❀
Habitat: SCREE   JULY
Trail: PCT ABOVE ROUND LAKE CIRQUE

The Greek word *gala* refers to milk; some species of *Galium* were used to curdle milk. This particular bedstraw has much showier fruits than most. They are delightful to photograph because of the way the tawny fruits catch the light. You will find this *Galium* growing with Rock Fringe (*Epilobium obcordatum*) and *Primula suffrutescens* on the PCT east-facing scree slopes.

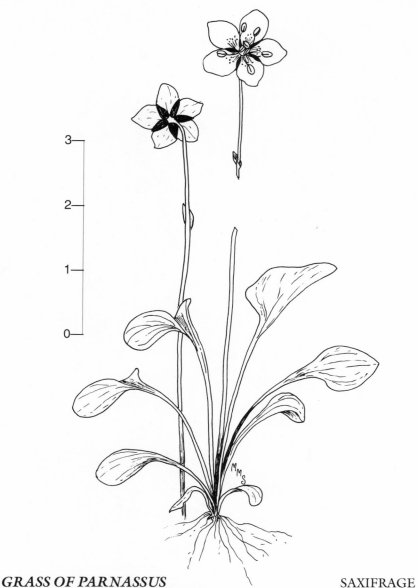

GRASS OF PARNASSUS   SAXIFRAGE
Parnassia palustris var. californica

Height: 10 in.   Perennial   ❀ **WHITE** ❀
Habitat: MOIST   JULY/AUGUST
Trail: GRAY EAGLE LODGE TRAIL TO LONG LAKE 🍃 NEAR LODGE SPRINGS
This plant is named *Parnassia* for Mt. Parnassus; *palustris* means marsh-loving. This plant blooms in late summer in wet places and is often found on the edge of lakes. The flowers are fairly simple to draw if you can find a dry log or rock to sit on while you sketch.

48

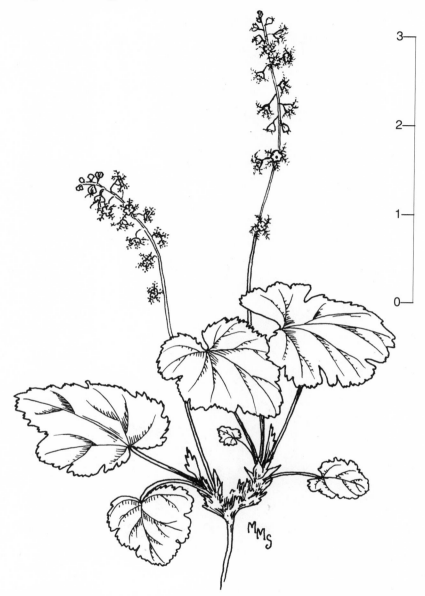

3 —
2 —
1 —
0 —

BISHOP'S CAP   ***Mitella breweri***   SAXIFRAGE

Height: To 12 in.   Perennial   ❀ **WHITE TO PALE GREEN** ❀
Habitat: MOIST   JUNE
Trail: ROUND LAKE TRAIL 🐾 NEAR SPRINGS

The origin of this name is the Greek *mitra*, meaning cap, which refers to the shape of the fruit. The greenish-white flower is an intricate structure good for close-up photography. Bishop's Cap is often found at the base of Alders or Dwarf Huckleberry.

SPREADING PHLOX   *Phlox diffusa*   PHLOX

Height: 3 in. mat   Perennial   ❀ **WHITE, PINK, LAVENDER** ❀
Habitat: ROCKS, DRY   JUNE
Trail: LONG LAKE TRAIL ❧ JUST ABOVE GRAY EAGLE LODGE

The Greek *phlox* means a flame; *diffusa* means spreading. This beautiful
cushion of fragrant flowers can be white, pink, or lavender. There is an area
along the Round Lake Trail above the mine where a "river" of phlox
perfumes the air in early June.

GRANITE GILIA   *Leptodactylon pungens*   PHLOX
ssp. pulchriflorum

Height: 3 to 8 in.   Perennial   ❀ **WHITE WITH PINK TINT** ❀
Habitat: ROCKY, DRY, SANDY   JUNE
Trail: BELOW LONG LAKE OUTLET

Translated from the Greek, the botanical name comes from *leptus*, which means narrow, and *dactylon*, meaning finger, because of the leaf lobing. *Pungens* means sharp-pointed, and *pulcher* stands for beautiful and *florum* for flowers. Can you tell the difference between this plant and *Phlox diffusa*, the common spreading phlox? Look at the leaves and the twisted flower buds.

51

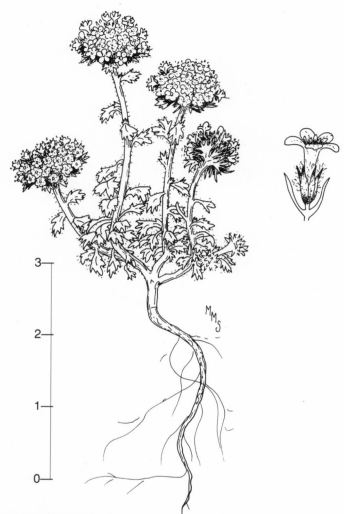

MMS

MANY-FLOWERED GILIA   *Ipomopsis congesta*   PHLOX
BALL-HEADED GILIA

Height: To 8 in.   Perennial   ❀ **WHITE** ❀
Habitat: SCREE   JULY
Trail: PCT ABOVE ROUND LAKE

The species name is obvious when you look at the crowded flowers on this flower head. *Ipomopsis congesta* is found on the Sierra crest growing with Sulphur Buckwheat (*Eriogonum umbellatum*), Balsam Root (*Balsam-orhiza sagittata*), and a prostrate form of Bitterbrush (*Purshia triden-tata*). These plants have adapted to this harsh environment with low growth, insulating hairs, reflective white surfaces, and long taproots.

DWARF CHAMAESARACHA NIGHTSHADE
Chamaesaracha nana

Height: To 4 in. Perennial ❀ **WHITE** ❀

Habitat: GRAVEL JULY

Trail: PCT 🌿 WEST OF WHITE RHYOLITE OUTCROP

This little white flower, found growing in the middle of the PCT, looks like a tomato flower, but don't eat the fruit. Tomatoes, potatoes, and Deadly Nightshade are all relatives. The name is of Greek origin, *chamae* meaning low and *saracha*, a genus of South America. The species, *nana*, means dwarf.

SANDWORT	PINK	CAPITATE SANDWORT

SANDWORT
Arenaria kingii var.
glabrescens

PINK

CAPITATE SANDWORT
Arenaria congesta

JULY	❀ WHITE ❀	JULY
Height: To 8 in.	Perennial	8 in.
Habitat: DRY		DRY GRAVEL SLOPES

Trail: BETWEEN SILVER LAKE AND LONG LAKE 🐾 IN GRAVEL

The genus name is from the Latin *arena,* meaning sand, in which this plant often grows. Sandwort looks a bit like the bridal bouquet flower Baby's Breath, which is not surprising since they are both in the Pink or Carnation family. My students remember the botanical name because of the airy appearance of the plant . . . airy arenaria. *Arenaria congesta* refers to the crowded flower heads.

54

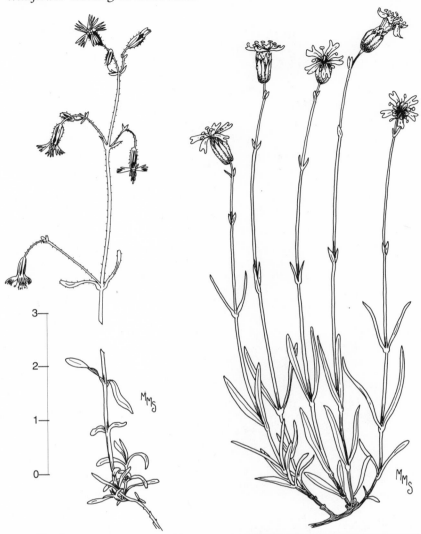

LEMMON'S CATCH-FLY   PINK   **DOUGLAS'S CATCH-FLY**
CAMPION *Silene lemmonii*   *Silene douglasii*

JULY	❀ WHITE ❀	JULY
Height: 10 in.	Perennial	8 in.
Habitat: GRAVEL, DRY		GRAVEL, DRY
Trail: GRASS LAKE TO LONG LAKE		LONG LAKE TRAIL TO SILVER LAKE

Plants of the Carnation or Pink family have opposite leaves at the swollen nodes. (The node is where you would break a carnation stem.) *Silene lemmonii* has four narrow, linear lobes to the petals and nodding flowers. Tiny gnats can become trapped in the viscid secretion that is noticeable on the calyx of the flower. *S. douglasii* has creamy white two-lobed petals with two small scalelike appendages at the base of each petal.

55

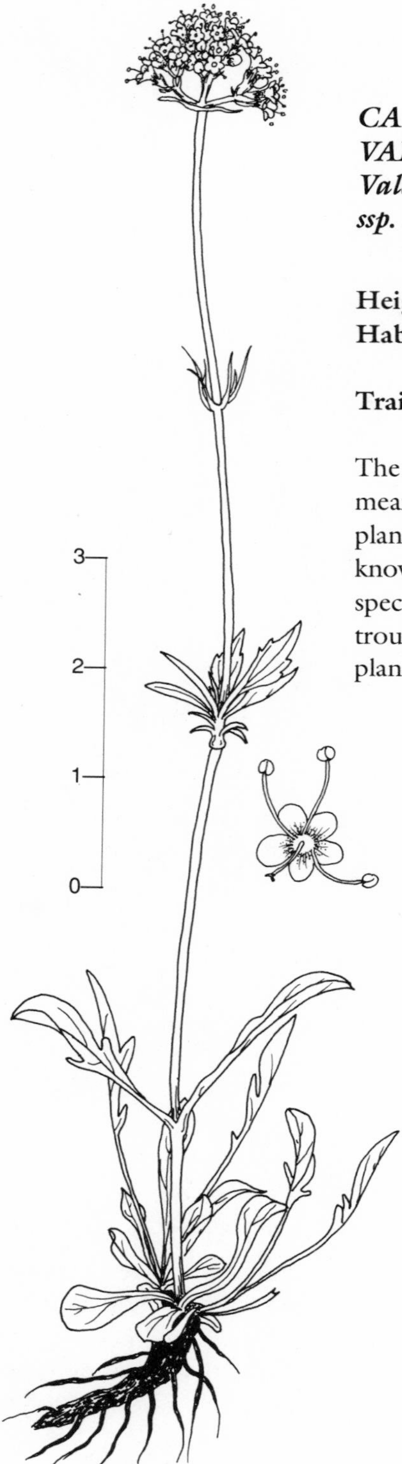

CALIFORNIA VALERIAN

VALERIAN

Valeriana capitata ssp. californica

❀ **WHITE** ❀

Height: To 1 ft. Perennial
Habitat: SHADE, MOIST OR DRY JULY/AUGUST
Trail: ROUND LAKE TRAILHEAD
❧ NEAR PARKING AREA

The medieval Latin word *valere* means to be healthy and refers to the plant's medicinal properties. It was known to the Indians, who used a species of Valerian to treat stomach troubles. Valerian is a late-blooming plant that is pretty in the garden.

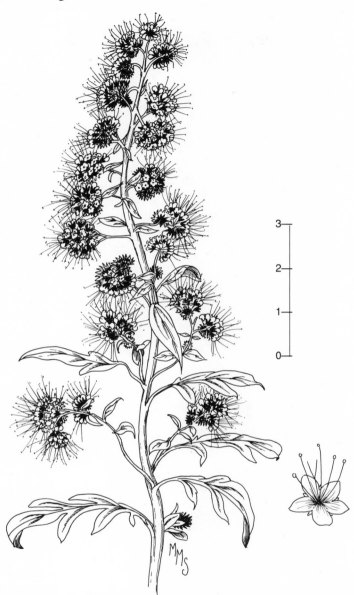

VARI-LEAF PHACELIA   *Phacelia heterophylla*   WATERLEAF

Height: 2 ft.   Perennial   ❀ **GREENISH-WHITE** ❀
Habitat: DRY GRAVEL   JUNE/JULY
Trail: GRAY EAGLE LODGE TRAILHEAD TO SMITH LAKE

The Greek word *phakelos*, a bundle, refers to the clustered flowers. *Hetero* means varied, and *phylla* is leaf. In the illustration you can see the variability of the leaf shapes. Notice also the exserted stamens and the two-pronged style that is typical of the genus *Phacelia*.

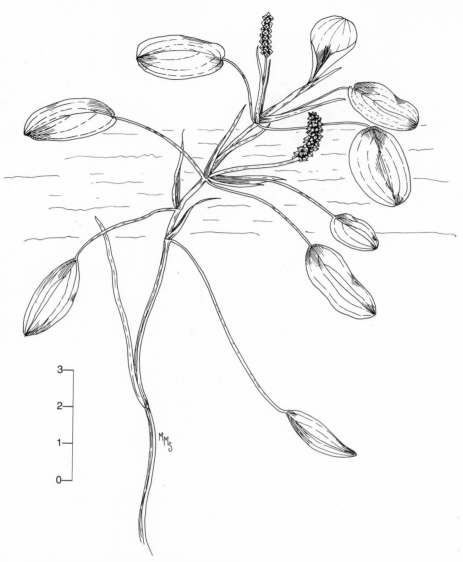

VARIOUS-LEAVED PONDWEED   PONDWEED
Potamogeton gramineus

Height: To 5 ft.   Aquatic   ❀ **GREENISH-WHITE** ❀
Habitat: LAKE   AUGUST
Trail: GRASS LAKE
     🌿 ACROSS THE BRIDGE FROM LAKES BASIN CAMPGROUND

Pondweed is found in many shallow lakes in the area. The floating leaves are leathery and the submerged leaves are thin. The leaves are an important food source for waterfowl and turn rosy-red in fall. The rhizomes are edible. Pondweed grows with Buckbean (*Menyanthes trifoliata*).

58

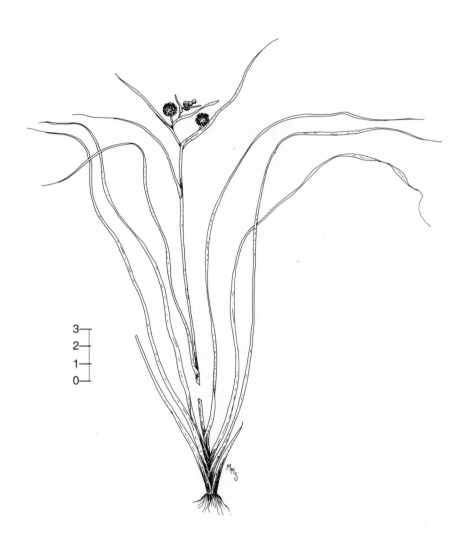

BUR-REED *Sparganium multipedunculatum* BUR-REED

Height: To 4 ft. long   Aquatic   ❀ **CREAMY-WHITE** ❀
Habitat: PONDS   AUGUST
Trail: ROUND LAKE TRAIL 🐾 AT POND BEYOND BEAR LAKE OVERLOOK
Bur-reed has very long reedlike leaves that lie on top of the water. In August a flowering head bearing creamy flowers pokes out of the water. The thickened base of the stem and the tubers on the rhizome are edible.

59

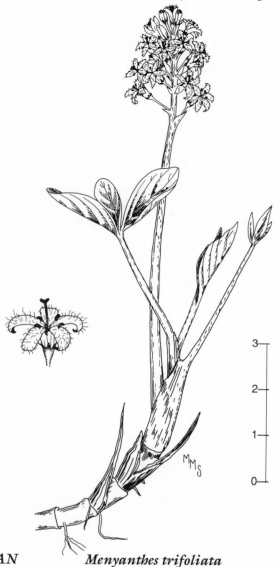

BUCKBEAN   *Menyanthes trifoliata*   GENTIAN

Height: To 15 in.   Aquatic   ❀ **WHITE** ❀

Habitat: LAKE   JULY

Trail: GRASS LAKE 🍂 FROM BRIDGE NEAR CAMPGROUND
        AROUND THE NORTH SIDE

The Greek *men* means month and *anthos* is flower, referring to the long blooming time of Buckbean. The species name, *trifoliata*, refers to the three leaflets. Look closely at the hairs on the petals. This plant is interesting to photograph for scenery or in close-up. The root is edible if boiled in water that is changed several times. Buckbean also grows in the Swiss Alps.

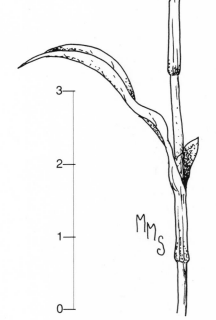

LADIES' THUMB   BUCKWHEAT
BISTORT
Polygonum bistortoides

❀ **WHITE** ❀

Height: To 2 ft.   Perennial
Habitat: MOIST MEADOWS   JULY
Trail: MEADOWS NEAR GRASS LAKE
   🍃 BELOW LONG LAKE OUTLET

The genus *Polygonum*, from the Greek, can be broken down into *poly*, meaning many, and *gonu*, meaning knee or joint, referring to the jointed stems of this genus. These joints are usually covered with a papery sheath. Bistort had several Indian uses; the leaves and roots were edible if cooked and the seeds could be ground into flour.

61

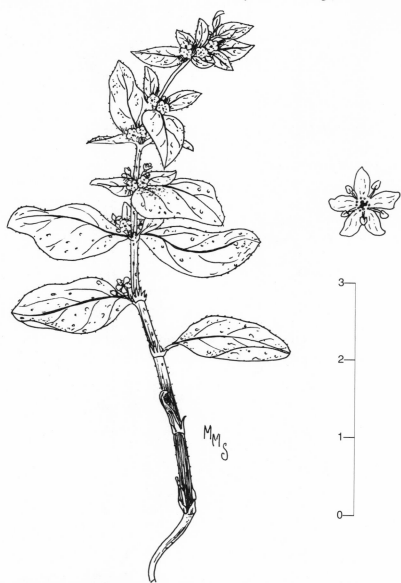

DAVIS'S KNOTWEED   *Polygonum davisiae*   BUCKWHEAT

Height: 8 to 12 in.   Perennial   ❀ **WHITE** ❀
Habitat: GRAVEL SLOPES   JULY
Trail: SILVER LAKE TO ROUND LAKE 🍃 ON NORTH-FACING SLOPES
This Knotweed always provokes interest as it emerges from the ground a
few weeks after the snow melts, usually in late May, because of the bright
red stems. During the summer the plant's small flowers and ordinary
foliage are not particularly noticeable. However, in late August the stems
and leaves turn red again and give a real autumn feeling to the mountains.

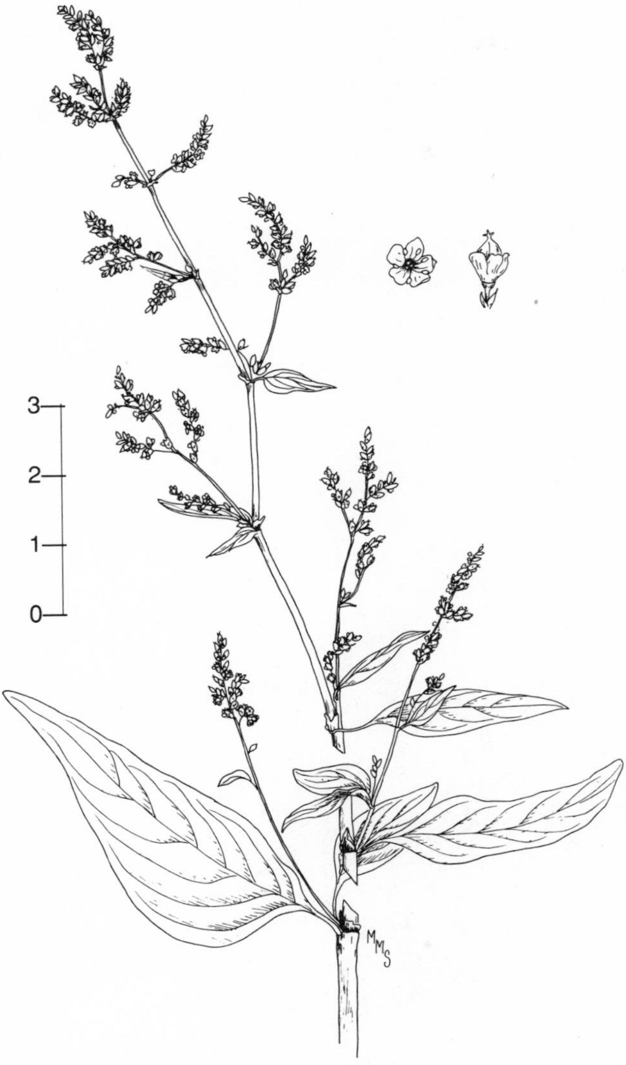

ALPINE KNOTWEED ***Polygonum*** BUCKWHEAT
MOUNTAIN LACE ***phytolaccaefolium***

Height: 3 to 5 ft. Perennial ❀ **WHITE** ❀
Habitat: ROCKS, MOIST JULY
Trail: SILVER LAKE TO PCT TRAIL
❧ ALONG SPRINGS FROM THE PCT ABOVE MUD LAKE

The species name can be broken down to make it less overwhelming. The name *Phytolacca* refers to the plant Pokeweed and *folia* is leaf. This plant has leaves like Pokeweed, an eastern plant. It is easy to see the papery sheaths on the joints of this large *Polygonum*. Mountain Lace is beautiful near the PCT spring garden between Helgramite Lake and the PCT.

SHASTA KNOTWEED   *Polygonum shastense*   BUCKWHEAT

Height: 4 in.   Perennial   ❀ **WHITE** ❀

Habitat: GRAVEL SLOPES   JULY/AUGUST

Trail: ROUND LAKE TRAIL; PCT ABOVE ROUND LAKE

Observe the thickened joints and notice the papery sheath that often covers a part of the joint; this should help you recognize the genus *Polygonum*. Look at the delicate flower, with a pink midvein on the petal. This plant grows prostrate on the ground and sprawls rather than forming a mat.

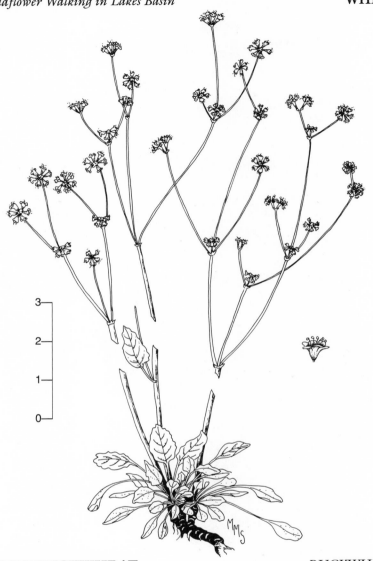

NUDE BUCKWHEAT   BUCKWHEAT
Eriogonum latifolium ssp. nudum

Height: To 1½ ft.   Perennial   ❀ **WHITE** ❀
Habitat: GRAVEL   JULY
Trail: BEAR LAKE TRAILHEAD
      🐌 ON LAKES BASIN CAMPGROUND ENTRY ROAD

The species, *latifolium,* means wide leaf, and *nudum* refers to the nude or leafless stem. The flowers of Nude Buckwheat should be observed with a hand lens to see the tiny flowers that create the white-to-pink tinted puffs on top of the tall stems. This Buckwheat is common in dry places at lower elevations.

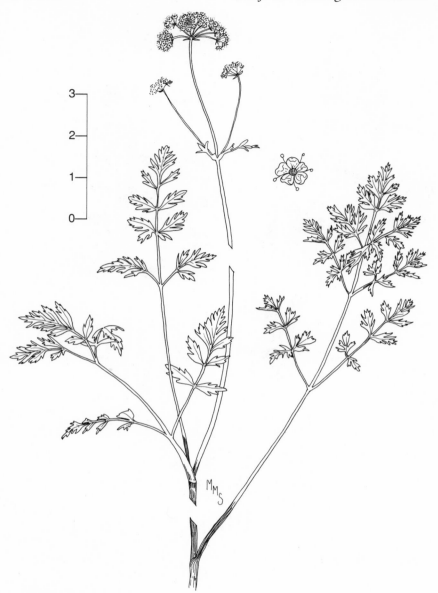

GRAY'S LOVAGE   *Ligusticum grayi*   CARROT

Height: To 2½ ft.   Perennial   ❁ **WHITE** ❁
Habitat: MEADOWS AND OPEN WOODS   JULY
Trail: GRAY EAGLE LODGE TO LONG LAKE ❧ NEAR LILY LAKE JUNCTION
Lovage is a delicate lacy plant that smells like celery and looks a bit like
Queen Anne's Lace. Don't eat members of this plant family; there are too
many poisonous members that are difficult to tell apart. This plant usually
grows in part shade, often with Snowberry (*Symphoricarpos acutus*).

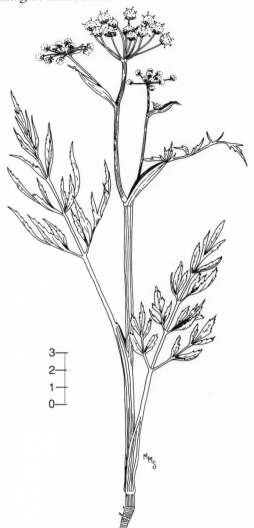

RANGER BUTTONS　*Sphenosciadium capitellatum*　CARROT
WHITE HEADS

Height: To 5 ft.　　　　Perennial　　　　❀ **WHITE** ❀
Habitat: MOIST　　　　　　　　　　　　JULY/AUGUST
Trail: GRAY EAGLE LODGE MEADOW

The genus is of Greek origin, from *sphenos,* meaning a wedge, and *sciadios,* an umbrella, referring to the shape. The species, *capitellatum,* means small-headed, referring to the "buttons." This plant is very poisonous. It somewhat resembles *Angelica breweri* and Cow Parsnip (*Heracleum lanatum*); but the individual flower heads, or "buttons," are more rounded than either of these other plants. All three plants are large members of the Carrot family.

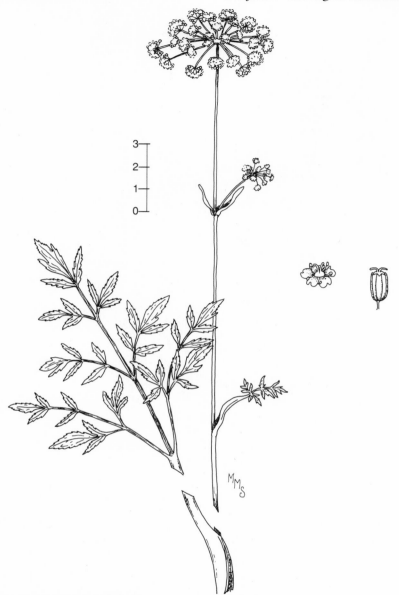

BREWER'S ANGELICA   *Angelica breweri*   CARROT

Height: To 5 ft   Perennial   ❀ WHITE ❀

Habitat: OPEN WOODS AND SLOPES   AUGUST

Trail: GRASS LAKE TO LONG LAKE; SIERRA BUTTES TRAIL

The genus name from the Latin, *Angelica*, refers to the plant's medicinal properties. The flowers and the large-size plant are similar to Cow Parsnip (*Heracleum lanatum*), but the leaves of the Cow Parsnip are much heavier and palmate-shaped. Angelica is spectacular on the Sierra Buttes trail.

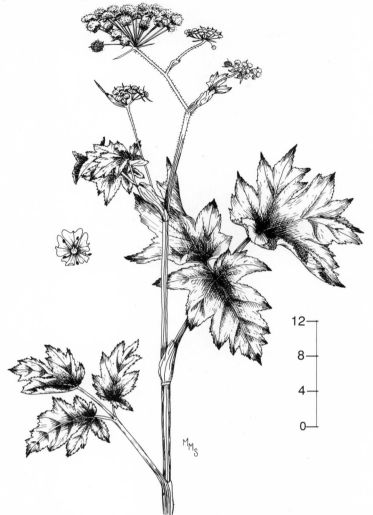

COW PARSNIP	*Heracleum lanatum*	CARROT

Height: To 5 ft.   Perennial   ❀ **WHITE** ❀
Habitat: MOIST   JULY
Trail: IN ASPEN NEAR GRASS LAKE

This large plant with its beautiful lacework of small flowers arranged in an umbel shape is named after Hercules, who supposedly first used this giant herb as a medicine. The root may be cooked and eaten, the stems peeled and eaten raw or cooked. Dry the plant and burn it to retrieve a salty ash. At lower elevations be careful not to confuse it with Poison Hemlock (*Conium maculatum*), which is also a large plant but has carrotlike leaves and purple spots on its stem. *Angelica breweri* and poisonous Ranger Buttons could also be confused with Cow Parsnip. Cow Parsnip is attractive as a background plant in a large garden.

YAMPA *Perideridia bolanderi*	CARROT	*PARISH'S YAMPA* *Perideridia parishii*
JULY	✿ **WHITE** ✿	JULY
Height: 1 to 1½ ft.	Perennial	1 ft.
Habitat: MEADOWS		MOIST MEADOWS

Trail: ROUND LAKE TRAIL 🌿 BEYOND GOLD LAKE LODGE

The edible tuberous root tastes starchy. The seeds can be cooked and eaten. But don't eat them until you are an expert at identifying the Carrot family. These plants, which look like a delicate Queen Anne's Lace, are responsible for the beautiful white cast of many mountain meadows and stream banks. *Perideridia bolanderi* has slightly longer terminal leaflets than *P. parishii*.

CORN LILY   *Veratrum californicum*   LILY

Height: To 5 ft.   Perennial   ❀ **WHITE** ❀
Habitat: MOIST   JULY
Trail: ROUND LAKE 🐾 NEAR GOLD LAKE LODGE

This plant resembles a cornstalk. However, all parts of the Corn Lily are poisonous. We often see large meadows of Corn Lily that never seem to bloom. They are waiting for ideal conditions, usually the right amount of moisture at the right time. They are reliably beautiful near the springs that supply Gold Lake Lodge. Peek into an individual flower and see the green V at the base of each petal.

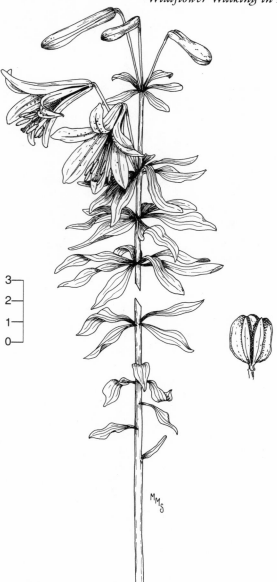

WASHINGTON LILY *Lilium washingtonianum* LILY

Height: 4 ft.   Bulb   ❀ **WHITE** ❀
Habitat: SLOPES, DRY   JULY
Trail: SOUTHEAST SLOPE OF MT. ELWELL

The Washington Lily looks like an Easter Lily and is very fragrant. The few places I have seen Washington Lily seem to be where deer cannot browse them, such as in the middle of a Manzanita thicket. We collected some seed at Lake Tahoe and four years later have the plants on a hot slope in our mountain garden.

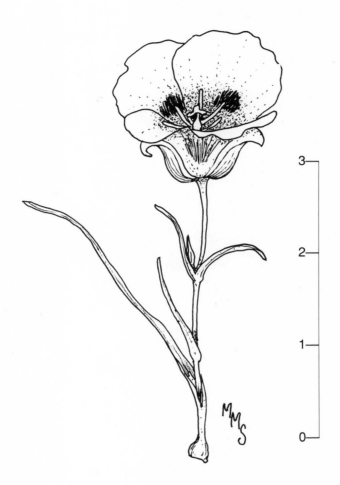

MARIPOSA LILY SEGO LILY	*Calochortus leichtlinii*	LILY

Height: 4 in.　　　　　　Bulb　　　　　❀ **WHITE** ❀

Habitat: SCREE　　　　　　　　　　　　JULY/AUGUST

Trail: PCT

The genus name, *Calochortus*, is of Greek derivation, from *kallos*, meaning beautiful, and *chortus*, meaning grass. Mariposa is Spanish for butterfly. On the PCT the plant is a dwarf because of the harsh environment. Mariposa Lily is also found in the rock garden near the junction of the Grass Lake to Long Lake trail and the Gray Eagle Lodge trail.

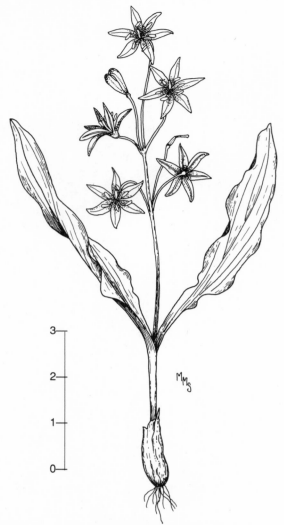

FAWN LILY   *Erythronium purpurascens*   LILY

Height: 7 in.   Bulb   ❀ **CREAM TO PALE YELLOW** ❀
Habitat: SLOPES, DRY   MAY/JUNE
Trail: FERN FALLS OVERLOOK

     🌰 ON GOLD LAKE HIGHWAY ACROSS BRIDGE

The species name, *purpurascens,* means becoming purple, in this case just a tint as the flowers age and wither. The plants' bulbs are buried as deep as ten inches in between large rocks, a good survival mechanism for a lovely garden plant. It takes about three years from seed to develop flowers. This is a good flower to sketch. There is an acre or two of Fawn Lily located along the beginning of the Sierra Buttes Lookout trail. The problem is that the plant blooms before the snow has completely melted off the trail.

WHITE BRODIAEA   LILY
Brodiaea hyacinthina
[Triteleia hyacinthina]

❀ WHITE ❀

Height: To 1½ ft.   Bulb
Habitat: MOIST   JULY/AUGUST
Trail: LILY LAKE
🐾 FROM GRAY EAGLE LODGE

The White Brodiaea or White Hyacinth looks like an onion but lacks the
typical onion odor. The flower is
united into a tube below the spreading
petal tips. White Hyacinth is common
at lower elevations.

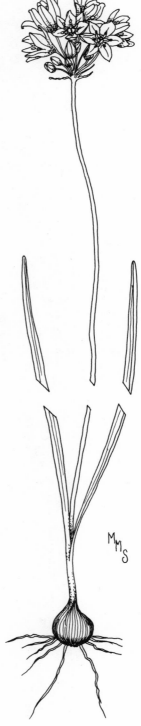

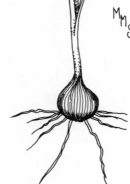

3—

2—

1—

0—

75

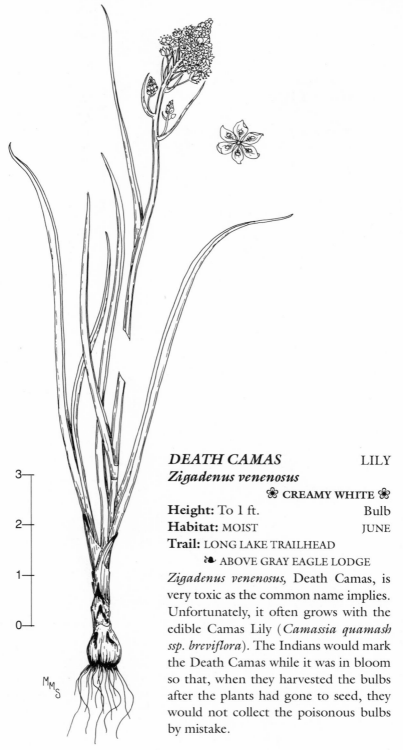

DEATH CAMAS   LILY
Zigadenus venenosus

❀ **CREAMY WHITE** ❀

Height: To 1 ft.   Bulb
Habitat: MOIST   JUNE
Trail: LONG LAKE TRAILHEAD
    🍃 ABOVE GRAY EAGLE LODGE

Zigadenus venenosus, Death Camas, is very toxic as the common name implies. Unfortunately, it often grows with the edible Camas Lily (*Camassia quamash ssp. breviflora*). The Indians would mark the Death Camas while it was in bloom so that, when they harvested the bulbs after the plants had gone to seed, they would not collect the poisonous bulbs by mistake.

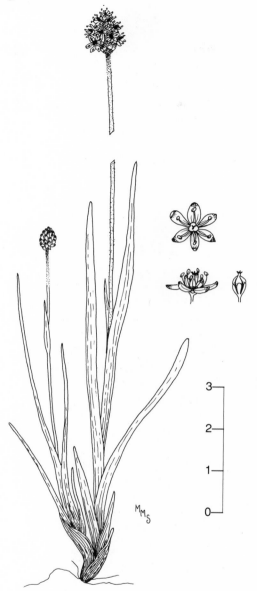

TOFIELDIA   *Tofieldia glutinosa ssp. occidentalis*   LILY

Height: To 8 in.   Perennial   ❀ **CREAMY WHITE** ❀
Habitat: MOIST   JULY
Trail: LONG LAKE TRAILHEAD
          ❧ AT END OF LAKES BASIN CAMPGROUND ROAD

Tofieldia glutinosa refers to the stickiness on the stem of the plant. Using your hand lens or a magnifying glass, you can see glands on the stem. Can you see the six tepals for each little lily flower? This plant is toxic.

77

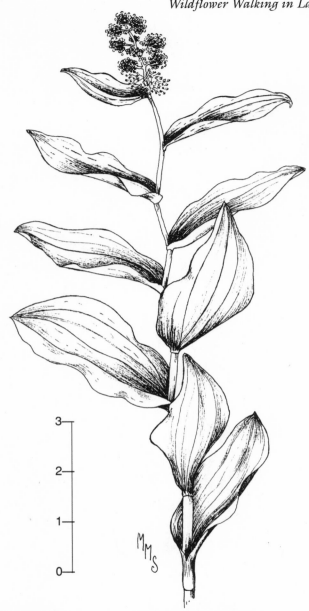

FAT SOLOMON   *Smilacina racemosa*   LILY
FALSE SOLOMON'S-SEAL

Height: To 2 ft.   Perennial   ❀ **WHITE** ❀
Habitat: WOODS   JUNE/JULY
Trail: NEAR INLET TO GRASS LAKE

Smilacina racemosa, Fat Solomon, has a heavier appearance than *S. stellata*. The species name refers to the branched racemose flower head. This is a good landscape plant for a dry shady garden.

STAR-LIKE   LILY
SOLOMON'S-SEAL
Smilacina stellata

❀ WHITE ❀

Height: To 2 ft.   Perennial
Habitat: WOODS, MOIST   JUNE/JULY
Trail: NEAR INLET TO GRASS LAKE

The species name, *stellata*, means star-
like, referring to the delicate flowers.
This whole plant has a more delicate
appearance than *S. racemosa* and it
grows in a more moist situation.

NEVADA LEWISIA   *Lewisia nevadensis*   PURSLANE

Height: 4 in.   Perennial   ❀ **WHITE** ❀
Habitat: MEADOWS, MOIST   JUNE
Trail: GRASS LAKE 🍂 SUNNY, MOIST GRAVEL AREAS NEAR ASPEN GROVES
Lewisia was named after Meriwether Lewis of the Lewis and Clark
expedition of the early 1800s. *Lewisia nevadensis* belongs to the same
genus as the state flower of Montana, *Lewisia rediviva*, or Bitterroot. The
Indians dried Lewisia roots, making them less bitter by peeling the outer
brown covering.

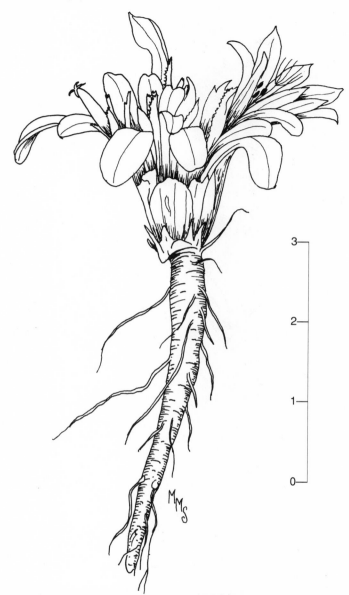

KELLOGG'S LEWISIA   *Lewisia kelloggii*   PURSLANE

Height: To 4 in.   Perennial   ❀ **WHITE TO PINK** ❀
Habitat: SCREE RIDGES   JULY
Trail: PCT ABOVE ROUND LAKE; SIERRA BUTTES LOOKOUT TRAIL
Beautiful Kellogg's Lewisia is a relative of Bitterroot (*Lewisia rediviva*),
the state flower of Montana. In the scree above Round Lake, along the
PCT, the showy flower is white, and on the Sierra Buttes trail it is pink. In
both cases it is on a slightly eastern slope just below the actual ridge.

81

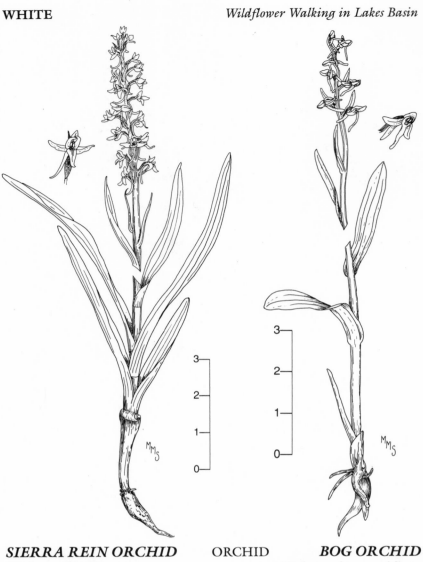

SIERRA REIN ORCHID   ORCHID   **BOG ORCHID**
Habenaria dilatata   *Habenaria sparsiflora*
JULY   ❀ WHITE ❀   JULY
Height: To 1½ ft.   Perennial   To 1 ft.
Habitat: MOIST   MOIST, SHADED
Trail: GRAY EAGLE LODGE MEADOW

The Latin word *habena* means rein of a horse, referring to the shape of the
spur petal, which is longer than the lip petal. *Dilatata* means spread out.
The orchids occur in many of the wet meadows that are easily damaged
when walked on, so try to observe these beautiful plants where they grow
along the trails. There are many spots along the Grass Lake to Long Lake
trail where springs cross the trail. You will find the Rein Orchid next to the
trail and the pale green Bog Orchid near it under willows or huckleberries.

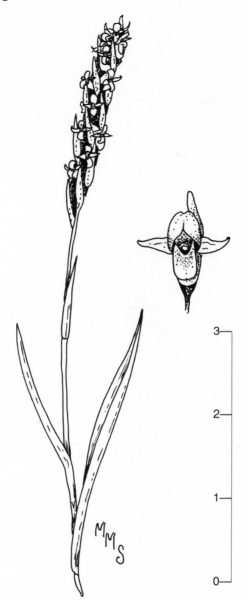

LADIES' TRESSES   *Spiranthes romanzoffiana*   ORCHID

Height: 3 to 5 in.   Perennial   ❀ **WHITE** ❀

Habitat: MOIST   JULY

Trail: GRASP LAKE 🍀 ON PENINSULA ON NORTH SIDE OF LAKE

The origin of *Spiranthes* is Greek, from *speira,* spiral, and *anthos,* flower. Notice the spiral pattern of the flowers on the stem. This plant also can be found in the wet areas below Long Lake outlet. The plant is quite rare.

WHITE-VEINED SHINLEAF   WINTERGREEN   *SIDEBELLS*
Pyrola picta   *Pyrola secunda*

JULY	❀ WHITISH ❀	JULY
Height: 8 in.	Perennial	6 in.
Habitat: WOODS, DRY		WOODS

Trail: ROUND LAKE TRAIL 🍀 IN SHADE OF RED FIRS

The genus name, *Pyrola*, means pearlike, and *picta* means decorated, referring to the prominent white veining on the leaves. *Pyrola picta ssp. dentata* (not illustrated), once called *P. pallida* because of the pale green wavy leaves, grows on the Sierra Buttes Lookout trail. *Pyrola secunda*, Sidebells or One-sided Wintergreen, is more delicate than *P. picta*. It grows under the pines near Grass Lake.

MACLOSKEY'S VIOLET   *Viola macloskeyi*   VIOLA

Height: 2 in.   Perennial   ❀ **WHITE** ❀
Habitat: MOIST   JUNE/JULY
Trail: GRASS LAKE 🍂 PENINSULA ON NORTH SIDE OF THE LAKE
This tiny white violet can form a dense mat with its creeping stolons and
thus can stabilize lake and stream banks. It is found in either sun or shade
as long as the soil is wet. Often it grows with little gold Tinker's Penny
(*Hypericum anagalloides*).

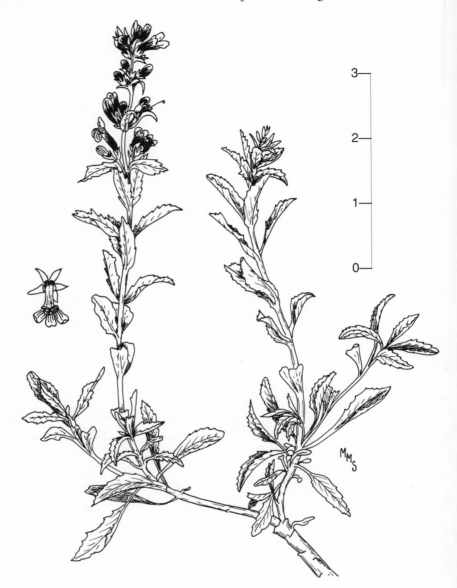

HOT-ROCK PENSTEMON   *Penstemon deustus*   FIGWORT

Height: 5 to 12 in.   Perennial   ❀ **WHITE** ❀
Habitat: ROCKS   JULY
Trail: GRASS LAKE TO LONG LAKE 🐾 ON ROCKS AFTER STREAM CROSSING
The origin of the name is Greek, from *pente*, meaning five, and *stemon*,
meaning stamens. The species name, *deustus*, means burned. As the
common name implies, this plant grows on hot rocks. Look inside the
flower at the delicate red nectar guides.

86

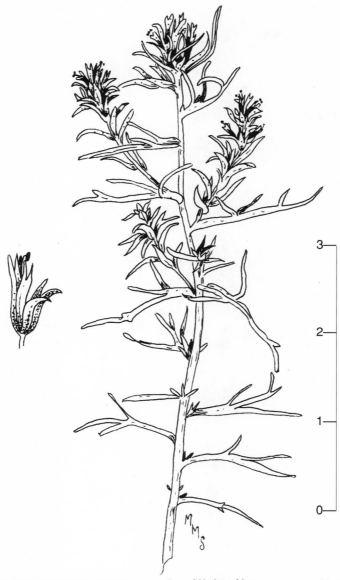

HAIRY PAINTBRUSH	*Castilleja pilosa* FIGWORT

Height: To 8 in.   Perennial   ❀ **WHITISH** ❀
Habitat: GRAVEL   JUNE/JULY
Trail: BEAR LAKE TRAIL 🐾 ABOVE BEAR LAKE

The species name, *pilosa*, means hairy. Hairy Paintbrush is one of those plants about which my students would say, "This isn't a paintbrush, is it?" The offwhite, dusty-pink flower with little black stigma protruding certainly doesn't look like the typical paintbrush, but the shape of the flowering head gives it away. This is a good hand-lens plant.

87

LONG-STALKED CLOVER   *Trifolium longipes*   PEA

Height: 7 in.   Perennial   ❀ **WHITE** ❀
Habitat: MOIST   JUNE/JULY
Trail: GRAY EAGLE LODGE TO LONG LAKE 🍃 AT CREEK CROSSING
The botanical name is derived from the Latin *tres*, meaning three, and
folium, meaning leaf. *Longipes*, the species name, refers to the long stalk or
stem. The flowers are upright until they have been pollinated, after which
they droop. Clover leaves can be steamed and eaten, and a tea can be made
from dried flower heads.

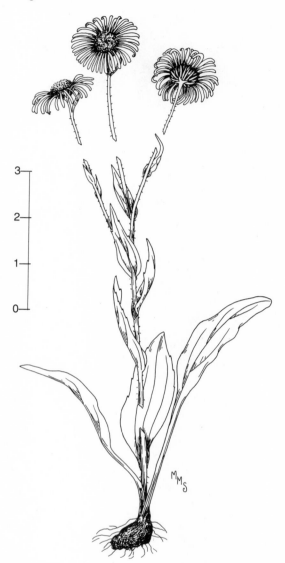

COULTER'S DAISY   *Erigeron coulteri*   COMPOSITE

Height: 8 to 12 in.   Perennial   ❀ **WHITE** ❀
Habitat: MOIST   JULY
Trail: GRASS LAKE TO LONG LAKE

This tidy white daisy grows in fairly deep shade near streams. It is easy to
tell from an *Aster* by looking at the underside of the flower. Notice that all
the green bracts on *Erigeron* are the same length (see illustration), whereas
the bracts on *Aster* overlap like shingles, giving a messy appearance. Asters
usually have many flower heads to a stem.

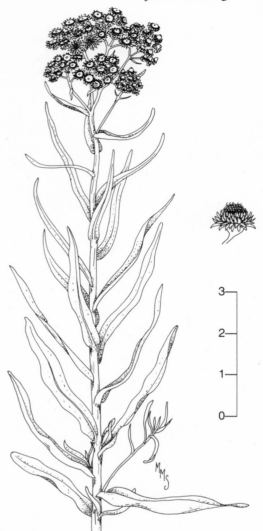

PEARLY EVERLASTING   COMPOSITE
Anaphalis margaritacea

Height: To 2 ft.   Perennial   ❀ WHITE ❀
Habitat: OPEN WOODS   AUGUST
Trail: GRASS LAKE 🌿 NEAR CAMPGROUND

Anaphalis means everlasting, and *margaritacea* means pearly. This plant dries nicely if hung upside down so the stems don't wilt. I have used the dried flowers as wreaths on Christmas cards. They have a pungent aroma whether fresh or dried. The flowers seem to be whiter and larger the farther north in California and Oregon they grow. Both the Swiss Edelweiss and the Pearly Everlasting are in the Cudweed tribe of the Composite family, characterized by strawlike, everlasting flowers.

90

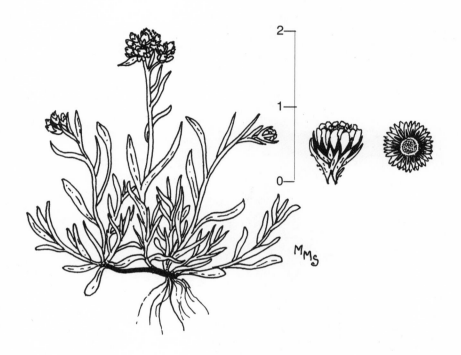

PUSSY TOES   *Antennaria rosea*   COMPOSITE
ROSY EVERLASTING

Height: 6 in.   Perennial   ❀ **WHITE-PINK** ❀
Habitat: DRY   JULY
Trail: LONG LAKE TRAIL ❧ NEAR OUTLET OF LONG LAKE

The genus is from the Latin word *antenna*, because the pappus hairs of the male flowers have swollen tips that resemble the antennae of a butterfly. The species name refers to the pink tint of the flower. There is another Pussy Toes in Lakes Basin, *Antennaria corymbosa*, that lacks the pink cast. This plant is closely related to the Swiss Edelweiss and the Pearly Everlasting (*Anaphalis margaritacea*). It is a beautiful garden plant because of the silver mat foliage and the little pinkish-white flowers.

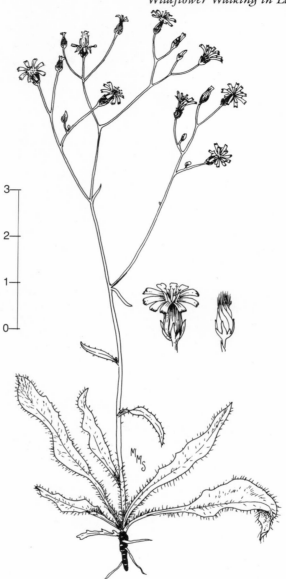

WHITE-FLOWERED HAWKWEED   COMPOSITE
Hieracium albiflorum

Height: 15 in.   Perennial   ❀ **WHITE** ❀
Habitat: OPEN WOODS   JULY
Trail: GRASS LAKE TO LONG LAKE ❧ NEAR THE CREEK CROSSING

The Greek word *hierax* means hawk. An ancient belief was that hawks used the sap (a milky juice) of Hawkweed to sharpen their eyesight. *Albiflorum* translates to white flower. This plant is a member of the Dandelion tribe in the Composite family.

YARROW   ***Achillea lanulosa***   COMPOSITE

Height: 2 ft.   Perennial   ❀ **WHITE** ❀
Habitat: MEADOWS   AUGUST
Trail: ROUND LAKE TRAIL 🐾 NEAR GOLD LAKE LODGE

This plant was named for the ancient Greek warrior Achilles, who is said to have used it medicinally to stop the flow of blood and for healing cuts and bruises. These curative properties are responsible for some of the other common names: Soldier's Woundwort, Bloodwort, Staunchgrass, and Staunchweed. The Indians used Yarrow for toothaches, headaches, and stomach aches. The species name refers to the woolly leaves.

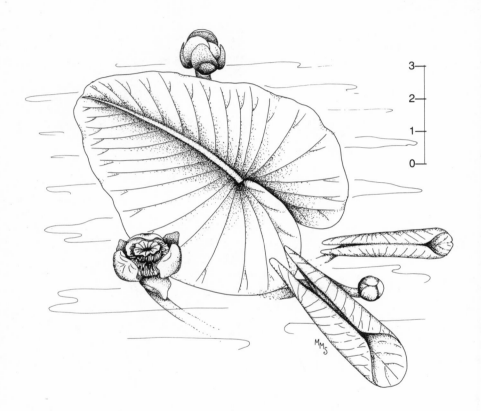

YELLOW POND LILY   *Nuphar polysepalum*   WATER LILY
COW LILY

Height: Varies with pond depth   Aquatic   ❀ **YELLOW** ❀
Habitat: PONDS AND SHALLOW LAKES   JULY
Trail: GRASS LAKE; LILY LAKE

Nuphar is an Arabic name. The species, *polysepalum*, means many-sepaled. The yellow flowers have from five to twelve sepals. The petals are very similar to the numerous stamens. The best place to see Pond Lilies is on the northern peninsula of Grass Lake. The seeds and roots were used by the Indians.

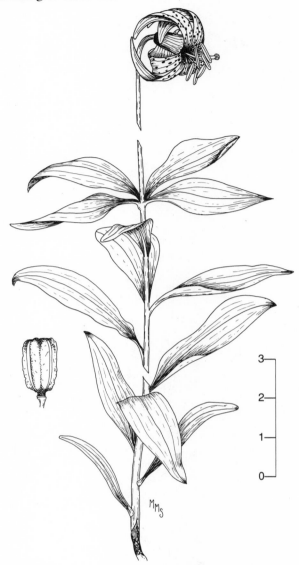

LEOPARD LILY   *Lilium pardalinum*   LILY
TIGER LILY, TURK'S CAP LILY

Height: To 7 ft.   Bulb   ❀ **ORANGE** ❀
Habitat: MOIST   JULY
Trail: GRASS LAKE TO LONG LAKE TRAIL

Pardalinum means leopardlike. The height of Leopard Lily varies from two to seven feet. As long as the petals recurve on themselves, however, you have this one species of Leopard Lily in Lakes Basin. It is very prevalent throughout the region wherever there is moisture.

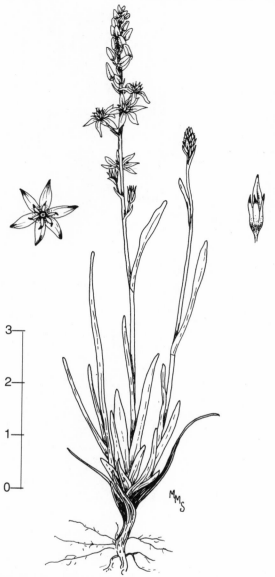

BOG-ASPHODEL   *Narthecium californicum*   LILY

Height: To 22 in.   Perennial   ❀ **YELLOW** ❀
Habitat: MOIST   JULY
Trail: LONG LAKE TRAIL ❧ NEAR GRAY EAGLE LODGE SPRINGS

Bog-asphodel is fairly rare south of Lakes Basin. This bright yellow
member of the Lily family has a creeping root stock and is quite prevalent
in the northern part of the Lakes Basin region. Bog-asphodel will be found
growing with another member of the Lily family, *Tofieldia glutinosa ssp.
occidentalis.*

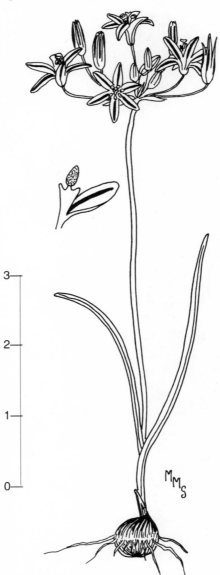

GOLDEN BRODIAEA   *Brodiaea lutea var. analina*   LILY
MOUNTAIN PRETTY   *[Triteleia lutea var. analina]*
  FACE

Height: 5 to 8 in.   Bulb   ❀ **YELLOW** ❀
Habitat: DRY   JUNE/JULY
Trail: LAKES BASIN CAMPGROUND ❧ IN GRAVEL AREAS

Lutea refers to the yellow of the flower. Look closely at the flower and spot the forked filament with its blue or yellow anther between the forks. The Indians harvested Brodiaea bulbs.

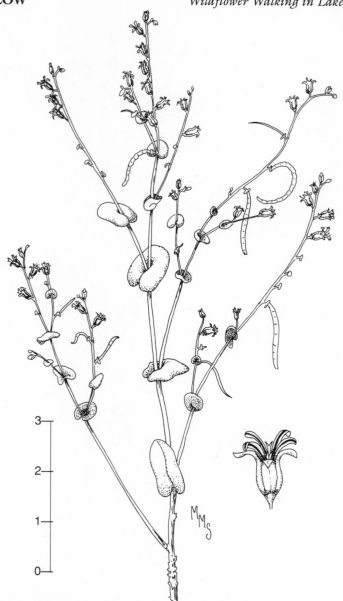

JEWEL FLOWER   *Streptanthus tortuosus*   MUSTARD

Height: 1 to 2 ft.   Annual   ❀ **VIOLET TO YELLOW** ❀

Habitat: ROCKS, DRY   JULY

Trail: GRASS LAKE TO LONG LAKE ❧ JUST AFTER THE STREAM CROSSING

Streptanthus is Greek in origin, from *streptas,* meaning twisted, and *anthos,* meaning flower, a reference to the petals. The leaves are more noticeable than the flowers. They are chartreuse and wrap around the stem the way Miner's Lettuce does. Don't sample this plant; its edibility is unknown.

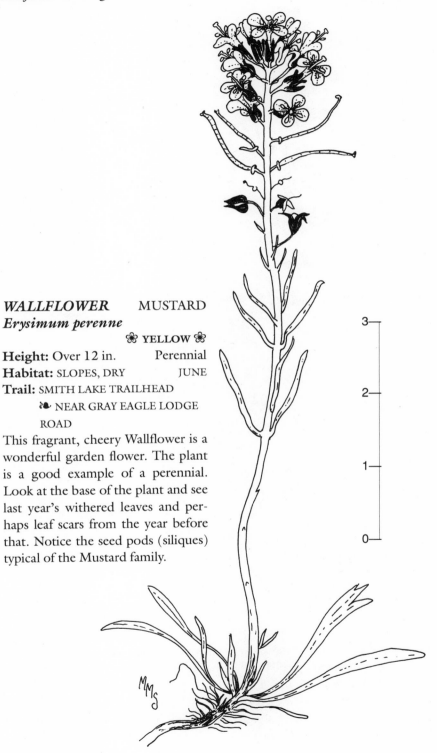

WALLFLOWER MUSTARD
Erysimum perenne

❀ YELLOW ❀

Height: Over 12 in.   Perennial
Habitat: SLOPES, DRY   JUNE
Trail: SMITH LAKE TRAILHEAD
    ❧ NEAR GRAY EAGLE LODGE
    ROAD

This fragrant, cheery Wallflower is a wonderful garden flower. The plant is a good example of a perennial. Look at the base of the plant and see last year's withered leaves and perhaps leaf scars from the year before that. Notice the seed pods (siliques) typical of the Mustard family.

3—
2—
1—
0—

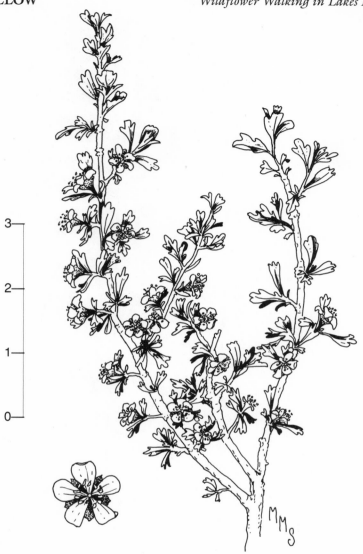

ANTELOPE BRUSH BITTERBRUSH   *Purshia tridentata*   ROSE

Height: To 6 ft.   Shrub   ❀ **YELLOW** ❀
Habitat: SCREE   JUNE
Trail: PCT

Bitterbrush, normally a good-sized shrub, is a dwarf when it grows in the harsh environment on the PCT. Perhaps grazing by deer is also responsible for its being only about a foot tall here. The species name refers to the three teeth at the tip of each silvery-gray leaf. Pale yellow Bitterbrush can be quite showy growing along Highway 89, on southwest-facing banks, between Truckee and Sierraville.

WATER-PLANTAIN   RANUNCULUS
BUTTERCUP   *Ranunculus alismaefolius*

Height: 7 in.   Perennial   ❀ **YELLOW** ❀
Habitat: MEADOWS, MOIST   JUNE
Trail: GRASS LAKE ❧ NEAR OUTLET

The genus name, *Ranunculus*, is derived from *rana*, meaning frog. This Water-plantain Buttercup, like the frog, is always found in moist areas. Most Buttercups have a palmate or crowfoot pattern to their leaves; however, this leaf is entire like that of the Water-plantain, hence its common name. Western Buttercup (*Ranunculus occidentalis var. eisenii*) can be found in meadows.

101

FAN-LEAF CINQUEFOIL
Potentilla flabellifolia

GRACEFUL CINQUEFOIL
Potentilla gracilis
ssp. nuttallii

ROSE

❀ YELLOW ❀

FAN-LEAF CINQUEFOIL		GRACEFUL CINQUEFOIL
JULY		JULY
Height: 8 in.	Perennial	To 1½ ft.
Habitat: MEADOW, MOIST		MEADOW, MOIST

Trail: UPPER HELGRAMITE LAKE ON SOUTH SIDE; ROUND LAKE TRAIL

Potentilla, from the Latin *potens*, powerful, refers to the plant's medicinal properties, such as tannins, that stop bleeding. *Flabellifolia* refers to the fanlike foliage. The flower is dark yellow. Notice the heavy stems and the leaf scars at the base of the plant from last year, indicating a perennial plant. The other species, *gracilis*, means graceful or slender. Note the palmate shape of the leaves in contrast to the pinnate shape of the leaves of *Potentilla glandulosa*.

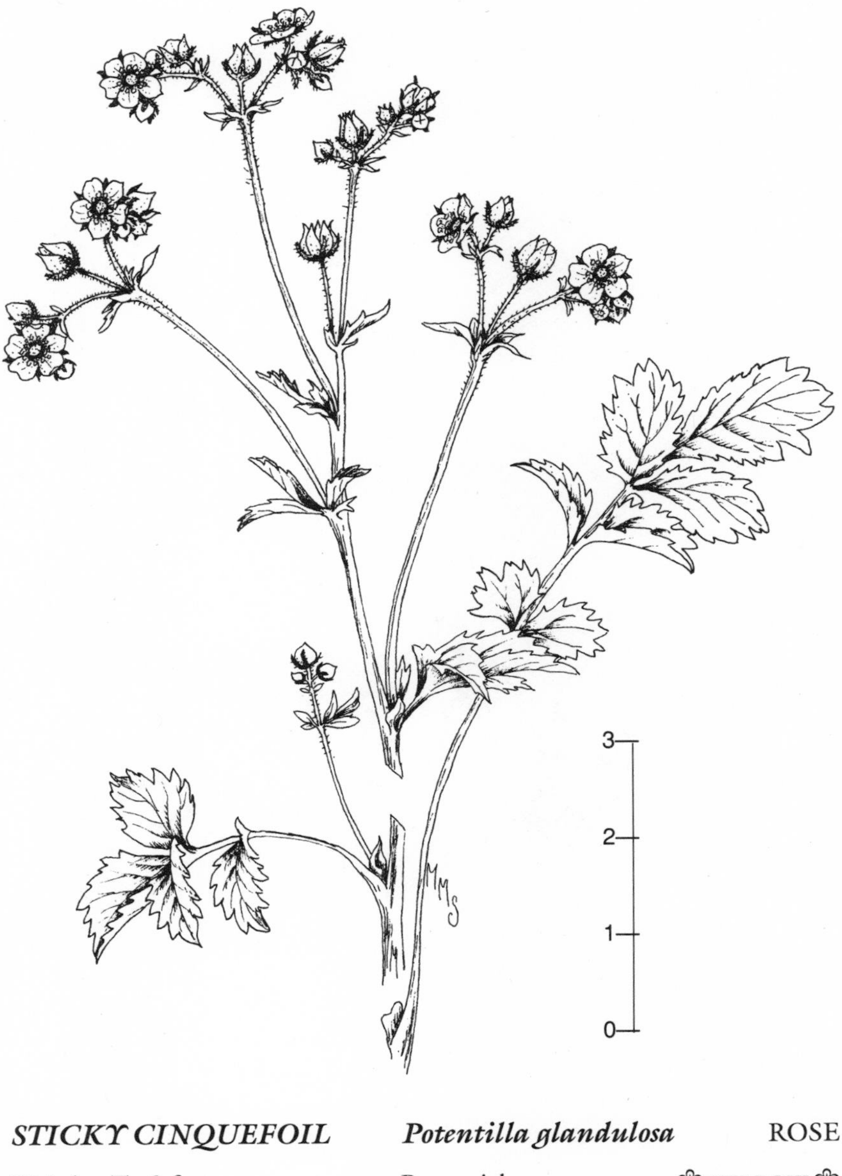

STICKY CINQUEFOIL ***Potentilla glandulosa*** ROSE

Height: To 2 ft. Perennial ❀ **YELLOW** ❀

Habitat: GRAVEL FLATS JULY

Trail: ROUND LAKE TRAIL ❧ BEYOND GOLD LAKE LODGE

The species name refers to the glands on the upper part of the stem near the flower, which you can see with a hand lens. The common name, Cinquefoil, translates to foliage of five. This *Potentilla* has pinnate leaves and strawberrylike flowers. It is very common in the Sierra.

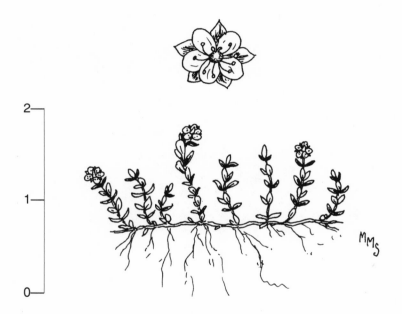

TINKER'S PENNY   *Hypericum anagalloides*   HYPERICUM

Height: Mat   Perennial   ❀ YELLOW ❀
Habitat: MOIST   JULY
Trail: GRASS LAKE 🐾 ON PENINSULA ON NORTH SIDE

These flowers look like small pieces of gold dropped on a bright green carpet. You will find Tinker's Penny growing with other delicate beauties, like the blue Hiker's Gentian (*Gentiana simplex*) and the bright yellow Primrose Mimulus (*Mimulus primuloides*), at the water's edge on the rocky peninsula on the north side of Grass Lake. This flower is a miniature of the garden Hypericum.

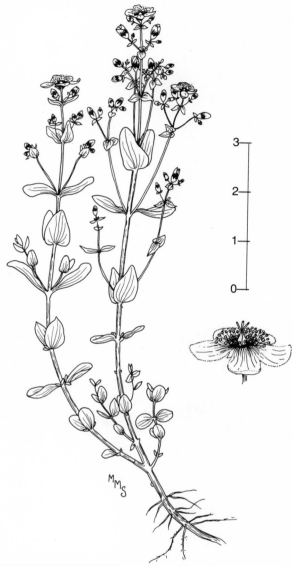

SCOULER'S HYPERICUM   *Hypericum*   HYPERICUM
ST. JOHN'S WORT   *formosum var. scouleri*

Height: 12 to 20 in.   Perennial   ❀ **YELLOW** ❀
Habitat: MOIST MEADOWS   JULY/AUGUST
Trail: GRAY EAGLE LODGE TO LONG LAKE ❧ NEAR LODGE SPRING
St. John's Wort will remind you of the garden variety *Hypericum*. Get out a hand lens and look at the black dots on the margins of the leaves and sepals. It is an attractive plant, but not nearly as robust as the invasive Klamath Weed (*Hypericum perforatum*), which can be seen growing along Gold Lake Road between Bassetts and the Sardine Lake turnoff.

105

DELICATE YELLOW BUCKWHEAT
MARUM-LEAVED BUCKWHEAT
Eriogonum marifolium

BUCKWHEAT

Height: 6 in. Perennial ❀ **YELLOW** ❀
Habitat: GRAVEL JULY
Trail: LAKES BASIN CAMPGROUND ❧ IN GRAVEL AREAS

Marum-leaved Buckwheat is smaller than the other species in this area. The flowers are pale yellow when compared with the bright Sulphur Buckwheat. The plant forms a mat up to about eight inches across. The leaves are downy on the underside and green on top. Marum-leaved Buckwheat is very common throughout the region.

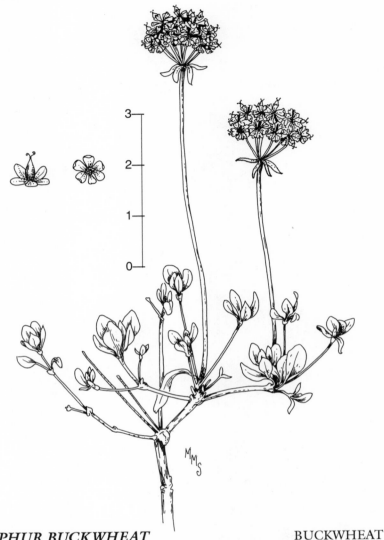

SULPHUR BUCKWHEAT   BUCKWHEAT
Eriogonum umbellatum ssp. polyanthum

Height: 8 in.   Perennial   ❀ **YELLOW** ❀
Habitat: GRAVEL   JULY
Trail: PCT SCREE ❧ ABOVE ROUND LAKE CIRQUE

This is probably the best known of the mountain buckwheats. It is very common in the Tahoe area and along Highway 89 in hot spots, along with Bitterbrush (*Purshia tridentata*) and Woolly Mule Ears (*Wyethia mollis*). Sulphur Buckwheat is very showy on the PCT scree with its bright yellow, sometimes almost chartreuse flowers that develop a rust color as they age. The bracts just below the flower head on Sulphur Buckwheat are more prominent than those on Marum-leaved Buckwheat.

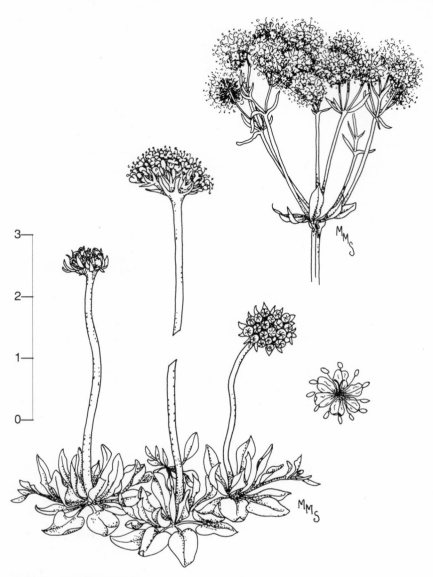

BEAR BUCKWHEAT   *Eriogonum ursinum*   BUCKWHEAT

Height: To 12 in.   Perennial   ❁ **YELLOW** ❁

Habitat: ROCKS   JULY

Trail: GRASS LAKE TO LONG LAKE ❧ NEAR STREAM CROSSING

Bear Buckwheat has pale yellow fluffy flower balls when young. As the flowers mature the flower head becomes more umbel-like (see the illustration) and ages to a delicate rose color. The Bear Buckwheat is so pretty in the rock garden near the stream crossing mentioned above that this is often a photo and snack stop.

3 —
2 —
1 —
0 —

TWINBERRY HONEYSUCKLE   HONEYSUCKLE
Lonicera involucrata

Height: To 3 ft.   Shrub   ❀ **YELLOW FLOWERS, RED BRACTS** ❀
Habitat: MOIST   JUNE/JULY
Trail: GRASS LAKE TRAIL TO LONG LAKE ❧ BEFORE CREEK CROSSING

The species name, *involucrata*, refers to the papery covering around the seed. The two showy persistent bractlets look like reddish flowers. Because Twinberry Honeysuckle appears to be in bloom over a long period it is a good landscape plant. The flowers look like typical honeysuckle flowers. *Lonicera conjugialis* can be found in moist areas near Bear Lake. It is an inconspicuous small shrub. The fruits of both species attract birds.

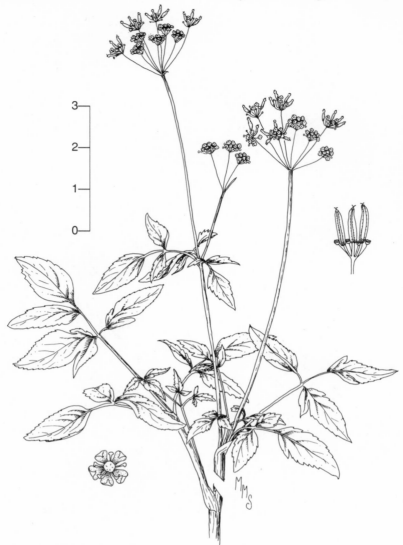

WESTERN SWEET-CICELY *Osmorhiza occidentalis* CARROT

Height: 15 to 30 in.   Perennial   ❀ YELLOW ❀
Habitat: WOODS   JULY
Trail: LONG LAKE TRAIL FROM GRAY EAGLE LODGE
           🐌 IN WOODS BEYOND GRAVEL FLATS

The botanical name is derived from the Greek *osme*, meaning odor, and *rhiza*, root. The plant smells like licorice. The seeds are very important in identifying different members of the Umbel or Carrot family. Western Sweet-Cicely has tiny yellow flowers. *Osmorhiza chilense*, Sweet Cicely, is a more delicate plant, with tiny white flowers about half the size of *O. occidentalis*, and grows in shade.

110

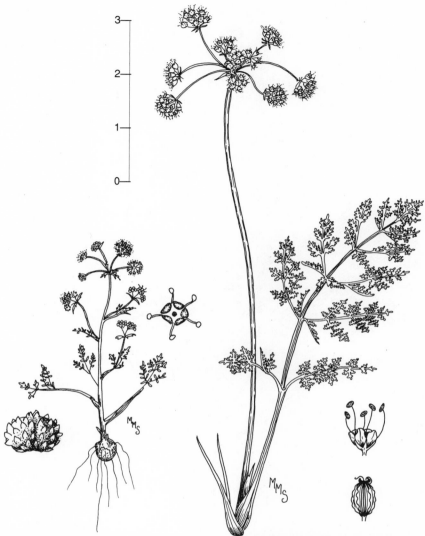

TUBEROUS SANICLE
Sanicula tuberosa   CARROT

TEREBINTH'S PTERYXIA
Pteryxia terebinthina
var. californica

JUNE	❀ YELLOW ❀	JUNE
Height: 5 in.	Perennial	8 in.
Habitat: SLOPES		GRAVEL, DRY

Trail: BEAR LAKE TRAILHEAD ❧ NEAR LAKES BASIN CAMPGROUND ENTRY

The genus name is derived from the Latin *sanare*, to heal, and the species name is descriptive of the root. Tuberous Sanicle probably contains alkaloids. *Pteryxia* (pronounced "ter-ix-ia") *terebinthina* has showier flowers and greener, more fernlike foliage than Sanicle. These plants are found together and are early bloomers.

111

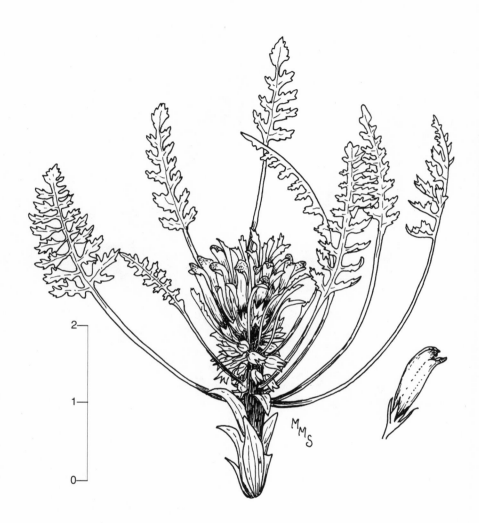

PINE WOODS LOUSEWORT
Pedicularis semibarbata

FIGWORT

Height: 2 to 6 in.   Perennial   ❀ YELLOW ❀

Habitat: WOODS, DRY   JUNE

Trail: SMITH LAKE TRAILHEAD 🍃 OUTSIDE GRAY EAGLE LODGE GATES

Pediculus is the Latin word for louse. Wort is the Old English word for plant. Whether this plant attracted or repelled lice does not seem to be known. The flowers nestle down in fernlike foliage and have a protruding beaked upper lip.

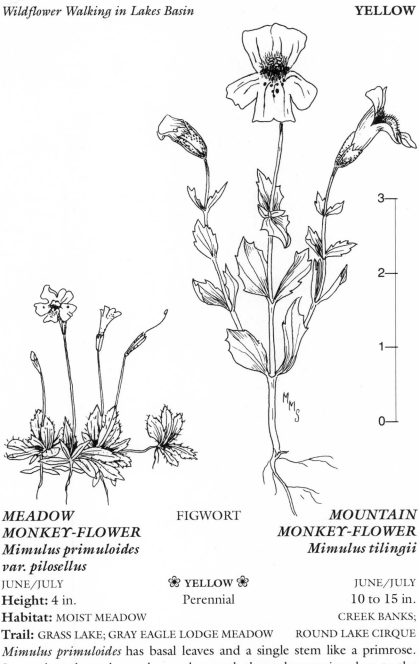

**MEADOW
MONKEY-FLOWER**
*Mimulus primuloides
var. pilosellus*

FIGWORT

**MOUNTAIN
MONKEY-FLOWER**
Mimulus tilingii

JUNE/JULY

❀ **YELLOW** ❀

JUNE/JULY

Height: 4 in.

Perennial

10 to 15 in.

Habitat: MOIST MEADOW

CREEK BANKS;

Trail: GRASS LAKE; GRAY EAGLE LODGE MEADOW   ROUND LAKE CIRQUE

Mimulus primuloides has basal leaves and a single stem like a primrose. Some plants have downy leaves that catch the early morning dew, to the delight of photographers. *Mimulus tilingii* is often found at the edges of streams and springs. The leaves of this species and of Musk Monkey-flower (*Mimulus moschatus*) both feel slimy or cool to the touch. The difference is that *M. tilingii* has an irregular-shaped flower, whereas *M. moschatus*, not illustrated, has a more symmetrical or circular flower.

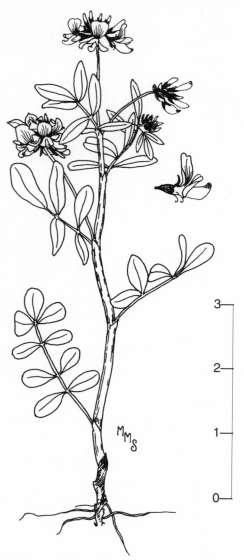

NARROW-LEAVED LOTUS *Lotus oblongifolius* PEA
MEADOW HOSACKIA

Height: 7 to 10 in.   Perennial   ❀ **YELLOW** ❀
Habitat: MOIST   JULY
Trail: GRASS LAKE TO LONG LAKE
    ❧ ABOVE THE STREAM CROSSING IN WET AREAS

This pretty lotus flower has a yellow banner and white lower wings that are adjacent to the keel. When a bee lands on the wings of the pea flower, the keel splits open and deposits pollen on the bee. Try this with your finger on a lupine flower and see the golden pollen pop out of the keel.

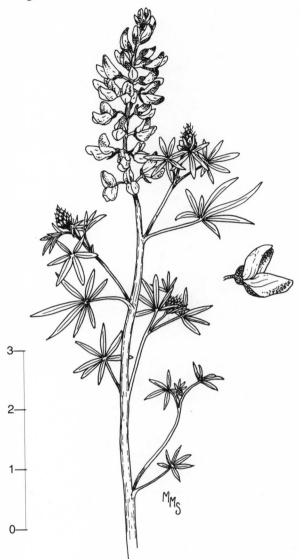

ANDERSON'S LUPINE   *Lupinus andersonii*   PEA

Height: 15 in.   Perennial   ❀ **YELLOW, WHITE, LAVENDER** ❀
Habitat: WOODS, OPEN, GRAVEL, DRY   JUNE/JULY
Trail: LONG LAKE TO SILVER LAKE; UPPER ROUND LAKE TRAIL

The plant has several color variations; the yellow and the lavender plants are both pale. The botanical name is derived from the Latin *lupus*, a wolf. Members of the Pea family take nitrogen from the air and put it into the soil. Pull up a weedy Clover (same plant family) from a lawn, press the nitrogen nodules on the root, and see the colored stain the nitrogen leaves on your fingers.

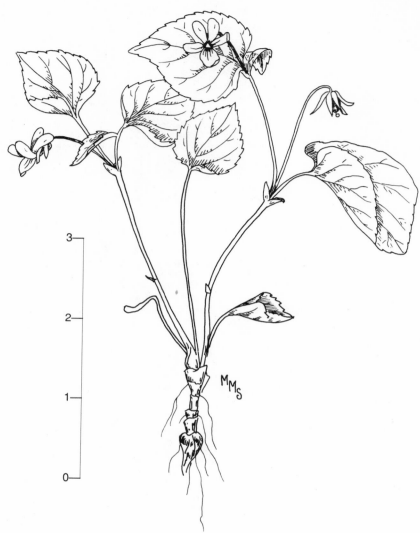

STREAM VIOLET *Viola glabella* VIOLA
SMOOTH YELLOW VIOLET

Height: 8 in. Perennial ❀ **YELLOW** ❀
Habitat: MOIST JUNE
Trail: GRASS LAKE INLET

The species name, *glabella*, means smooth, referring to the leaves, which in all *Viola* species are edible. The flowers of all violets are pretty used in salads or to decorate a cake. Stream Violet often grows with Meadow Rue (*Thalictrum fendleri*) and Clover (*Trifolium longipes*). Stream Violet can also be found growing at sea level in Redwood forests.

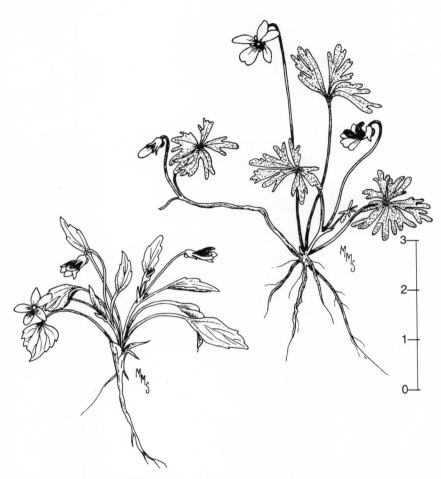

MOUNTAIN VIOLET	VIOLA	**SHELTON'S VIOLET**
Viola purpurea		*Viola sheltonii*

MAY/JUNE	❀ YELLOW ❀	MAY/JUNE
Height: 7 in.	Perennial	5 to 7 in.
Habitat: DRY		DRY GRAVEL

Trail: BEAR LAKE TRAILHEAD

🐌 ON LAKES BASIN CAMPGROUND ENTRY ROAD

Mountain Violet has purple on the backs of the upper petals and purple veins on the lower petals. The flowers of Shelton's Violet are similar to the Mountain Violet. Both violets bloom early and grow in the same dry, rocky, slightly shaded environment. The leaves of Shelton's Violet look similar to the leaves of Steer's Head (*Dicentra uniflora*), and the two plants are often found growing together.

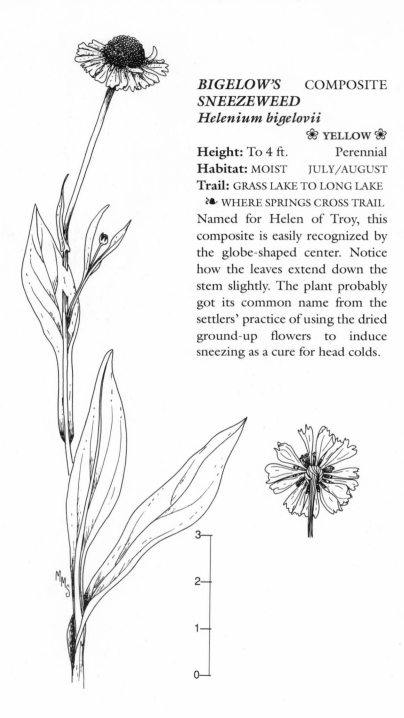

BIGELOW'S SNEEZEWEED
COMPOSITE
Helenium bigelovii

❀ **YELLOW** ❀

Height: To 4 ft.   Perennial
Habitat: MOIST   JULY/AUGUST
Trail: GRASS LAKE TO LONG LAKE
❧ WHERE SPRINGS CROSS TRAIL
Named for Helen of Troy, this composite is easily recognized by the globe-shaped center. Notice how the leaves extend down the stem slightly. The plant probably got its common name from the settlers' practice of using the dried ground-up flowers to induce sneezing as a cure for head colds.

TARWEED COMPOSITE
BOLANDER'S MADIA
Madia bolanderi

❀ YELLOW ❀

Height: To 3 ft. Perennial
Habitat: MOIST JULY/AUGUST
Trail: GRASS LAKE TO LONG LAKE

🐾 WHERE SPRINGS CROSS TRAIL
Use your hand lens to look at the glands on the stem, which are responsible for the stickiness and the aroma of this lovely Tarweed. Notice the two types of flowers in a composite flower head in the illustrated glossary inside the front cover.

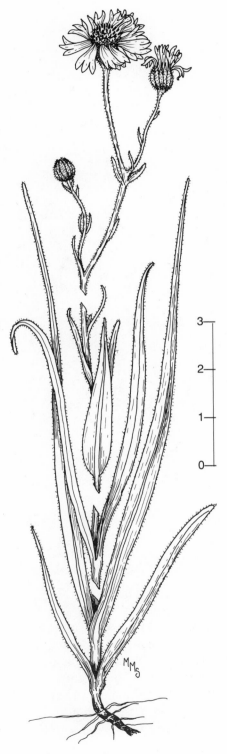

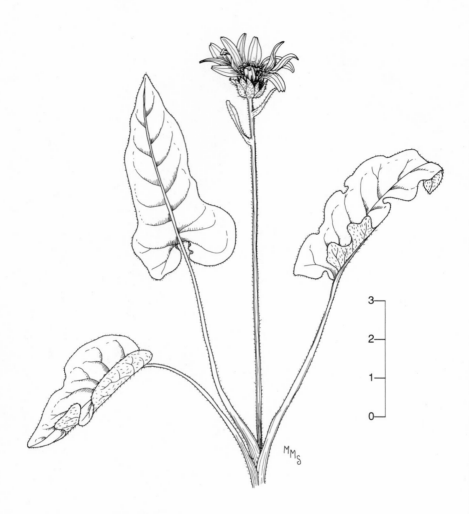

BALSAM ROOT   *Balsamorhiza sagittata*   COMPOSITE

Height: To 2 ft.   Perennial   ❀ **YELLOW** ❀

Habitat: SCREE   JULY

Trail: PCT CREST 🐾 ABOVE ROUND LAKE

The species name, *sagittata*, means arrowlike. The young Balsam Root plant has dense hairs on the underside of the leaves, giving a paler appearance. A similar species, Deltoid Balsam Root (*Balsamorhiza deltoidea*), is green on both leaf surfaces and occurs in the gravel flats on the Long Lake Trail. Both species have roots and stems that are edible when cooked; the seeds are also edible.

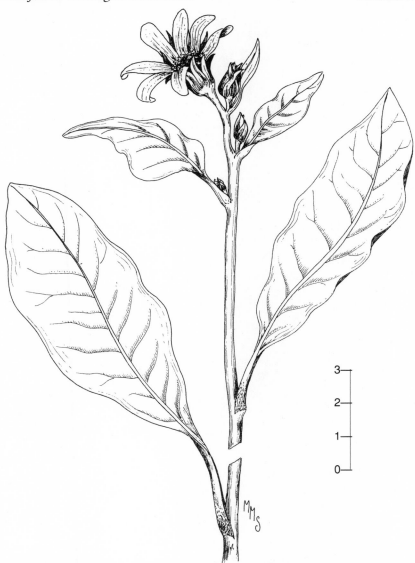

MOUNTAIN MULE EARS　　　*Wyethia mollis*　　COMPOSITE
WOOLLY MULE EARS

Height: 2 to 3 ft.　　　　　Perennial　　　　❀ **YELLOW** ❀
Habitat: GRAVEL FLATS; WOODS, OPEN　　　　　　　JULY
Trail: ROUND LAKE 🐾 NEAR GOLD LAKE LODGE

The species name, *mollis*, refers to the soft, hairy young leaves. Look for last year's leaf skeletons with just the veins remaining. They are beautiful in a winter arrangement. This very common mountain plant can be seen along Highway 89 between Truckee and Sierraville. Woolly Mule Ears has edible seeds.

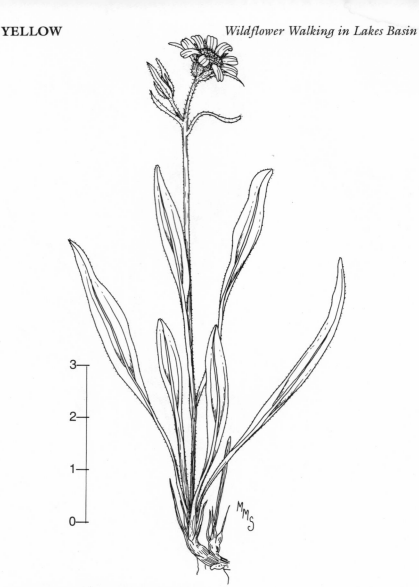

CALIFORNIA HELIANTHELLA   COMPOSITE
Helianthella californica var. nevadensis

Height: To 2 ft.   Perennial   ❀ **YELLOW** ❀
Habitat: GRAVEL FLATS   JULY
Trail: GRAY EAGLE LODGE TRAIL TO LONG LAKE
    🍀 BEYOND LILY LAKE JUNCTION

The plant is sometimes called the California Sunflower. The genus name is derived from the Greek *helios,* sun, and *anthos,* flower. *Helianthella* is the diminutive of *Helianthus.* This plant is more delicate and has narrower leaves than either Woolly Mule Ears (*Wyethia mollis*) or Balsam Root (*Balsamorhiza sagitatta*).

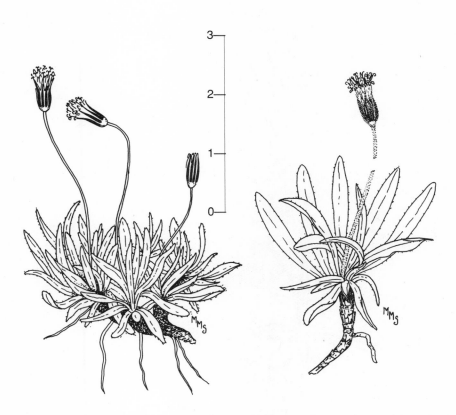

SILVER	COMPOSITE	GREEN-LEAVED

SILVER RAILLARDELLA
Raillardella argentea

COMPOSITE

GREEN-LEAVED RAILLARDELLA
Raillardella scaposa

JULY

❀ YELLOW ❀
Perennial

JULY
4 to 11 in.
SCREE

Height: To 4 in.
Habitat: SCREE
Trail: PCT NEAR THE WHITE ROCK OUTCROP

The species name, *argentea*, meaning silver, refers to the white silky leaves. *Raillardella scaposa*, Green-leaved Raillardella, grows to eleven inches high. The species name, *scaposa*, describes the leafless flowering stalk that arises from a basal cluster of leaves. Observe the glands and hair on the scape.

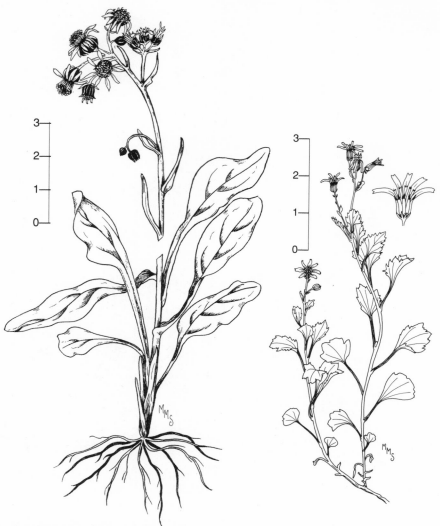

GROUNDSEL   COMPOSITE   *FREMONT'S GROUNDSEL*
Senecio integerrimus var. exaltatus   *Senecio fremontii*

JUNE	❀ YELLOW ❀	JULY/AUGUST
Height: 2 ft.	Perennial	To 10 in.
Habitat: WOODS, OPEN		ROCKS
Trail: SMITH LAKE TRAILHEAD, BEFORE		LONG LAKE ON NW CORNER,
GRAY EAGLE LODGE GATES		AT BASE OF ROCKY CLIFFS

The species name, *integerrimus*, means undivided, referring to the spatulate leaves. Groundsel is an early bloomer. Many groundsels have a black dot at the tip of each involucral bract. *Senecio fremontii* has just been located after six years of searching in the area. How many other plants do you suppose there are in Lakes Basin that we have not yet found?

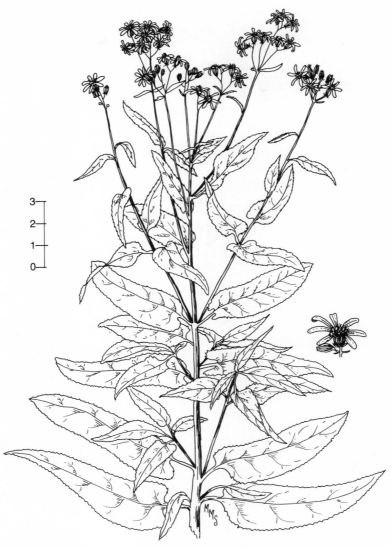

GROUNDSEL   *Senecio triangularis*   COMPOSITE
OLD MAN'S BEARD

Height: To 6 ft.   Perennial   ❀ **YELLOW** ❀

Habitat: MOIST MEADOWS   JULY

Trail: ROUND LAKE TRAIL 🐾 BY GOLD LAKE LODGE

The genus name is derived from the Latin *senex*, meaning old man, because of the white pappus (thistledown) on the seeds. The species name, *triangularis*, refers to the leaf shape. The individual flowers of Groundsel are unimpressive, but the masses of Groundsel growing with Corn Lily (*Veratrum californicum*), *Lupinus latifolius*, and Indian Paintbrush (*Castilleja miniata*) make a perfect picture.

LAWLESS ARNICA   *Arnica diversifolia*   COMPOSITE

Height: To 14 in.   Perennial   ❀ **YELLOW** ❀
Habitat: SLOPES, MOIST   JULY
Trail: ROUND LAKE 🦶 IN CIRQUE WITH RED HEATHER

The genus *Arnica* is easy to learn to recognize. Unlike most members of the Composite or Daisy family, *Arnica* has leaves that are opposite each other on the stem. They have a wonderful fresh smell when you rub the foliage. At the Round Lake Mine look up the hill. Perhaps you can spot the yellow cascade of *Arnica* near the small Mountain Hemlocks. Rock-hop over to the flowers for great photos.

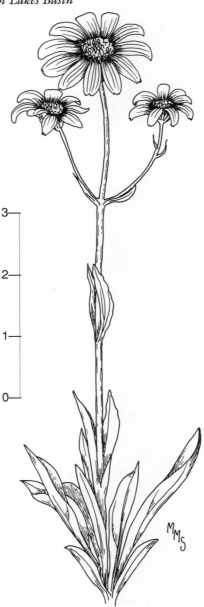

TWIN ARNICA   *Arnica sororia*   COMPOSITE

Height: 12 in.   Perennial   ❀ **YELLOW** ❀
Habitat: DRY SLOPES   JULY/AUGUST
Trail: SIERRA BUTTES LOOKOUT

Arnica comes from the Greek word *arnakis*, meaning lambskin; it refers to the texture of the leaves, which are a silvery gray in color. This cheery plant greets you as soon as you start your ascent up the exposed slope to the Sierra Buttes Lookout.

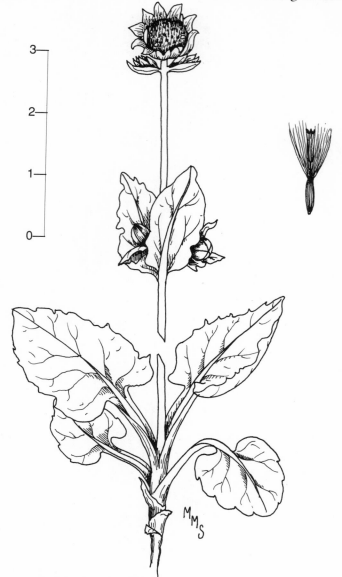

RAYLESS ARNICA   *Arnica discoidea var. alata*   COMPOSITE

Height: To 2 ft.   Perennial   ✿ **YELLOW** ✿
Habitat: WOODS, DRY   JULY
Trail: GRASS LAKE TO LONG LAKE

The species, *discoidea*, means rayless. Notice the difference betweeen this
species and the two species of *Arnica* on the preceding pages. In reality,
using a hand lens, you can see a multitude of tiny flowers in this large
flower head, each one with its own floral parts. Rayless Arnica is found
about half a mile down the trail to Long Lake.

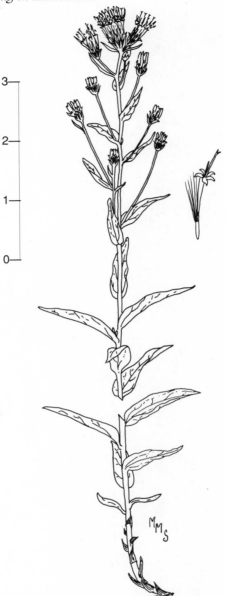

BREWER'S GOLDEN ASTER *Chrysopsis breweri* COMPOSITE

Height: 2 ft.   Perennial   ❀ **YELLOW** ❀
Habitat: SLOPES, DRY   JULY/AUGUST
Trail: LAKES BASIN CAMPGROUND

The botanical name is from the Greek *chryso*, meaning golden, and *opsis*, meaning appearance, referring to the blossom. This late-blooming plant is very common in dry woods and on slopes. It is a pleasant surprise to see these little golden flowers blooming after other flowers have gone to seed.

COMMON DANDELION
Taraxacum officinale

COMPOSITE

Height: 15 in.   Perennial   ❀ **YELLOW** ❀
Habitat: MEADOWS   JUNE
Trail: GRAY EAGLE LODGE 🌿 ALONG ROAD TO LODGE

The Dandelion is in the Chickory tribe of the Composite family. All members of this tribe have a milky juice in the stem. The young leaves are edible. A German friend of mine tells of picking Dandelion greens for German soldiers during World War II.

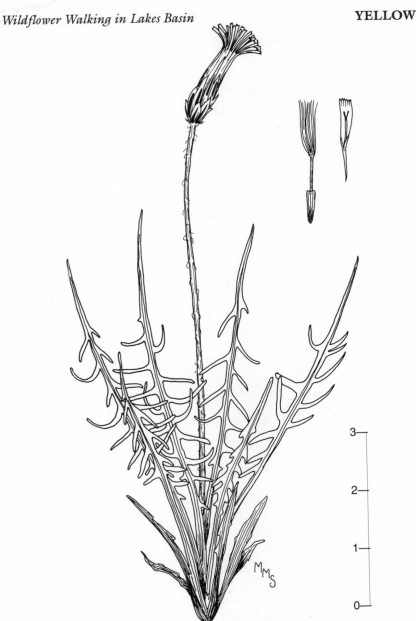

SPEAR-LEAVED AGOSERIS   *Agoseris retrorsa*   COMPOSITE

Height: 15 in.   Perennial   ❀ **YELLOW** ❀
Habitat: DRY SLOPES   JULY
Trail: LONG LAKE TO MT. ELWELL; GOLD LAKE ROAD
Notice that the lancelike leaves are retrorse, meaning bent back or turned
downward. The phyllaries or bracts of the involucre (somewhat like sepals
on most flowers) are in two sets or layers. The Dandelion tribe has only
ray flowers. See the illustrated glossary inside front cover.

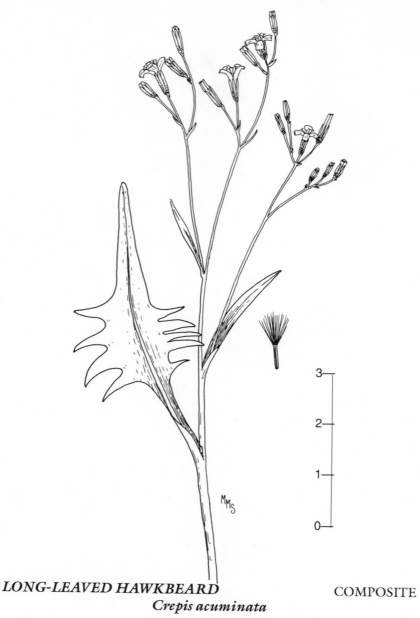

LONG-LEAVED HAWKBEARD
Crepis acuminata

COMPOSITE

Height: 15 to 20 in.   Perennial   ❀ YELLOW ❀
Habitat: DRY   JULY
Trail: GRAY EAGLE LODGE ENTRY ROAD

The species name, *acuminata*, means gradually tapering to a sharp point, which describes the leaf shape. Like the Dandelion, *Crepis* will have milky juice if the stem is broken or a leaf is torn. This species can have as many as forty flowering heads on one plant.

NODDING MICROSERIS   *Microseris nutans*   COMPOSITE

Height: To 8 in.   Perennial   ❀ **YELLOW** ❀

Habitat: WOODS OR MOIST PLACES   JULY

Trail: GRASS LAKE OUTLET

Of Greek origin, *micros* means small and *seris*, lettucelike. Lettuce and Nodding Microseris are both in the Chickory tribe of the Composite family. They have milky juice when you break the stem or tear a leaf, and they have only ray flowers. The roots are edible raw. The common name refers to the nodding bud.

SAGEWORT   *Artemisia norvegica var. saxatilis*   COMPOSITE
MOUNTAIN MUGWORT

Height: To 2 ft.   Perennial   ❀ **YELLOW** ❀

Habitat: SLOPES   AUGUST

Trail: BEAR LAKE TRAILHEAD

    ❧ ON LAKES BASIN CAMPGROUND ENTRY ROAD

This plant is named for the Greek god Artemis. The plant is very aromatic and might remind you of the lower elevation mugwort, *Artemisia douglasiana*. The Indians had a multitude of medicinal and ceremonial uses for the plants in the genus *Artemisia*. Some species of *Artemisia* cause vomiting if taken internally.

MEADOW GOLDENROD   COMPOSITE
Solidago canadensis ssp. elongata

Height: To 3 ft.   Perennial   ❀ **YELLOW** ❀
Habitat: SLOPES, MEADOWS   AUGUST
Trail: LAKES BASIN CAMPGROUND

The botanical name is derived from the Latin *solidus*, which means to make whole or strengthen, and *ago*, referring to the plant's medicinal properties. This late-blooming perennial is pretty in the wild garden blooming with asters, but Goldenrod is invasive. Many people think Goldenrod causes hay fever, but if you look with a hand lens you will see it has sticky pollen that can't blow; so perhaps it is the mold spores dotting the dried grasses that cause the fall hay fever.

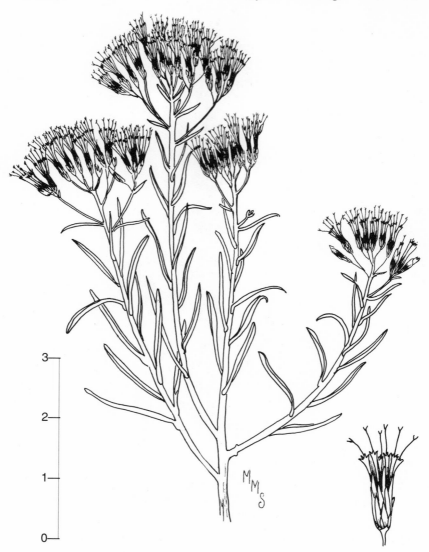

WHITE-STEM RABBIT BRUSH

Chrysothamnus nauseosus ssp. albicaulis

COMPOSITE

Height: 2 ft. Shrub ❀ **YELLOW** ❀

Habitat: SCREE AUGUST/SEPTEMBER

Trail: PCT SCREE AT CREST

The genus name is of Greek origin, from *chryso*, meaning gold, and *thamnos*, meaning shrub. The subspecies *albi* (albino), meaning white, and *caulis*, meaning stem, refers to the common name. Photographers delight in catching a Rabbit Brush in bloom in the foreground with the golden Aspen in the background. Indians used the bright flowers as a yellow dye.

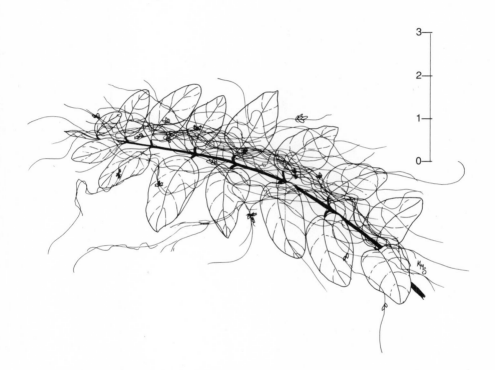

DODDER   *Cuscuta suksdorfii*   DODDER
          ssp. subpedicellata

Height: Depends on host   Clinging   ❀ **ORANGE-YELLOW STEMS** ❀
                                  parasite

Habitat: RED FIR FOREST   AUGUST

Trail: LONG LAKE TRAIL TO MT. ELWELL

Dodder is a true parasite and lacks chlorophyll, hence cannot manufacture its own food. The tiny flowers are waxy-white, but the orange-yellow tangle is much more noticeable. You will find it growing on *Aster*, *Apocynum*, and many other perennials in late summer.

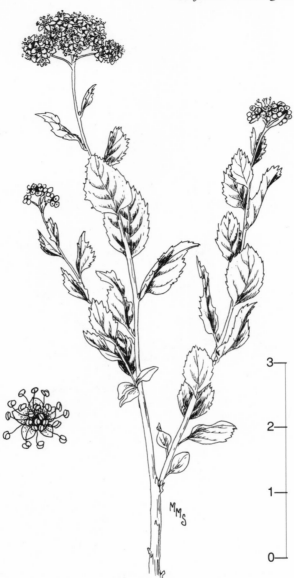

MOUNTAIN SPIRAEA   *Spiraea densiflora*   ROSE

Height: To 3 ft.   Shrub   ❀ PINK ❀

Habitat: ROCKY, OFTEN MOIST   JULY

Trail: TARN BETWEEN LONG LAKE AND SILVER LAKE

Spiraea is of Greek origin and means wreath or band. These are wonderful garden plants. Notice the delicate appearance of the flowering head, due to the protruding stamens. *Spiraea densiflora*, with rounded or capitate flower clusters, is a smaller, more compact shrub than Douglas's Spiraea, with its whiplike branches and long racemes of flowers.

138

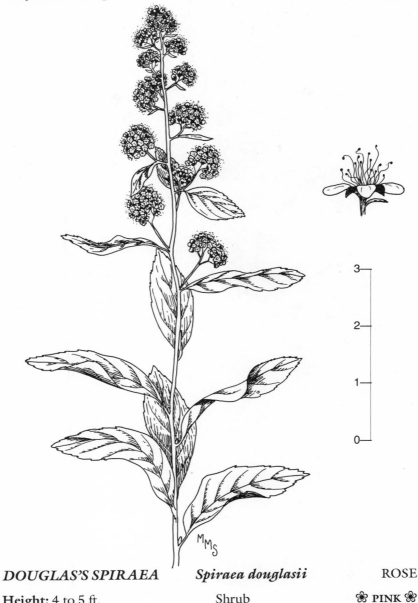

DOUGLAS'S SPIRAEA   *Spiraea douglasii*   ROSE

Height: 4 to 5 ft.   Shrub   ❀ **PINK** ❀
Habitat: WOODS, MOIST   JULY
Trail: SARDINE LAKE CAMPGROUND

Douglas's Spiraea grows in Sardine Lake campground and is threatened by flooding from the beaver ponds. Although it grows in very wet areas here, it also does well in Bay Area gardens in dry shade and in Tahoe gardens in sun with some water. This plant is not supposed to grow naturally any farther south in the Sierra than Plumas County, so perhaps we have extended the range to include Sierra County.

139

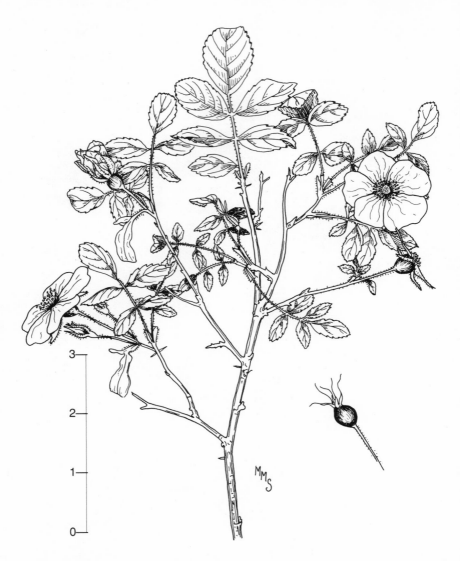

PINE ROSE	***Rosa pinetorum***	ROSE

Height: 3 to 4 ft.   Shrub   ❀ PINK ❀
Habitat: OPEN WOODS   JULY
Trail: GRAY EAGLE LODGE TO LILY LAKE

The beautiful pink, fragrant *Rosa pinetorum* is found only at the lower elevations in Lakes Basin. The rose hips are edible. The citrus-tasting hips are nice for nibbling or in tea. To grow the rose from seed, grind the hip between two bricks, which should slightly scratch the seeds before they are planted. Or nibble the rose hips until just the hard seeds are left; put them in a cup, pour boiling water on them, let soak ten hours, and plant.

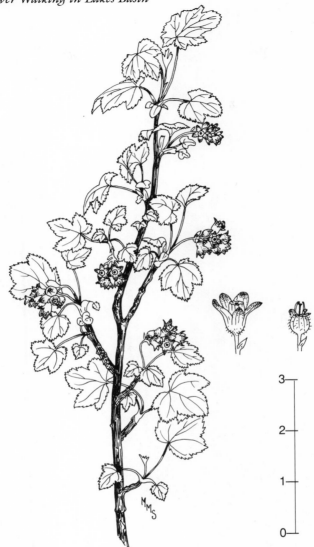

SIERRA CURRANT   *Ribes nevadense*   SAXIFRAGE

Height: 5 ft.   Shrub   ✤ **PINK** ✤
Habitat: MOIST   JUNE
Trail: GRASS LAKE TO LONG LAKE 🐾 BEFORE CREEK CROSSING
The deep rose clusters of flowers on the Sierra Currant appear early in the spring, just after the snow melts. The dark fruits of the currant are bitter, but not barbed like Sierra Gooseberry. Gooseberry bushes have spines on their branches but not always on their fruit, while the currants lack spines on either the branches or the fruit. This is a wonderful plant for a mountain garden. It does not need much water and is available at nurseries in the Tahoe area.

141

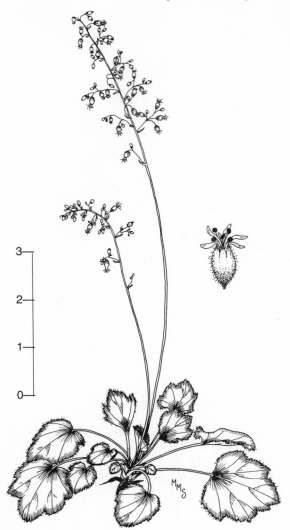

PINK HEUCHERA   SAXIFRAGE
ALUMROOT   *Heuchera rubescens var. glandulosa*

Height: 10 in.   Perennial   ❀ PINK ❀
Habitat: DRY, ROCKY   JULY
Trail: HELGRAMITE LAKE TO PCT ❧ AT SPRING GARDEN IN ROCKS

Pink Heuchera is a photographer's delight with the delicate wandlike flowering stalks against massive rocks or the pink flowers against the sky. You can buy many species of Heuchera in nurseries. There is a common garden plant called Coral Bells (*Heuchera sanguinea*) whose species name tells you the flower is blood-red. It is native to Arizona and Mexico and hybridizes with our California Heuchera when the two grow in the garden together. The young leaves of Heuchera are edible.

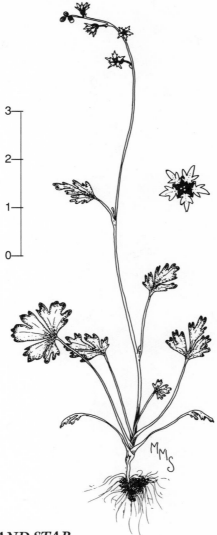

PINK WOODLAND STAR
Lithophragma parviflora

SAXIFRAGE

Height: 7 in. Perennial ❀ **PINK** ❀

Habitat: GRAVEL, DRY MAY/JUNE

Trail: BEAR LAKE TRAILHEAD

🦋 LAKES BASIN CAMPGROUND NEAR ENTRY ROAD

The botanical name is of Greek origin, from *lithos*, meaning rock, and this plant grows in rocky areas. Pink Woodland Star, along with its early spring companions, *Viola sheltonii*, *V. purpurea*, Steershead (*Dicentra uniflora*), and the Sierra Gooseberry (*Ribes roezlii*), blooms while the soil is still moist from the melting snow. Its gravelly habitat becomes hot and dry by mid-June.

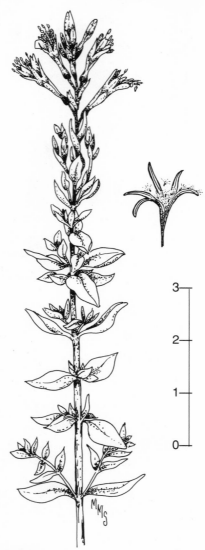

CALIFORNIA FUCHSIA   EVENING PRIMROSE
Zauschneria californica ssp. latifolia

Height: 4 to 14 in.   Perennial   ❀ **RED** ❀
Habitat: ROCKS   AUGUST
Trail: GRAY EAGLE LODGE TO LONG LAKE

The subspecies, *latifolia*, refers to the wide leaves. The mountain *Zauschneria* has wider, greener leaves than the plants of lower elevations. This is a wonderful garden plant that will attract hummingbirds. It is very easy to grow and is available from nurseries at Tahoe. You will find California Fuchsia growing in the rocks above Upper Helgramite Lake as well as along the trail below Long Lake.

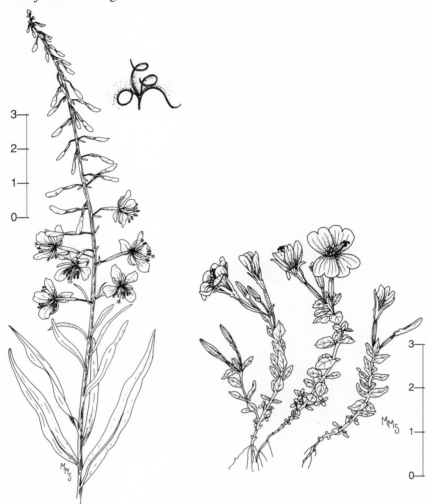

FIREWEED	EVENING PRIMROSE	**ROCK-FRINGE**
Epilobium angustifolium		*Epilobium obcordatum*
JULY	❀ PINK ❀	JULY
Height: 2 to 6 ft.	Perennial	To 6 in.
Habitat: MOIST WOODS, MEADOWS		SCREE
Trail: BELOW BEAR LAKE		PCT ABOVE ROUND LAKE

The genus is derived from the Greek *epi*, upon, and *lobos*, a pod. The flower sits on the ovary (or seed pod), which looks like the stem to the flower but is much too rigid. Notice the X-shaped stigma. *Angustifolium* means narrow-leaved. Young stems are edible raw or cooked. The seeds are attached to thistledown and are carried by the wind to colonize new areas where the soil is bare, such as it is after a fire. The species *obcordatum* refers to the heart-shaped petals of Rock-fringe. This excellent rock-garden plant is found on steep east slopes near the white rocks along the PCT.

145

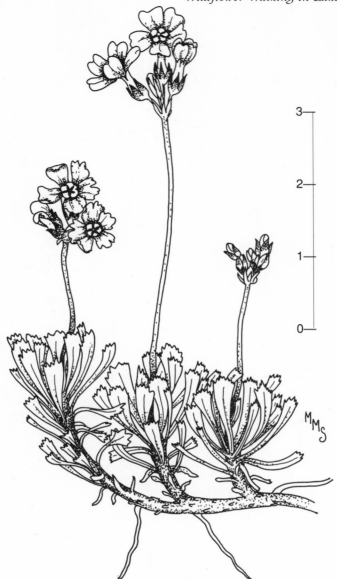

SIERRA PRIMROSE *Primula suffrutescens* PRIMROSE

Height: To 4 in. Perennial ❀ **PINK-ROSE** ❀

Habitat: SCREE JULY

Trail: PCT ABOVE ROUND LAKE

Sierra Primrose is a photographer's delight, cascading off the eastern edge of the PCT like a bright pink waterfall. Get closer and observe the yellow throat of the Primula. The botanical name can be translated thus: *primus* means first (it blooms early) and *suffrutescens*, woody at the base. You find primula only at high elevations.

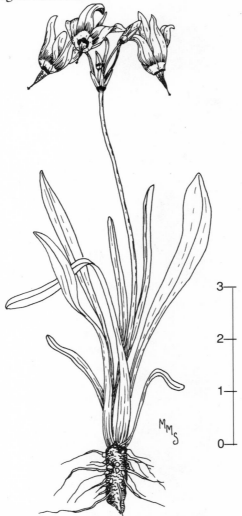

SHOOTING STAR   *Dodecatheon alpinum*   PRIMROSE
MOSQUITO BILLS

Height: 10 in.   Perennial   ❀ **PINK** ❀
Habitat: MOIST MEADOWS   JUNE
Trail: NEAR TRAILHEAD TO LONG LAKE
        ❧ IN AREA OF SPRINGS ABOVE GRAY EAGLE LODGE

The genus, *Dodecatheon*, is derived from the Greek *dodeca*, twelve, and *theos*, god, and is the name given by Pliny to the Shooting Star as being under the care of the twelve leading gods. In the drawing notice the small bulblets on the root, and the four petals and the enlarged stigma tip in the flower; these are the key characteristics of this species. If you missed the Shooting Stars at the Long Lake trailhead you may find them in bloom until mid-July at Upper Helgramite Lake.

147

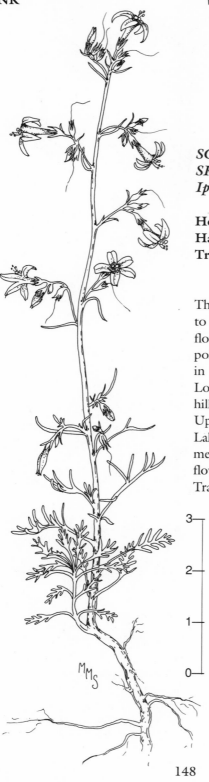

SCARLET GILIA   PHLOX
SKY ROCKET GILIA
Ipomopsis aggregata

❀ RED ❀

Height: 1½ ft.   Perennial
Habitat: GRAVEL FLATS   JULY
Trail: GRAY EAGLE LODGE TO LONG
    LAKE ❧ BEYOND LILY LAKE
    JUNCTION

The species name, *aggregata*, refers
to the clustered flowers. Many red-
flowered plants are hummingbird-
pollinated. Besides the plants found
in the gravel flats garden on the
Long Lake Trail, there is a beautiful
hillside of Scarlet Gilia between
Upper Salmon Lake and Horse
Lake. The foliage has been used
medicinally. Scarlet Gilia has a pink
flower along the Winnemucca Lake
Trail on Carson Pass.

3—

2—

1—

0—

MMS

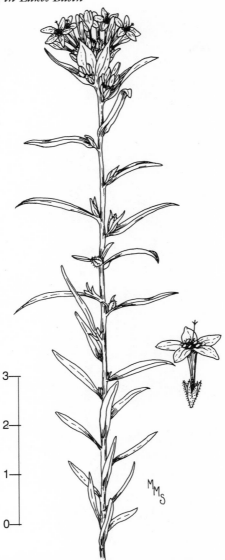

APRICOT COLLOMIA   *Collomia grandiflora*   PHLOX
LARGE-FLOWERED COLLOMIA

Height: 10 in.   Annual   ❀ **PINK-SALMON** ❀
Habitat: SCREE   JULY
Trail: PCT FLATS ❧ SOUTH OF WHITE ROCK OUTCROP

The genus name is derived from the Greek *kolla*, because of the muci-
laginous seeds. The species name you can interpret for yourself. This is a
very showy flower, partly because of its size but also because the color is
unusual in our mountain flora. It makes me wonder if there is a special
pollinator. Apricot Collomia is fairly rare in Lakes Basin. It seems to be
more prevalent at slightly lower elevations.

149

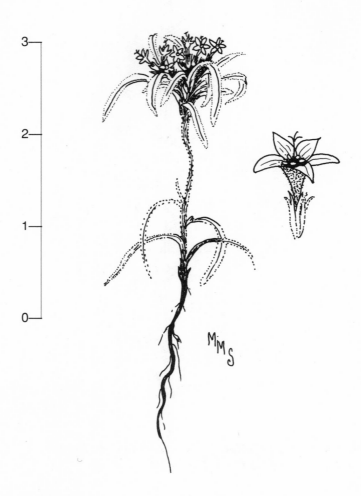

NARROW-LEAVED COLLOMIA *Collomia linearis* PHLOX

Height: 4 in.   Annual   ❀ **PINK** ❀
Habitat: GRAVEL FLATS   JUNE/JULY
Trail: LONG LAKE TRAIL 🐾 AFTER LILY LAKE JUNCTION
The species name refers to the linear leaves of this "belly flower" (you have
to lie on your belly to see it). While you are lying there, be sure to notice
the glands that cover the stem and leaves.

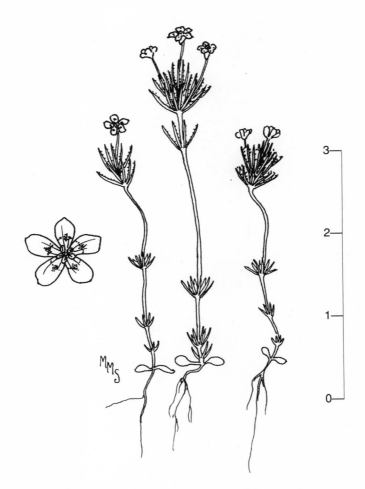

| **WHISKER-BRUSH** | *Linanthus ciliatus* | PHLOX |

Height: 4 in.　　　　　　Annual　　　　　❀ **PINK** ❀
Habitat: GRAVEL FLATS, DRY　　　　　　JUNE/JULY
Trail: GRAY EAGLE LODGE TO LONG LAKE
　　🐾 BEYOND LILY LAKE JUNCTION

The Greek *linon* means flax and *anthos*, flower. The species, *ciliatus*, refers to the hairy edges of the leaves. Observe this colorful little annual with a hand lens to see the leaf hairs and the pretty yellow center of the flower. As an example of how common names get started, a friend who leads hikes calls this plant "tutu" because of the ballerina-skirt appearance of the leaves. At least forty people now use this as the common name.

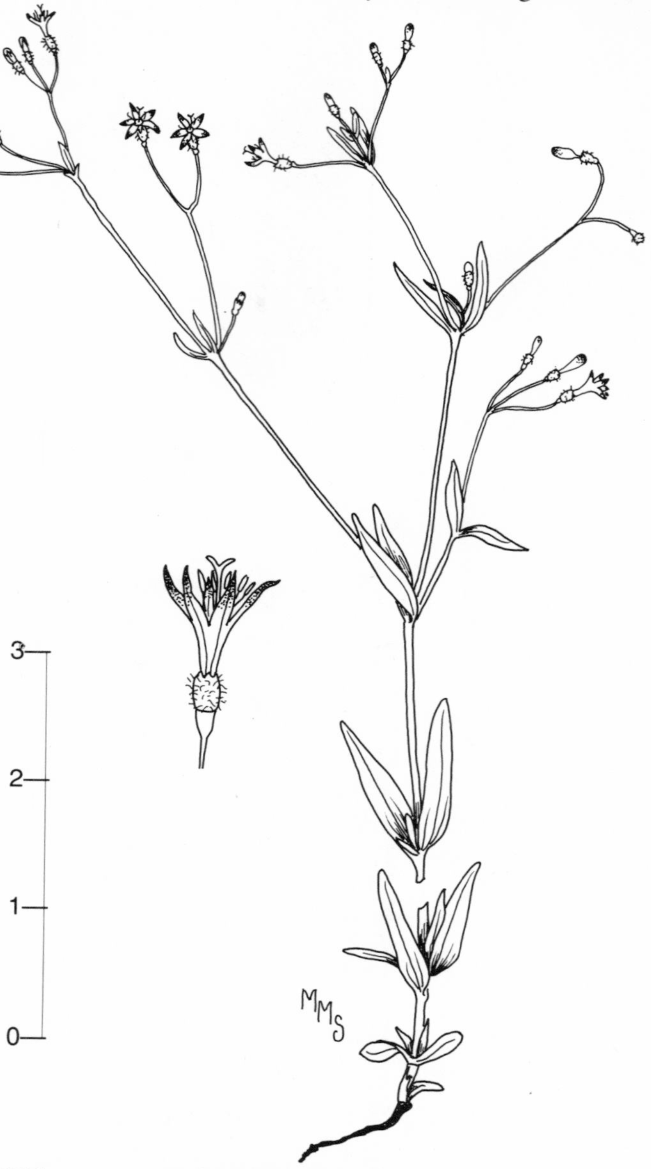

KELLOGGIA ***Kelloggia galioides*** MADDER

Height: To 10 in. Perennial ❀ **PINK-WHITE** ❀

Habitat: SLOPES, DRY JULY/AUGUST

Trail: LONG LAKE TRAIL ❧ NEAR GRAY EAGLE LODGE

This plant was named for Dr. A. Kellogg, the pioneering California botanist and a founder of the California Academy of Sciences in San Francisco. He was born in 1813 and died in 1887. The species name indicates that the plant resembles Bedstraw, or *Galium*. This delicate plant has pinkish flowers and blooms later than most of the Lakes Basin plants.

MALLOW   *Sidalcea oregana ssp. spicata*   MALLOW
SPIKE CHECKER

Height: 2 ft.   Perennial   ❀ **PINK** ❀
Habitat: MOIST   JULY
Trail: ROUND LAKE TRAIL 🌿 IN MEADOW AFTER GOLD LAKE LODGE
The subspecies name, *spicata*, describes the spiked shape of the flowering
stalk. Observe the anther column, typical of the Mallow family; the
filaments of the numerous stamens are fused together, resembling the
center of the Hollyhock, to which the plant is related. Usually the leaves of
this plant family look like maple leaves, but the upper leaves of this *Sidalcea*
are deeply lobed.

153

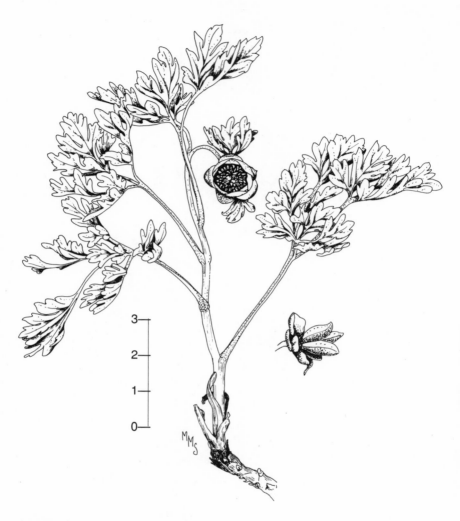

PEONY   *Paeonia brownii*   PEONY

Height: 8 to 14 in.   Perennial   ❀ **MAROON** ❀
Habitat: SLOPES, MEADOWS   JUNE
Trail: GROUNDS OF GOLD LAKE LODGE; NORTH OF ROUND LAKE
      TRAIL AFTER RED FIR FOREST IN STEEP MEADOW

The coarse blue-green foliage and interesting seed pod are more visible than the heavy, rounded maroon flower, which usually is drooping and hidden in the foliage. The Peony is an early bloomer, although along the Round Lake Trail it may bloom until mid-June because of the north-facing slope.

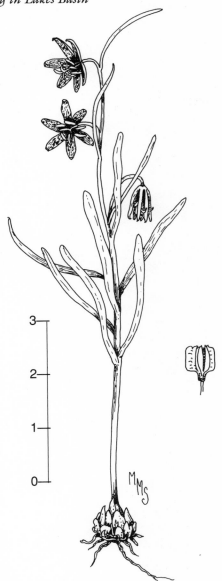

PURPLE FRITILLARY   *Fritillaria atropurpurea*   LILY
SPOTTED MOUNTAIN BELLS

Height: To 1 ft.   Bulb   ❀ **MAROON** ❀
Habitat: DRY SLOPES, OPEN WOODS   JULY
Trail: ROUND LAKE ❧ NEAR BEAR LAKE OVERLOOK

The Latin *fritillus* means a dice box, referring to the checkered flowers, and *atropurpurea* means dark purple. This plant appears to have six petals. The sepals and petals are alike and are called tepals. It is strange to see this delicate flower growing with the buckwheats in hot gravel areas.

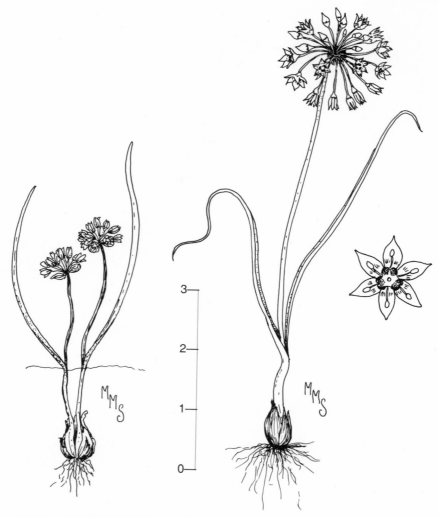

RED *or* DWARF SIERRA ONION   LILY   *SIERRA ONION*
Allium obtusum   *Allium campanulatum*

JUNE/JULY   ❀ PINK ❀   JUNE/JULY
Height: 2 to 3 in.   Bulb   4 to 11 in.
Habitat: GRAVEL FLATS   GRAVEL FLATS
Trail: LONG LAKE TRAIL FROM GRAY EAGLE LODGE
       ❧ NEAR LILY LAKE JUNCTION

Both onions are quite small; you will probably smell them before you see
them. They are edible. *Allium* is Greek for garlic. The species name,
obtusum, refers to the blunt, rounded tip of the petals on this small onion.
The species name of the larger onion, *campanulatum*, refers to the bell
shape of the flower.

SWAMP ONION   LILY   **FLAT-STEMMED ONION**
Allium validum   *Allium platycaule*

JUNE/JULY   ❀ PINK ❀   JUNE/JULY

Height: To 3 ft.   Bulb   6 in.

Habitat: MEADOWS, WET   GRAVEL, MOIST

Trail: LONG LAKE TRAIL FROM GRASS LAKE 🍃 IN WET SUNNY AREAS

Indians used the juice of onions as a treatment for bee stings. These onions grow in moist situations and both of them are very showy. The largest of the Sierra onions is *Allium validum*, meaning strong. Cut some of the leaves and stuff your just-caught trout or add zip to your freeze-dried dinners. *Allium platycaule* refers to the flat stem. The only location where the Flat-stemmed Onion has been found is near the spring along the trail below Long Lake outlet.

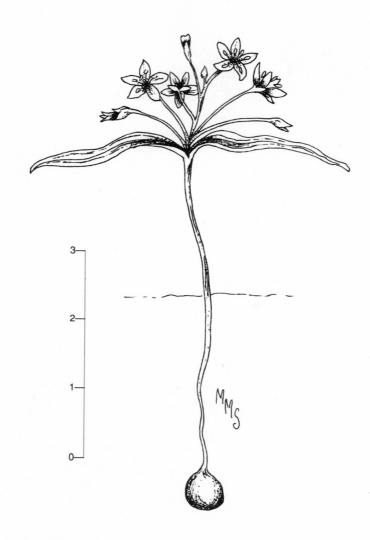

THREE-LEAVED LEWISIA   *Lewisia triphylla*   PURSLANE

Height: 4 in.   Corm   ❀ **PINK** ❀

Habitat: MOIST, GRAVEL FLATS   MAY/JUNE

Trail: SOUTHEAST SIDE OF GRASS LAKE

This delicate little Lewisia varies between two and three leaves. Two other species of Lewisia have been found in the area. They are *L. nevadensis* and *L. kelloggii*, both illustrated on pages 80–81.

158

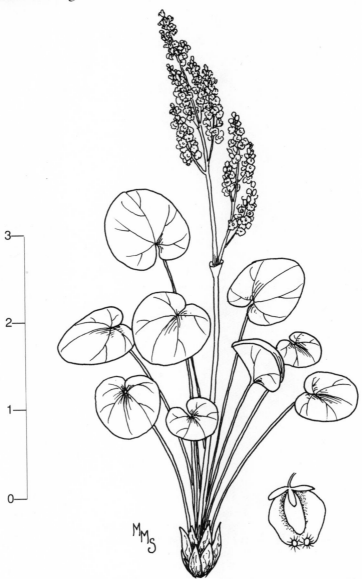

MOUNTAIN SORREL   *Oxyria digyna*   BUCKWHEAT

Height: 10 in.   Perennial   ❀ **PINK TO GREEN** ❀

Habitat: ROCKS   JULY

Trail: UPPER ROUND LAKE CIRQUE

The genus name is derived from the Greek *oxus*, meaning sour. *Digyna* means with two pistils. Nibble a leaf to relieve your thirst; it will remind you of sour grass. The leaves and stem are edible. I have not found this plant on any of the trails, but only when hiking cross-country in the cirques above Round Lake and Upper Helgramite Lake.

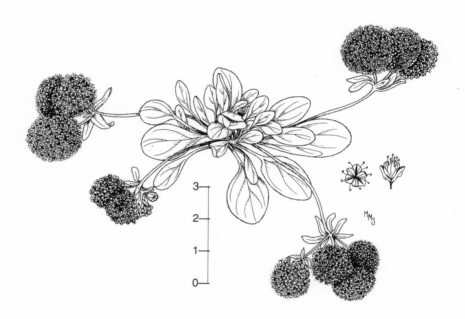

LOBB'S BUCKWHEAT   *Eriogonum lobbii*   BUCKWHEAT

Height: To 8 in.   Perennial   ❀ PINK ❀

Habitat: GRAVEL SLOPES   JULY/AUGUST

Trail: PCT ❧ ABOVE ROUND LAKE;

SIERRA BUTTES LOOKOUT ❧ ON EAST-FACING SCREE

The Greek word *erio* means wool, and *gonu* means knee or joint. Some species are hairy at the nodes. Lobb's Buckwheat has soft, fuzzy silver-white leaves that insulate the plant as it sprawls on hot rocks. This plant is particularly beautiful about halfway up the trail to Sierra Buttes Lookout. The color and puffy shape may remind you of a large Pussy Paw (*Calyptridium umbellatum*), although they are not related except in sharing hot habitats. The seeds of Lobb's Buckwheat can be ground into flour.

PUSSY PAWS   *Calyptridium umbellatum*   PURSLANE

Height: 7 in.   Perennial   ❀ **PINK TO WHITE** ❀
Habitat: DRY   JUNE
Trail: LAKES BASIN CAMPGROUND

Calyptridium is from the Greek word *kaluptra*, meaning a cap or covering, because of the way the petals close over the capsule in age. *Umbellatum* refers to the umbrella shape of the flowering head. You will notice
that the flower heads are on the ground in the morning, stand upright
during the day, and return to the ground at night. Is this to escape the
surface heat during the day? Pussy Paws range from rosy pink to creamy
white; the darkest pink I have seen is on the north side of Highway 49 just
above Sierra City.

RED MOUNTAIN HEATHER   *Phyllodoce breweri*   HEATH

Height: To 12 in.   Shrub   ❀ **PINK** ❀
Habitat: ROCKS, MOIST   JUNE/JULY
Trail: LONG LAKE TRAIL BELOW LAKE OUTLET; ROUND LAKE CIRQUE

Phyllodoce is the Greek name of a sea nymph. The plant is usually found near moisture. Red Heather—actually magenta in color—cascades down through the Mountain Hemlocks and beautiful yellow *Arnica* on the hillside above Round Lake. It is worth a little rock-hopping to get close to this hillside garden.

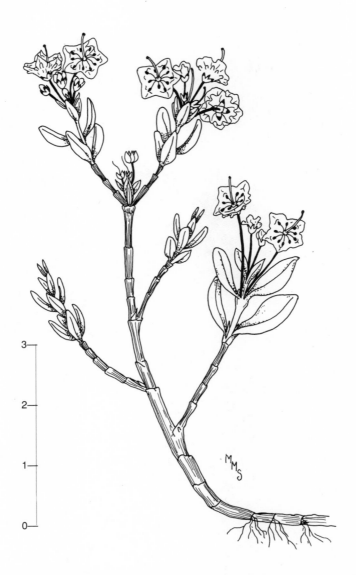

BOG LAUREL *Kalmia polifolia var. microphylla* HEATH

Height: 5 in. Shrub ❀ **PINK** ❀
Habitat: MOIST JUNE
Trail: SILVER LAKE TO PCT 🌿 NEAR UPPER HELGRAMITE LAKE
This delightful little lake liner has a clever pollinating mechanism. When an insect lands on the edge of the cup-shaped petal, the petal bends slightly and releases the anther from a depression in the petal. The filament, acting as a spring, tosses the pollen from the anther onto the insect.

PINE-MAT MANZANITA   *Arctostaphylos nevadensis*   HEATH

Height: To 9 in. with 3 ft. spread   Shrub   ❀ **WHITE TO PALE PINK** ❀
Habitat: MONTANE CHAPARRAL SLOPES   MAY/JUNE
Trail: BEAR LAKE 🐾 BETWEEN BEAR AND LONG LAKES

The genus name is derived from the Greek *arctos,* meaning bear, and *staphyle*, a bunch of grapes, referring to the hanging fruit. Bears and other animals do eat the fruit, and, in fact, the germination of the seed is more reliable if it has been processed with digestive acids to remove the waxy covering on the seed. Manzanitas are wonderful landscape shrubs, particularly effective when low-growing and taller species are used together.

GREENLEAF MANZANITA   *Arctostaphylos patula*   HEATH

Height: 5 ft.   Shrub   ❀ **PALE PINK** ❀
Habitat: MONTANE CHAPARRAL AND SLOPES   MAY/JUNE
Trail: BEAR LAKE ❧ BETWEEN BEAR AND LONG LAKES

The cooked ripe berries make good juice. Crush the berries, add an equal amount of scalding water, and allow the solids to settle. The dried fruit can be ground into meal. Try sucking the sweet nectar from the flowers—although occasionally you might get a peppery ant with the nectar. The upright Greenleaf Manzanita is particularly attractive in combination with the prostrate Pine-mat Manzanita.

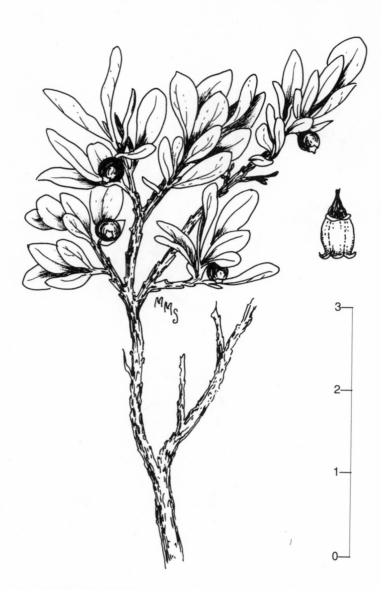

DWARF HUCKLEBERRY   *Vaccinium arbuscula*   HEATH

Height: 1 to 2 ft.   Shrub   ❀ WHITE-PINK ❀

Habitat: MOIST   JUNE

Trail: BEAR LAKE 🐾 AROUND THE EDGE OF BEAR LAKE

The species name, *arbuscula*, means like a small tree. Dwarf Huckleberry and Bilberry both grow in moist areas, and have tasty berries and beautiful fall color. Bear Lake has a rosy ring of Dwarf Huckleberry at the lake's edge in September.

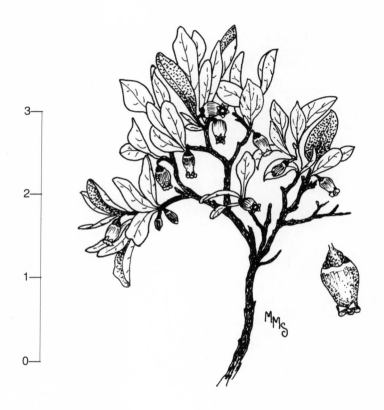

SIERRA BILBERRY   ***Vaccinium nivictum***   HEATH

Height: 8 in.   Shrub   ❀ **WHITE-PINK** ❀
Habitat: MOIST   JUNE
Trail: IN ASPEN BETWEEN LAKES BASIN CAMPGROUND AND GRASS LAKE
Nivictum refers to snow. This diminutive huckleberry grows in wet spots
throughout the campground. It grows with One-sided Wintergreen (*Pyrola secunda*) in moist areas under Alders and Aspen. Look for the little
blueberries at the end of summer.

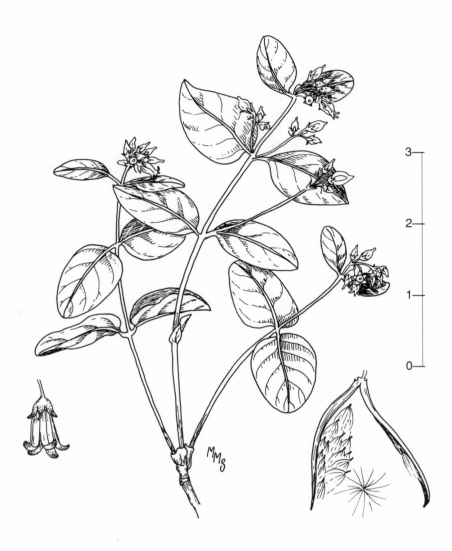

DOGBANE	*Apocynum androsaemifolium*	DOGBANE

Height: 1½ ft.   Perennial   ❀ PINK ❀

Habitat: DRY   JULY/AUGUST

Trail: GRASS LAKE TO LONG LAKE

This Dogbane has bell-shaped flowers. The herbage is poisonous to stock and humans. It has a milky, rubbery juice. The Indians used the soft dry fibers from the stems for weaving. The Dogbane is profuse beside the path just after the Grass Lake outlet.

COLUMBINE   *Aquilegia formosa*   RANUNCULUS
DOVES, GRANNY BONNETS,
EAGLES

Height: To 3 ft.   Perennial   ❀ **RED** ❀
Habitat: MOIST   JULY
Trail: GRAY EAGLE LODGE TRAIL TO LONG LAKE ❧ NEAR LODGE SPRINGS
The genus name is derived from the Latin *aquila*, meaning eagle, because
of the five clawlike nectar spurs. The species, *formosa*, means beautiful.
This popular plant grows in many places throughout the West and so has
many common folk names. Columbine is easy to grow from seed and will
attract hummingbirds to your garden.

169

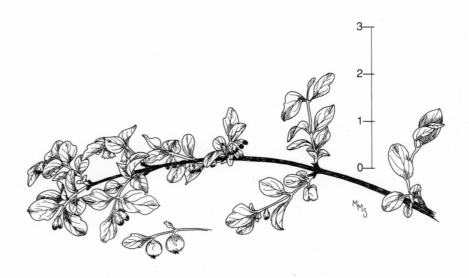

CREEPING SNOWBERRY   HONEYSUCKLE
Symphoricarpos acutus

Height: To 3 ft.   Shrub   ❀ PINK ❀
Habitat: WOODS, MOIST   JULY
Trail: LONG LAKE
        ❧ BETWEEN GRAY EAGLE LODGE AND GRASS LAKE JUNCTION

Symphoreo, of Greek origin, meaning to bear together, and *karpos*, meaning fruit, refer to the clusters of white berries. The leaves, which can be lobed or entire on the same plant, contain saponin, a poison. Snowberry resembles Honeysuckle, to which it is related. Creeping Snowberry is not very noticeable and the variability of the leaves can make it hard to identify.

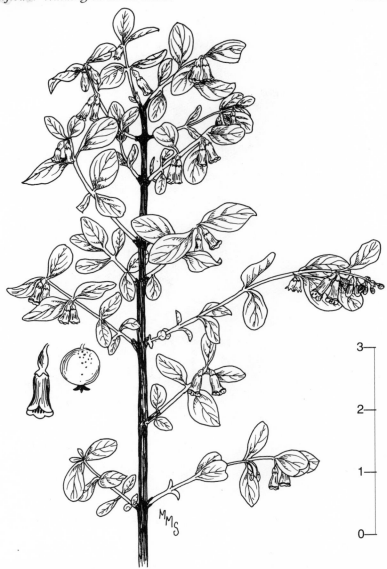

MOUNTAIN SNOWBERRY HONEYSUCKLE
SNOWBERRY *Symphoricarpos vaccinioides*

Height: To 4 ft. Shrub ❀ **PINK** ❀
Habitat: GRAVEL, DRY JULY
Trail: PCT

Symphoricarpos vaccinioides has leaves and little bell-like flowers that look like Huckleberry (*Vaccinium*). The fruit, from which the common name is derived, is white, pulpy, and poisonous. Our only sighting of this plant was on the PCT west of the white rock outcrop. This plant is very common on Carson Pass on the Winnemucca Lake trail.

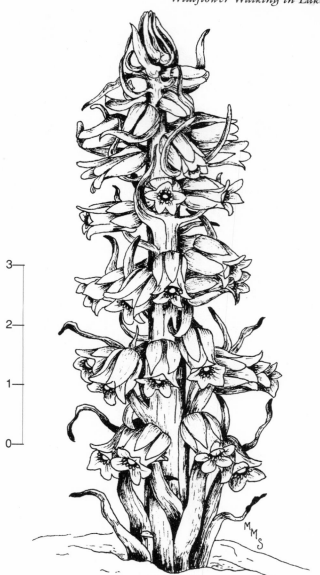

SNOW PLANT *Sarcodes sanguinea* WINTERGREEN

Height: To 15 in.   Saprophytic herb   ❀ **RED** ❀
Habitat: WOODS   JUNE
Trail: ROUND LAKE TRAIL

The origin of the botanical name is Greek, from *sarx*, meaning flesh, and *oeides*, meaning like; *sanguinea* means blood-red. It is thought that the saprophyte lacks chlorophyll and lives on dead organic material. This plant follows the snowmelt and makes a good photograph when the sun's rays highlight it in an otherwise dark forest.

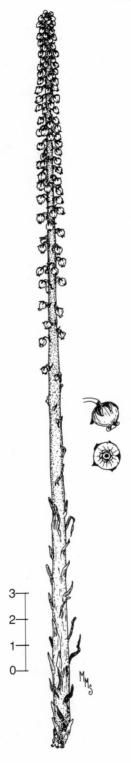

PINEDROPS   WINTERGREEN
Pterospora andromedea   ❀ PINK ❀

Height: To 3 ft.   Herbaceous root-parasite
Habitat: WOODS   JULY/AUGUST
Trail: SILVER LAKE ❧ IN FRONT OF THE
          SILVER LAKE SIGN

The botanical name is of Greek origin, from *pteros*, wing, and *spora*, seed. The stalks are purple-brown to reddish, clammy-pubescent; the flowers are urn-shaped, white to red. Old stalks are beautiful in flower arrangements (don't collect them in public areas). Be sure they are thoroughly dry, and tap out any remaining seeds.

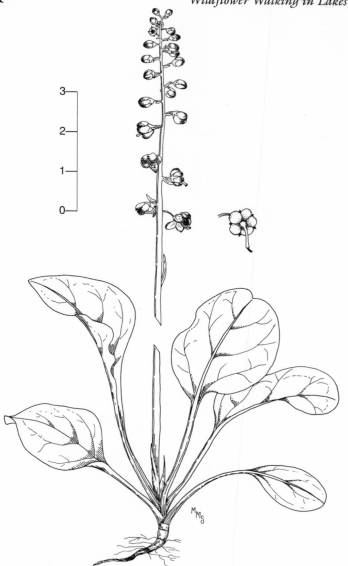

GINGER-LEAF PYROLA
Pyrola asarifolia var. purpurea
WINTERGREEN

Height: To 8 in.   Perennial   ❀ PINK ❀
Habitat: MOIST, SHADE   JULY/AUGUST
Trail: PACKER LAKE PICNIC AREA; ROUND LAKE TRAIL

This *Pyrola* has foliage like the Wild Ginger, whose botanical name is *Asarum*. It is the prettiest of the four *Pyrola* species growing in this region. It has large lush green leaves and beautiful pink flowers. You will find it on Round Lake Trail where the springs cross the trail in the deep shade of the Alder thickets.

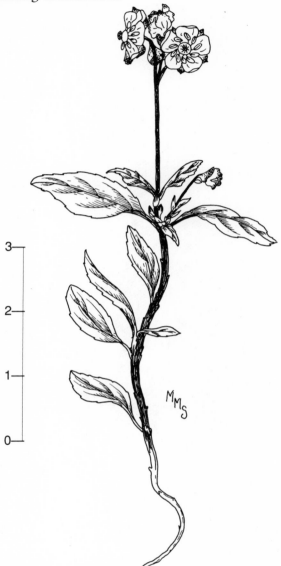

PIPSISSEWA   *Chimaphila menziesii*   WINTERGREEN
LITTLE PRINCE'S PINE

Height: 8 to 10 in.   Perennial   ❀ **WHITE-PINK** ❀
Habitat: WOODS   JULY
Trail: ROUND LAKE 🍂 IN RED FIR FOREST

The origin of this name is from the Greek *cheima*, meaning winter, and *philein*, to love, pertaining to the Wintergreen family. This species has white flowers that age to pink. *Chimaphila umbellata var. occidentalis*, or Western Prince's Pine, found in more open woods, has between three and seven pink flowers. Little Prince's Pine has up to three flowers.

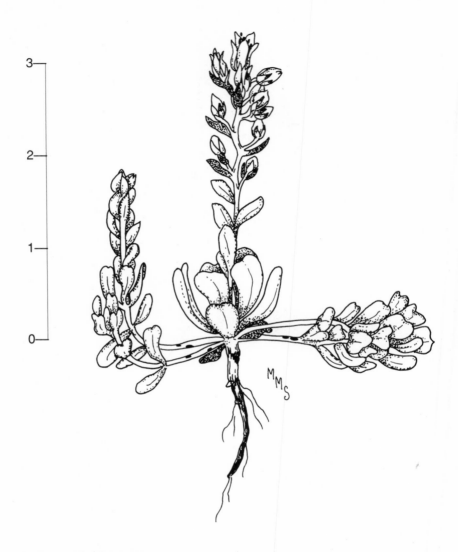

STONECROP, HOUSELEEK   *Sedum obtusatum*   STONECROP

Height: 5 in.   Perennial   ✿ **PINKISH** ✿
Habitat: ROCKS   JULY
Trail: LONG LAKE, GRASS LAKE, GRAY EAGLE LODGE TRAIL JUNCTION
The Latin word *sedum* means to assuage, and *obtusatum* refers to the leaf
shape. The fleshy, succulent plant appears to be pink, although the flowers
start out yellow and fade to pink. The young leaves and plants are edible.

176

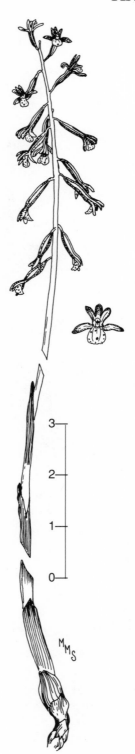

SPOTTED CORAL ROOT ORCHID
Corallorhiza maculata

❀ RED ❀

Height: To 13 in.   Perennial
Habitat: WOODS, RED FIR   JULY
Trail: ROUND LAKE TRAIL

❧ IN THE DARK WOODS

The genus name is of Greek origin, from
korallion, meaning coral, and *rhiza*, root,
and refers to the shape of the root. *Maculata* means spotted. Look at the spots on
the lower petal. The Striped Coral Root
(*Corallorhiza striata*) has stripes on the
petals instead of spots. This plant is toxic.

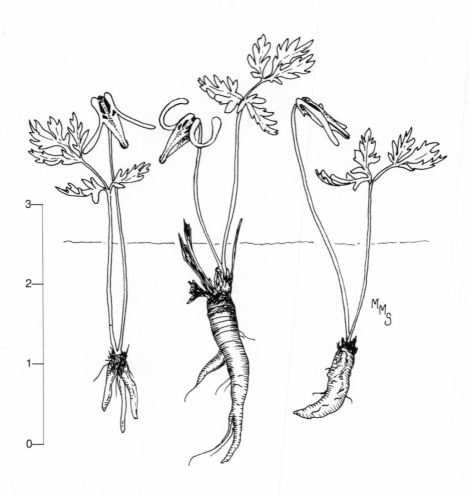

STEER'S HEAD	*Dicentra uniflora*	FUMITORY

Height: To 3 in.   Perennial   ❀ **PINK** ❀
Habitat: GRAVEL   MAY/JUNE
Trail: ROUND LAKE TRAIL 🍂 IN VICINITY OF DOGWOOD

This botanical name translates easily from the Greek *di*, two, and *kentron*, meaning spur: two spurs for the "horns." *Uniflora* means single flower. Steer's Head follows the snowmelt. The blue-green leaves are hard to find. If you see the yellow Shelton's Violet, whose leaves resemble Steer's Head, you are in the right habitat at the right time of the year to spot *Dicentra*.

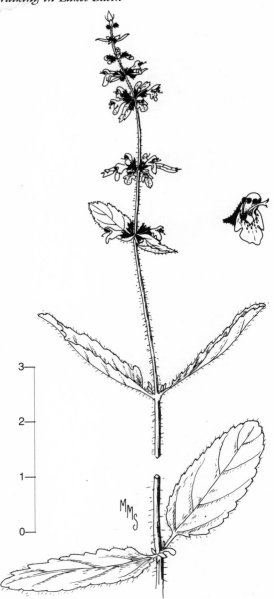

| **HEDGE NETTLE** | *Stachys rigida* | MINT |

Height: 1½ ft.　　　　　Perennial　　　　❀ **PINK** ❀
Habitat: SHADE, MOIST　　　　　　　　　　JULY
Trail: LONG LAKE TRAIL 🐾 AFTER LILY LAKE JUNCTION

Most members of the Mint family have aromatic foliage, square stems, and opposite leaves and are often invasive if used in the garden. *Stachys* means spike and *rigida* is also spike. Hedge Nettle has a beautiful little flower that should be observed with a hand lens.

179

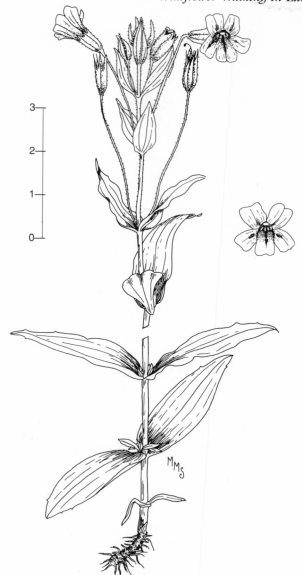

LEWIS'S MONKEY FLOWER   *Mimulus lewisii*   FIGWORT

Height: 2 ft.   Perennial   ❀ **PINK** ❀
Habitat: MOIST   JULY
Trail: ROUND LAKE 🍂 ROUND LAKE CIRQUE; PCT SPRING
Lewis's Monkey Flower, with its long blooming period and beautiful
flowers, is a good candidate for the garden. Its water requirements are the
same as those for Pansies and Columbine. Look into a flower and observe
the yellow ridges that guide insects to the nectar, thereby pollinating the
flower.

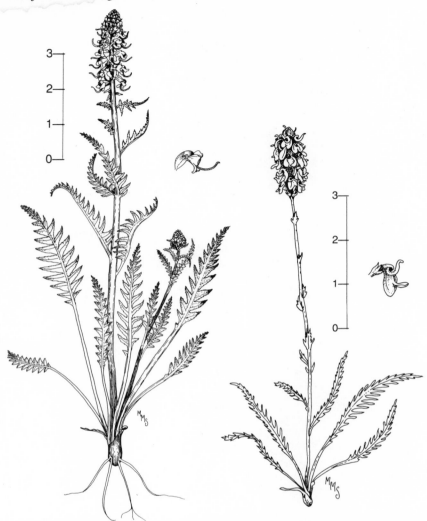

ELEPHANT HEADS FIGWORT *LITTLE ELEPHANT HEADS*
Pedicularis groenlandica   *Pedicularis attolens*

JULY	❀ PINK ❀	JULY
Height: 6 in. to over 14 in.	Perennial	6 to 12 in.
Habitat: MOIST		MOIST

Trail: UPPER HELGRAMITE LAKE ❧ ABOVE SILVER LAKE

The flower really does look like an elephant's head with ears and a trunk. This unusual flower can turn a whole meadow pink. It grows with the Alpine Shooting Star (*Dodecatheon alpinum*) and Bog Laurel (*Kalmia polifolia var. microphylla*). *Pedicularis attolens* is a more delicate plant. The species name, *attolens*, means upraised, referring to the little twisted trunk. Both species grow in Gray Eagle Lodge meadow, where they bloom earlier in the summer than at Upper Helgramite Lake.

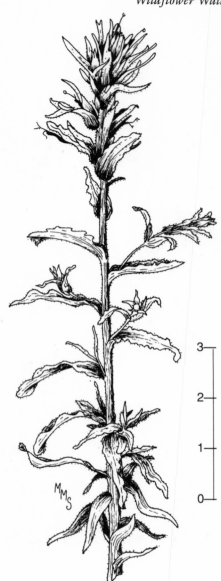

WAVY-LEAF PAINTBRUSH   *Castilleja applegatei*   FIGWORT
APPLEGATE'S PAINTBRUSH

Height: 12 in.   Perennial   ❀ **RED** ❀
Habitat: SLOPES AND MEADOWS; DRY   JULY
Trail: ROUND LAKE ❧ BEYOND GOLD LAKE LODGE IN SUN

Castilleja, named for a Spanish botanist, is a partial parasite, often growing in close proximity to grasses or sagebrush. Notice the wavy leaves on Applegate's Paintbrush. Lupine and Paintbrush, with their contrasting colors of blue and red, are often found growing together.

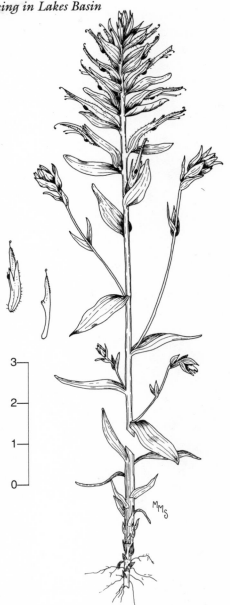

GIANT RED PAINTBRUSH   **Castilleja miniata**   FIGWORT

Height: To 3 ft.   Perennial   ❀ **RED TO MAGENTA** ❀
Habitat: SLOPES AND MEADOWS; MOIST   JULY
Trail: ROUND LAKE ❧ MEADOW ABOVE GOLD LAKE LODGE

Giant Red Paintbrush is very showy growing with Corn Lilies and other moisture-loving plants near the spring that supplies Gold Lake Lodge. The species name, *miniata*, means cinnabar-red. The magenta form of this paintbrush is not often found in the Lakes Basin region

PRIDE OF THE MOUNTAIN Penstemon newberryi FIGWORT
NEWBERRY'S PENSTEMON

Height: 8 to 20 in.   Perennial   ❀ **MAGENTA** ❀
Habitat: ROCKS   JUNE/JULY
Trail: ROUND LAKE TRAIL ❧ BELOW ROUND LAKE

Long-blooming Newberry's Penstemon is probably the first mountain penstemon you will recognize. Pride of the Mountain, another common name, often grows along highways and is especially beautiful on Interstate 80 between Soda Springs and Cisco. It grows well in a dry mountain garden and is available at Lake Tahoe nurseries.

184

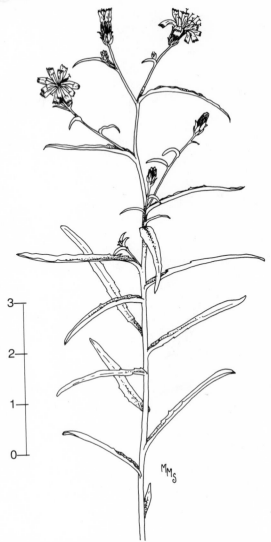

NARROW-LEAVED STEPHANOMERIA   COMPOSITE
Stephanomeria tenuifolia

Height: 12 in.   Annual   ❀ **PINK-LAVENDER** ❀
Habitat: SLOPES, DRY   AUGUST
Trail: ROUND LAKE TRAIL 🦫 BELOW MINE

This late-blooming member of the Composite family is an unusual color
for the Chickory or Dandelion tribe. It has milky juice when a leaf is torn,
and there are only ray flowers, no disk or center flowers. These qualities
put *Stephanomeria* into the Dandelion tribe. It is not as abundant in Lakes
Basin as it is along the sandy roadsides in Yosemite between Crane Flat and
May Lake in late summer.

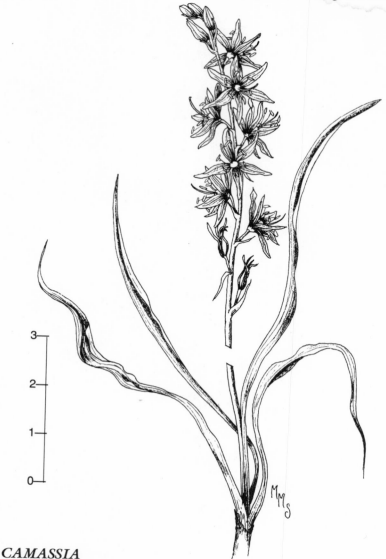

CAMASSIA
CAMAS LILY   *Camassia quamash ssp. breviflora*   LILY

Height: To 2 ft.   Bulb   ❀ **BLUE** ❀
Habitat: MOIST MEADOWS   JULY
Trail: BEAR LAKE 🐾 BELOW THE OUTLET ALONG THE CREEK

Camas means sweet in the Chinook Indian language, and the bulb was a major part of the Indian diet. The bulb would be steamed for twenty-four hours, then patted into cakes and dried. Wars were fought over territorial rights to the land where Camassia grows. Unfortunately, the Death Camas (*Zigadenus venenosus*) also grows in the same habitat and so the Death Camas had to be marked so it would not be harvested by mistake. Do not pick.

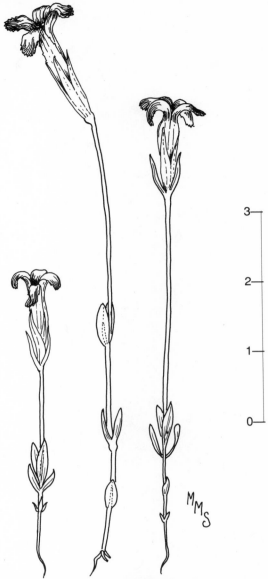

		3—
		2—
		1—
		0—

HIKER'S GENTIAN   *Gentiana simplex*   GENTIAN

Height: 4 to 6 in.   Annual   ❀ **BLUE** ❀
Habitat: MOIST   AUGUST
Trail: GRASS LAKE 🐾 ON NORTHERN PENINSULA

Hiker's Gentian is small in comparison with the host of Gentians in Switzerland. The blue Gentians are always a thrill to find because of their rich royal-blue flowers. The Sierra flora contains several Gentians, but this is the only one we have found in Lakes Basin. *Gentiana simplex* has an unbranched stem.

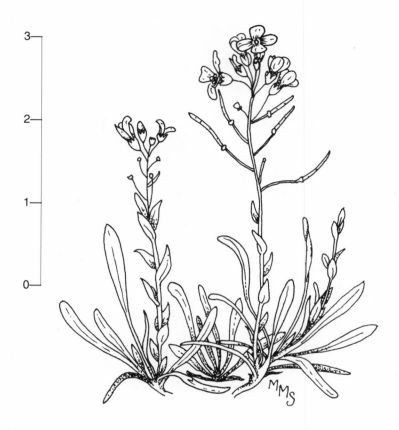

BREWER'S ROCK CRESS   *Arabis breweri*   MUSTARD

Height: 4 to 5 in.   Perennial   ❀ **PURPLE** ❀
Habitat: ROCK CREVICES   JUNE
Trail: GRASS LAKE TRAIL TO GRAY EAGLE LODGE
           🌣 IN ROCK GARDEN BY WATERFALL

This showy rock-garden plant grows below the creek crossing at the junction of the Grass Lake, Long Lake, and Gray Eagle Lodge trails. Some of the companion plants found in these large rocks are Bear Buckwheat (*Eriogonum ursinum*), Hot Rock Penstemon (*Penstemon deustus*), and another member of the Mustard family, Jewel Flower (*Streptanthus tortuosus*). Notice the long mustard-seed pod, called a silique, on the Jewel Flower and the Rock Cress.

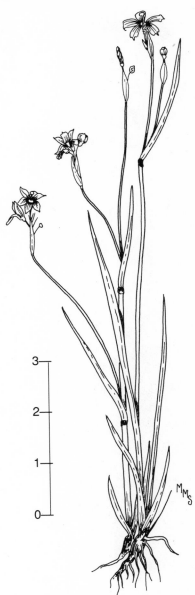

IDAHO BLUE-EYED GRASS   *Sisyrinchium idahoense*   IRIS

Height: 10 in.   Perennial   ❀ **BLUE** ❀
Habitat: MOIST   JUNE/JULY
Trail: LONG LAKE TRAIL ❧ NEAR SPRINGS BY GRAY EAGLE LODGE
The moist trail to Long Lake near Gray Eagle Lodge is the only place in
the Lakes Basin region where Blue-eyed Grass has been seen. The leaves
resemble those of iris. *Sisyrinchium bellum*, Blue-eyed grass, is common at
lower elevations and has a purplish flower.

189

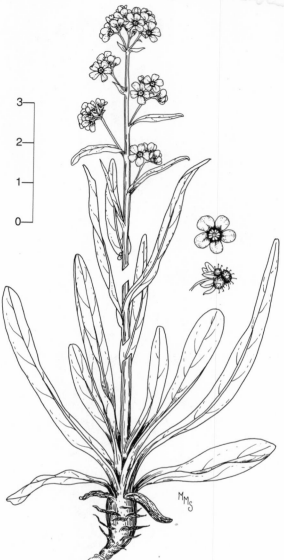

·*STICKSEED*   *Hackelia nervosa*   BORAGE
MOUNTAIN FORGET-ME-NOT

Height: To 1½ ft.   Perennial   ❀ **BLUE** ❀
Habitat: SLOPES   JUNE
Trail: LAKES BASIN CAMPGROUND ENTRY ROAD ❧ ON UPHILL SIDE

The prickles on the seed are responsible for the common name of Stickseed. The arrangement and shape of the prickles help to identify which kind of stickseed it is. In August you might have to spend time pulling Stickseed off your socks. Notice the white corona or crown in the center of the flower, typical of the Borage family.

LUNGWORT *Mertensia ciliata var. stomatechoides* BORAGE
MOUNTAIN BLUEBELLS,
LANGUID LADIES

Height: To 3 ft. Perennial ❀ **BLUE** ❀

Habitat: MOIST JULY

Trail: HELGRAMITE LAKE TO PCT SPRING GARDEN

Lungwort (an Old English common name) was once used to cure lung diseases. Wort, which appears so often in common names, is the Old English word for plant. With a hand lens, observe the papillate surface (little bumps) of the leaf. Mountain Bluebells are not common in Lakes Basin.

191

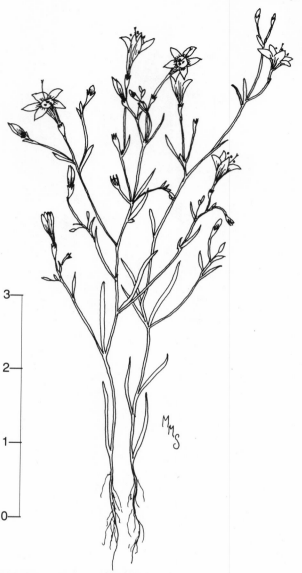

BRIDGE'S GILIA   *Gilia leptalea*   PHLOX

Height: To 5 in.   Annual   ❋ **LAVENDER-PINK** ❋
Habitat: OPENINGS IN WOODS   JUNE
Trail: ROUND LAKE ❧ ENTRY TO GOLD LAKE LODGE

This tiny annual looks like a lavender mist on the ground. It blooms while there is still moisture from the snowmelt. Very few annual plants can grow at the higher altitudes in the Sierra because the season is too short. Annuals need to grow, flower, attract a pollinator, and produce seed before the soil dries completely.

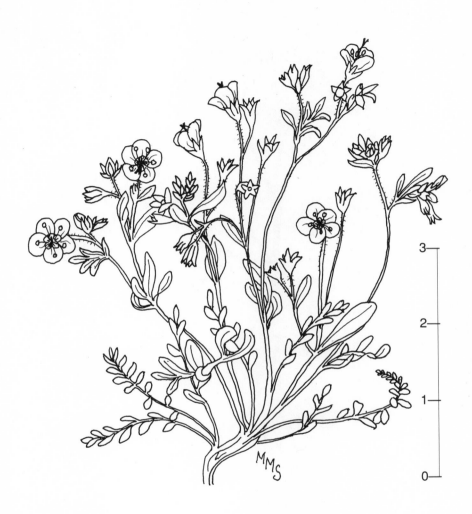

SHOWY POLEMONIUM *Polemonium pulcherrimum* PHLOX

Height: 5 to 10 in.   Perennial or Subshrub   ❀ **BLUE** ❀
Habitat: DRY, ROCKY, HIGH ELEVATION   JULY
Trail: SIERRA BUTTES LOOKOUT ABOVE TREES

Showy Polemonium usually grows in volcanic soil above 8,000 feet. In this case, start watching for it after you have left the forest behind. It looks like a small shrub with its rich green leaves and striking blue flowers nestled between the rocks and boulders just below the lookout.

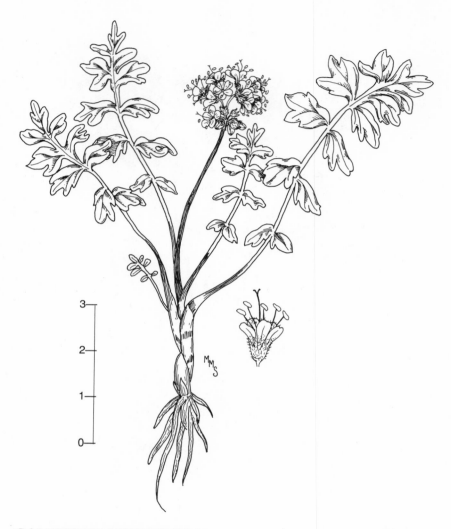

CALIFORNIA WATERLEAF
Hydrophyllum occidentale

WATERLEAF

Height: 8 to 10 in.   Perennial   ❀ LAVENDER ❀

Habitat: SLOPES, SOME SHADE   JUNE

Trail: LAKES BASIN CAMPGROUND ENTRY ROAD 🦎 ON UPHILL SIDE

The botanical name translates easily into *hydro*, water, and *phyllum*, leaf. This is the common name of the family. The flower is pale lavender. The young shoots can be eaten raw, but the roots must be cooked. You will find this plant growing with the Mountain Forget-me-not (*Hackelia nervosa*) on the entry road to the Lakes Basin Campground.

LOBB'S NAMA   *Nama lobbii*   WATERLEAF

Height: To 2 in.   Perennial   ❀ **BLUISH-PURPLE** ❀

Habitat: GRAVEL, DRY   JULY

Trail: PCT WEST OF WHITE RHYOLITE OUTCROP

Lobb's Nama is a tough little plant; it is growing through the asphalt in a friend's driveway at Lake Tahoe. The only place I have seen it in Lakes Basin is on a very hot and rocky south exposure. Lobb's Nama grows on the PCT with Mountain Snowberry (*Symphoricarpos vaccinifolia*) and *Chamaesaracha nana*.

BLUE WITCH *Solanum xantii var. montanum*   NIGHTSHADE
DEADLY NIGHTSHADE

Height: To 2 ft.   Shrub   ❁ **BLUE** ❁
Habitat: GRAVEL   JULY
Trail: PCT WEST OF WHITE RHYOLITE OUTCROPPING
Look closely at the blue flower and perhaps you can see the resemblance to
the tomato flower. Dwarf Chamaesaracha, located in this same area, is a
white flower growing right in the middle of the path. Both plants are in the
Solanaceae or Nightshade family, and both have poisonous fruits that look
like tiny tomatoes, which are also in the Nightshade family.

SQUAW CARPET   *Ceanothus prostratus*   BUCKTHORN
MAHALA MAT

Height: 10 in.   Shrub   ❀ **BLUE-LAVENDER** ❀
Habitat: GRAVEL   MAY/JUNE
Trail: LONG LAKE TRAIL 🐾 ABOVE GRAY EAGLE LODGE IN DRY CREEK BED
Prostratus refers to the matlike growth of this *Ceanothus*. The prostrate
branches can be three feet or more in length. The flowers vary from
blue-lavender to a pale lavender. The seeds have a red cast. To grow
Ceanothus you must treat the seed as if it has passed through a bird's
digestive tract so that the waxy seed coat is destroyed. Pour boiling water
over the seed and leave it in the water overnight; then plant the seed in a
mountain garden.

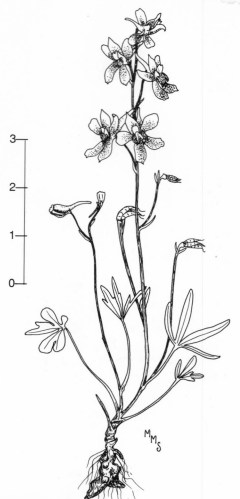

BILOBED DELPHINIUM   RANUNCULUS
LARKSPUR   *Delphinium nuttallianum*

Height: 12 in.   Perennial   ❀ BLUE ❀
Habitat: GRAVELLY   JUNE/JULY
Trail: BEAR LAKE TRAIL
        ᏋᎧ FROM LAKES BASIN CAMPGROUND ENTRY ROAD

Beautiful blue delphinium, so named because the bud resembles a dolphin, is a member of the Ranunculus or Crowfoot family. Notice the leaves are shaped like a crow's foot. The large blue petal-like structures have five outer sepals with the upper-most sepal a spur, and four small inner petals that have white edges. In other species these inner petals are often white. The seed pod is a five-chambered follicle containing shiny black seeds. *D. glaucum*, also in this area, is a five-foot Larkspur and is spectacular growing in moist areas in late July. Delphinium are very poisonous to cattle.

MONKSHOOD　　　***Aconitum columbianum***　　　RANUNCULUS

Height: To 5 ft.　　　　　Perennial　　　　❀ **BLUE** ❀
Habitat: MOIST　　　　　　　　　　　　　JULY
Trail: GRASS LAKE TO LONG LAKE TRAIL

This plant is extremely poisonous. The juice, containing the alkaloid aconitine, was used by the Greeks and Romans to poison their arrows. The flower has five large sepals, the upper ones forming the hood. They are generally blue-purple. Ours is pale blue. Monkshood is pollinated by bumblebees. This beautiful plant is related to Columbine (*Aquilegia formosa*) and Larkspur (*Delphinium sp.*).

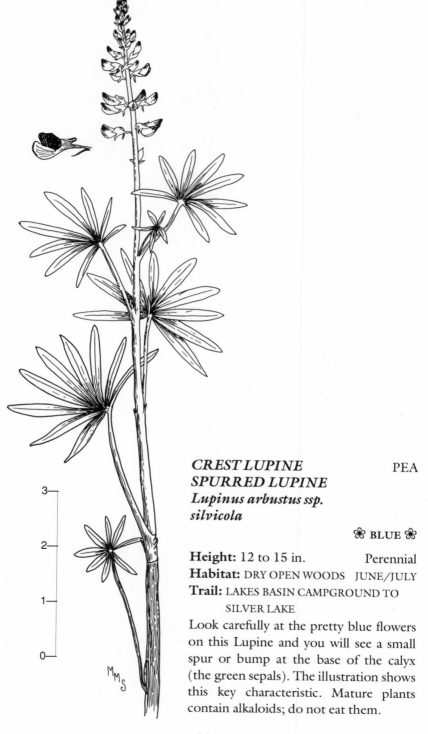

CREST LUPINE   PEA
SPURRED LUPINE
Lupinus arbustus ssp.
silvicola

❀ BLUE ❀

Height: 12 to 15 in.   Perennial
Habitat: DRY OPEN WOODS   JUNE/JULY
Trail: LAKES BASIN CAMPGROUND TO
       SILVER LAKE

Look carefully at the pretty blue flowers on this Lupine and you will see a small spur or bump at the base of the calyx (the green sepals). The illustration shows this key characteristic. Mature plants contain alkaloids; do not eat them.

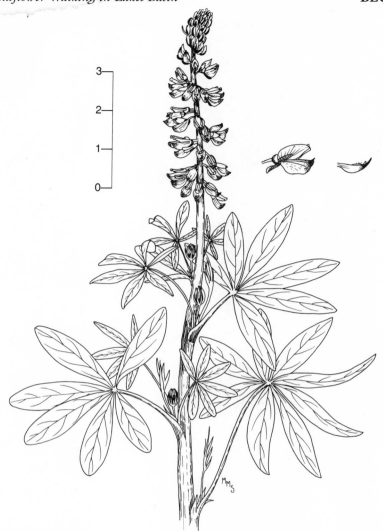

BOG LUPINE   *Lupinus latifolius*   PEA
BROAD-LEAF LUPINE, BLUEBONNETS

Height: To 5 ft.   Perennial   ❀ **BLUE** ❀
Habitat: MOIST   JULY
Trail: ROUND LAKE TRAIL ❧ ABOVE GOLD LAKE LODGE

This is the showiest of the lupines in this region. It is very similar to another large moisture-loving lupine, *Lupinus polyphyllus*, which is the parent of the garden Russell Lupine that the English hybridized. *Lupinus polyphyllus* has flowers that are stacked in parallel planes on the stem or verticilate, whereas the position of the flowers on Bog Lupine has a spiral appearance. There are several locations in Lakes Basin where you will see this beautiful Lupine.

201

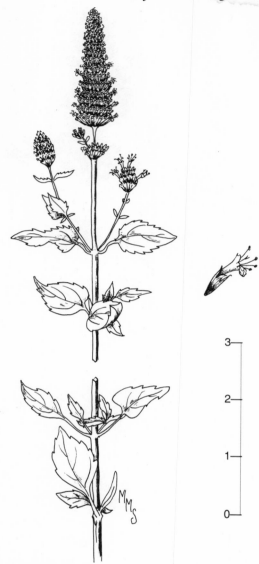

NETTLELEAF HORSEMINT *Agastache urticifolia* MINT HYSSOP

Height: 3 ft.   Perennial   ❀ **BLUE-PURPLE** ❀
Habitat: MEADOWS, WOODS, OPEN   JULY
Trail: ROUND LAKE ❧ NEAR GOLD LAKE LODGE

The genus, *Agastache*, is derived from the Greek word *agan*, meaning very much, and *stachys*, meaning a spike. The species, *urticifolia*, refers to the nettle-shaped leaves. The leaves soaked in hot water make a good tea or they can be used in stews. The seeds may be eaten raw or cooked. This might be a good garden plant, although it may be invasive.

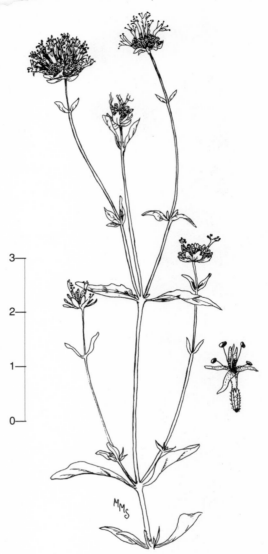

MOUNTAIN PENNYROYAL *Monardella odoratissima*   MINT

Height: To 12 in.   Perennial   ❀ **PALE LAVENDER** ❀

Habitat: SLOPES   JULY

Trail: ROUND LAKE TRAIL 🐾 NEAR GOLD LAKE LODGE

Pennyroyal makes a wonderful tea and becomes a staple for backpackers. It takes very few leaves to make a delightful brew. Or nibble a leaf to quench your thirst as you hike. *Lancet*, the medical journal, came out with an article several years ago reporting that *Monardella odoratissima*, when taken in quantity, could cause an abortion. The Indians knew of this property of Mountain Pennyroyal.

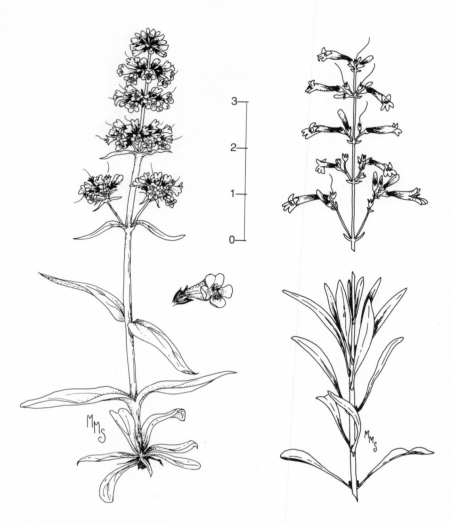

WHORLED PENSTEMON   FIGWORT   *GAY PENSTEMON*
Penstemon rydbergii var. oreocharis   Penstemon laetus ssp. roezlii

JULY   ❀ BLUE ❀   JULY
Height: To 10 in.   Perennial   To 10 in.
Habitat: DRY   GRAVEL, DRY
Trail: ROUND LAKE TRAIL 🌿 BEYOND GOLD LAKE LODGE

Whorled Penstemon grows at the edge of drying meadows. *Penstemon laetus ssp. roezlii* also grows in the meadow just beyond Gold Lake Lodge. The species, *laetus,* means bright or vivid. The penstemons are all good garden flowers and grow easily from seed in sandy soil.

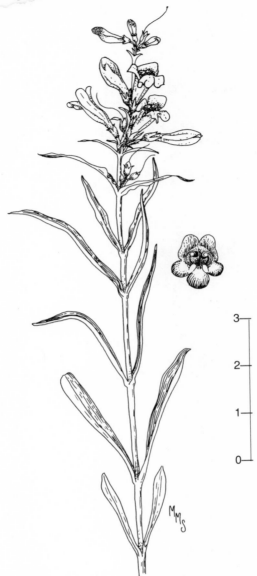

SHOWY PENSTEMON	***Penstemon speciosus*** FIGWORT
BEARD-TONGUE	

Height: 8 to 10 in.   Perennial   ✿ **BLUE** ✿
Habitat: DRY   JULY
Trail: ROUND LAKE ❦ BEYOND GOLD LAKE LODGE

This is the showiest of the blue penstemons. Look inside the throat of this flower and you will understand why penstemons are sometimes called beard-tongue. There are five stamens, one of which is sterile and has a fuzzy tip instead of an anther loaded with pollen.

205

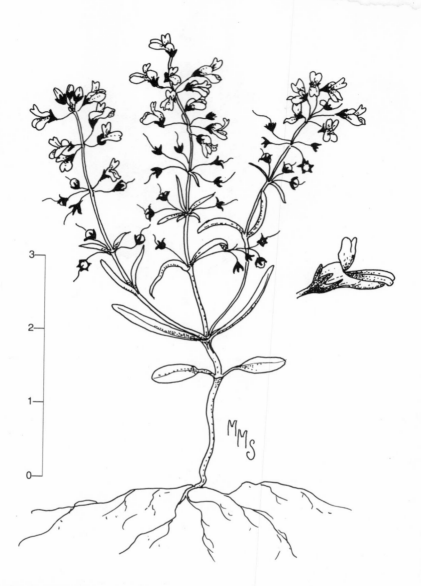

TORREY'S COLLINSIA   *Collinsia torreyi*   FIGWORT

Height: 3 to 9 in.   Annual   ❀ **BLUE-VIOLET AND WHITE** ❀
Habitat: WOODS, GRAVEL FLATS   JULY
Trail: ROUND LAKE TRAIL ❧ UNDER OPEN FOREST

This delicate plant can give the effect of a blue haze on the ground when it is prolific. A more diminutive relative of this Collinsia is Blue-eyed Mary (*Collinsia parviflora*). Look with the hand lens for the glands on the flower stems of Torrey's Collinsia.

WESTERN EUPATORIUM
COMPOSITE

Eupatorium occidentale

❀ LAVENDER-PINK ❀

Height: To 1½ ft.   Perennial
Habitat: ROCKY   JULY/AUGUST
Trail: LONG LAKE 🐾 ALONG
    WESTERN SHORE IN ROCKS

The species, *occidentale*, means western. The genus is derived from a Greek name, Eupator, who was King of Pontus and is said to have used this plant medicinally. *Eupatorium* is not common in this area. It has been seen only on the west shore of Long Lake. At first glance you may be reminded of a mint or spiraea.

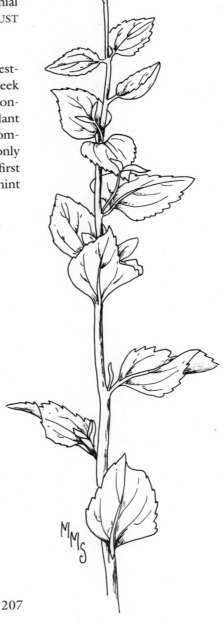

WANDERING DAISY COMPOSITE
Erigeron peregrinus var. angustifolius

Height: To 10 in.   Perennial   ❀ **LAVENDER** ❀
Habitat: MEADOWS   JULY
Trail: ROUND LAKE TRAIL ❧ BEYOND GOLD LAKE LODGE

This botanical name is derived from the Greek *eri,* meaning early, and *geron,* meaning old man. It refers to an early-flowering plant with hoary pubescence. Wandering Daisy is very common and a bit confusing because the bracts resemble those of the *Aster.* The bracts on *Erigeron* are usually very tidy. (See *Erigeron coulteri,* p. 89.) The bracts on *Aster* overlap one another like shingles and the tip of the bract often curls back on itself.

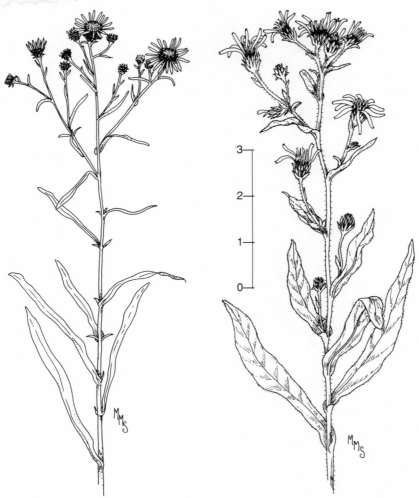

LONG-LEAVED ASTER   **SCRUFFY MOUNTAIN ASTER**
Aster adscendens   COMPOSITE   *Aster integrifolius*

JULY/AUGUST   ❀ **LAVENDER** ❀   JULY/AUGUST
Height: 1½ ft.   Perennial   To 1 ft.
Habitat: MEADOWS, DRY   DRY
Trail: GRASS LAKE; LAKES BASIN CAMPGROUND

Aster is the Greek word for star. Asters are usually late-blooming, have many flower heads, and therefore are good for landscape use. *Aster integrifolius* is a pretty blue hue but is a bit untidy, as the common name implies. The species name, *integrifolius*, refers to the entire leaf shape. Notice that the back of the flower head has overlapping green bracts that hold the flower together. These are called imbricated bracts and act something like shingles.

209

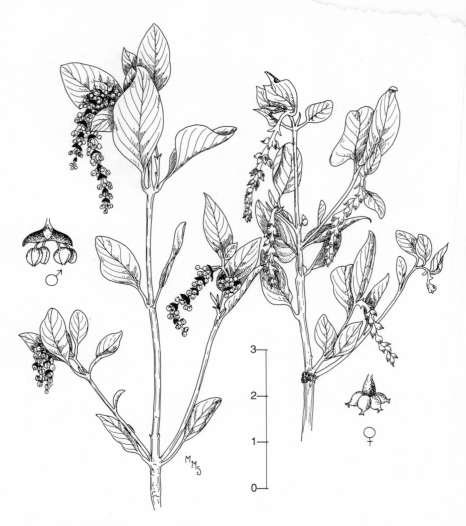

FREMONT'S SILK TASSEL BUSH   GARRYA
Garrya fremontii

Height: To 7 ft.   Shrub
Habitat: DRY SLOPES   MAY
Trail: LONG LAKE TRAIL FROM GRAY EAGLE LODGE
     🍃 NEAR DRY STREAMBED

Garrya looks like Manzanita except that it has long catkins and seed clusters. The Silk Tassel Bush is named for the long catkins (male flowers) that hang from the tips of the branches in early spring. The female bush has clusters of seeds that, at first glance, might be confused with Manzanita fruit; check the bark for identification, since the Manzanita bark will be reddish.

210

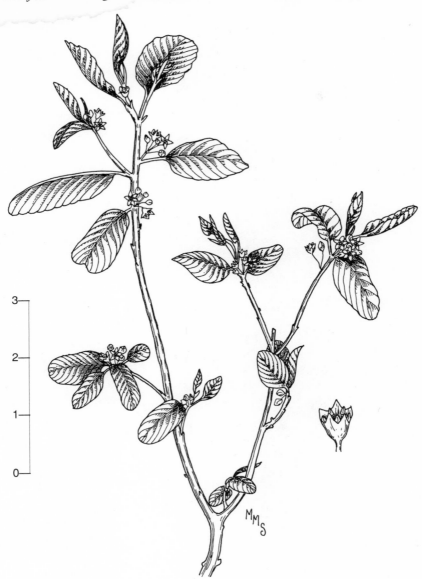

COFFEEBERRY, CASCARA
Rhamnus purshiana

BUCKTHORN

Height: 6 to 20 ft.   Shrub
Habitat: SLOPES
Trail: GRASS LAKE TO LONG LAKE

Cascara is a large shrub with smooth gray or brownish bark. It has elliptic to oblong leaves, 2 to 8 inches long, with prominent veination. The bark has medicinal uses and can be toxic to children.

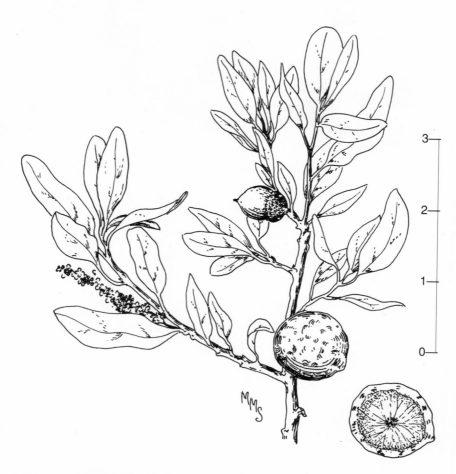

HUCKLEBERRY OAK   *Quercus vaccinifolia*   BEECH

Height: 5 ft.   Shrub
Habitat: MONTANE CHAPARRAL
Trail: BEAR LAKE TRAIL

The species name, *vaccinifolia*, refers to leaves like Huckleberry (*Vaccinium*). Can you find any acorns on this small oak? You probably will find some very decorative pink-spotted galls (see the illustration). Huckleberry Oak and Manzanita are the dominant shrubs of the montane chaparral habitat.

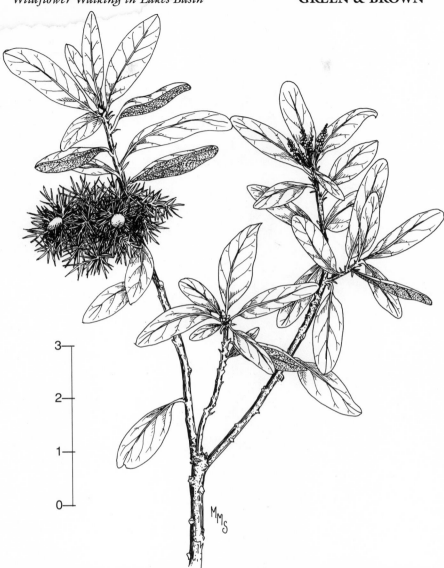

SIERRA CHINQUAPIN   *Castanopsis sempervirens*   BEECH

Height: 4 ft.   Shrub
Habitat: MONTANE CHAPARRAL
Trail: BEAR LAKE TO LONG LAKE

    🍂 ON SOUTH-FACING SLOPE BY BEAR LAKE

The Greek word *Castanea* means chestnut, and *opsis* means resembles. Chinquapin has a nut that ripens in September and can be eaten raw or roasted. Harvest it with thick gloves because it has a spiny outer coat. Often you will find only the empty husk. The underside of the leaf is golden.

213

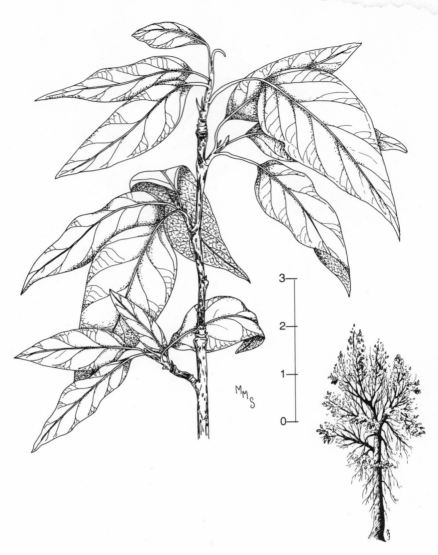

COTTONWOOD   ***Populus trichocarpa***   WILLOW

Height: To 125 ft.   Tree
Habitat: MOIST
Trail: SOUTH SIDE OF GRASS LAKE 🦋 NEAR INLET

The fall color of the Cottonwood is as beautiful as that of the Aspen. They are often found growing together along watercourses. Both Cottonwoods and Aspens are in the *Populus* genus. People object to Cottonwoods because of the messy way they disperse their seed in blowing cotton tufts. The Indians, however, found the Cottonwood useful because the inner bark was emergency food and the sap produced a brown dye.

214

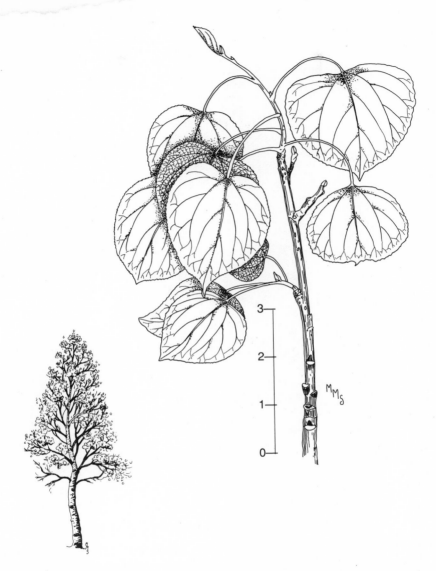

QUAKING ASPEN   *Populus tremuloides*   WILLOW

Height: To 60 ft.   Tree

Habitat: MOIST

Trail: SOUTH SIDE OF GRASS LAKE

There are very large Aspen along the Gold Lake Road. A photographer's delight is to catch the Aspen in their fall foliage against the Sierra Buttes, with bright yellow Rabbitbrush (*Chrysothamnus nauseosus*) in the foreground. The Aspen leaves tremble because of the flat petiole to the leaf. The inner bark is edible in an emergency.

LIGULATE WILLOW	WILLOW	*MACKENZIE'S WILLOW*
Salix ligulifolia		*Salix mackenziana*

Height: 3 to 12 ft.   Shrub   3 to 12 ft.

Habitat: MOIST   MOIST

Salix is the ancient Latin name of the willow. Willows are deciduous shrubs (leaves drop in the fall) and dioecious, meaning that the male and female flowers are borne on different plants. The male flower is the pussy willow bud that becomes yellow with pollen. The female flower is inconspicuous until it becomes swollen with seed and fluff (see *S. mackenziana*). We have at least four different willows in Lakes Basin. They were used by the Indians in basketry.

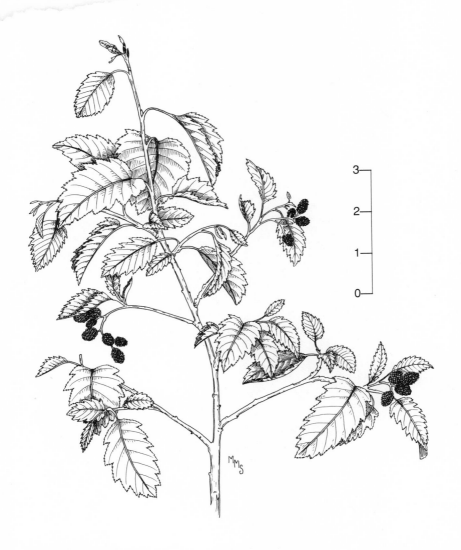

MOUNTAIN ALDER   *Alnus tenuifolia*   BIRCH

Height: To 14 ft.   Shrub
Habitat: MOIST
Trail: GRAY EAGLE LODGE ROAD

Alnus is the ancient Latin name for alder. *Tenuifolia* means slender-leaved. The Alder cone makes a pretty decoration on Christmas packages, in wreaths, or on placecards for Christmas dinner. If you are hiking cross-country and get stuck in the Alders, look under the branches for Twayblade (*Listera convallarioides*), a small white orchid with two opposite leaves. I have seen it in an Alder thicket on the Long Lake trail below Grass Lake.

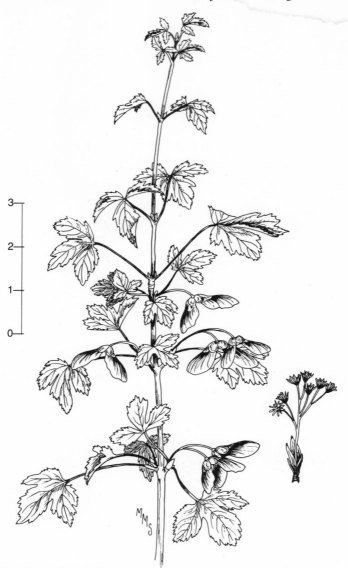

MOUNTAIN MAPLE   *Acer glabrum var. torreyi*   MAPLE

Height: To 10 ft.   Shrub
Habitat: SLOPES
Trail: GRASS LAKE TO LONG LAKE
   🦋 ON WEST-FACING SLOPES NEAR SPRINGS

Acer is the classical Latin name for Maple. *Glabra* means smooth, referring to the leaves. This plant should be used as a food source only in case of emergency. The inner bark can be eaten and the young shoots can be eaten like asparagus. Look for the flowers in early summer and the seed pods in late August.

218

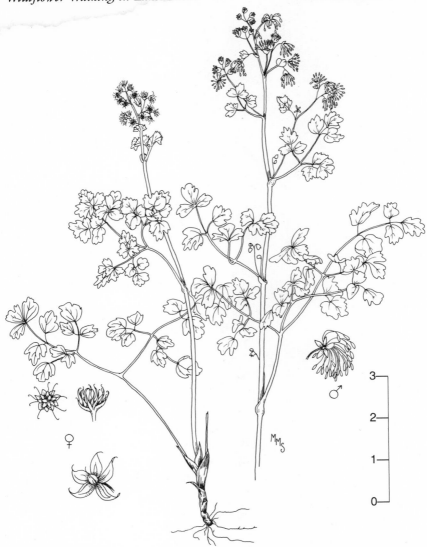

MEADOW-RUE   *Thalictrum fendleri*   RANUNCULUS

Height: To 3 ft.   Perennial

Habitat: WOODS, MEADOWS   JUNE/JULY

Trail: LONG LAKE TRAIL 🐾 IN WOODS NEAR LILY LAKE JUNCTION

The leaves of Meadow-rue resemble those of Columbine (*Aquilegia formosa*), another member of the Ranunculus family. This plant is dioecious, meaning that male and female flowers grow on two separate plants. If your Meadow-rue appears to have yellow flowers, that is really the pollen on the anthers of the male plant. The female plant will be nearby; her flowers don't show up much until you see the star shape in fruit. There are no true petals on either plant.

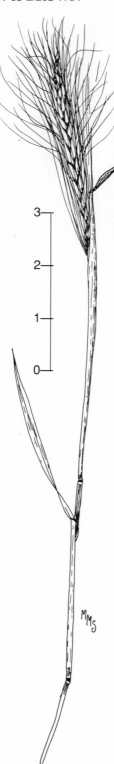

3

2

1

0

SQUIRRELTAIL GRASS   GRASS
Sitanion hystrix var.
californicum

Height: 7 in.
Habitat: DRY
Trail: LONG LAKE TO SILVER LAKE

This grass is lovely in August when it is
backlit by the sun. Be content with a photograph because the head of the grass shat-
ters (falls apart) easily in order to disperse
the seed. Notice the node, or bump, on
the stem of the grass; these joints are the
key characteristic that distinguishes a grass
from a sedge or a rush. Squirreltail Grass
also grows at low elevations.

SEDGE
Carex sp.

TIMOTHY GRASS
Phleum alpinum

RUSH
Juncus sp.

There are many sedges, grasses, and rushes growing in Lakes Basin. They are most often found in moist habitats around lakes and meadows. This little verse may help you remember the different characteristics of these grasslike plants: "sedges have edges, rushes are round, grasses have joints clear to the ground." The sedge leaf blade is like an iris leaf and is flat; the rush can be rolled between your fingers; the grass has bumps or joints on the stem as you run your finger down it. Children break the stem at this point and make grass whistles or nibble the sweet lower part of the stem.

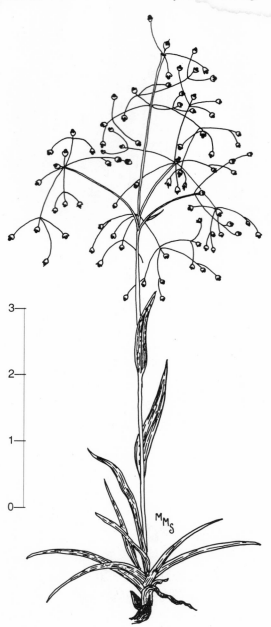

WOOD RUSH   *Luzula divaricata*   RUSH

Height: To 12 in.   Perennial   ❀ **BROWN** ❀
Habitat: SLOPES   JULY
Trail: PCT ABOVE ROUND LAKE CIRQUE

The species, *divaricata*, refers to the branching habit of the flower clusters. This pretty, delicate Wood Rush is found on dry ridges.

BRACKEN, BRAKE FERN
Pteridium aquilinum var. pubescens

FERN

Height: 2 ft.
Habitat: MEADOWS, OPEN WOODS
Trail: MOST LOW ELEVATION TRAILS

Bracken fern is the most common fern and covers large areas. It is too invasive to be considered for gardens. New foliage in the young fiddleneck stage is good raw or steamed and has an almond flavor. Old fronds may be poisonous in large amounts.

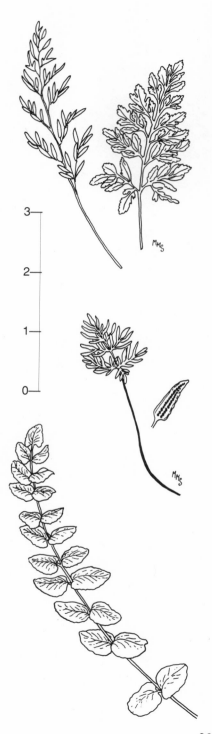

PARSLEY FERN   FERN
ROCK-BRAKE
Cryptogramma
acrostichoides

Height: 8 in.
Habitat: ROCKY

Parsley Fern is an interesting fern because of its two types of growth. The slightly taller type of growth is the fertile frond with its hidden sori. The green sterile or vegetative fronds look like parsley. The genus name is derived from the Greek *cryptos*, hidden, and *gramme*, line, because of the hidden sori.

INDIAN'S DREAM   FERN
CLIFF-BRAKE
Onychium densum

Height: 6 in.
Habitat: ROCKY

The genus name derives from the Greek *onychion*, meaning little claw. The sori on this small rock dweller are protected by the margins that are rolled to the underside of the frond. *Cheilanthes gracillima*, Lace Fern, can also be found in rock crevices.

BRIDGE'S   FERN
CLIFF-BRAKE
Pellaea bridgesii

Height: 7 in.
Habitat: ROCKY

Pellaea bridgesii will catch your eye, particularly on the Round Lake Trail just below the climb to the mine, where it grows at eye level in the south-facing rocks with New-berry's Penstemon.

FIVE FINGER FERN FERN
MAIDENHAIR FERN
Adiantum pedatum var.
aleuticum

Height: 1 ft.
Habitat: MOIST

Maidenhair Fern is found in the cascades below the creek crossing on the trail from Grass Lake to Long Lake. The genus, *Adiantum*, refers to the fern's ability to shed water. The Indians used the stems for the black portion of the design in their baskets.

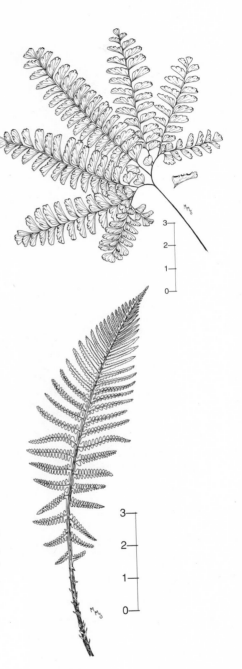

ALPINE LADY FERN FERN
Athyrium alpestre var.
americanum

Height: To 2 ft.
Habitat: MOIST

Alpine Lady Fern is found in moist places, usually at the base of large rocks, in Round Lake cirque. It dies back every year, leaving a bundle of old leaves clustered at the base of the plant. The brown sori on the back of the lacy fronds are round. If the sori are oblong or horseshoe-shaped, you may have Lady Fern (*Athyrium filix-femina*), which is similar but is a slightly larger plant.

DWARF JUNIPER   *Juniperus communis*   CYPRESS
var. montana

Height: 4 to 12 in.   Shrub
Habitat: ROCKY SLOPES
Trail: BETWEEN SILVER AND LONG LAKES

Dwarf Juniper is a beautiful mat-forming landscape shrub with blue-green new foliage. The Juniper berries are edible raw but better dried. There is another area of Dwarf Juniper about half a mile below Long Lake outlet, but it is not common in the Lakes Basin region.

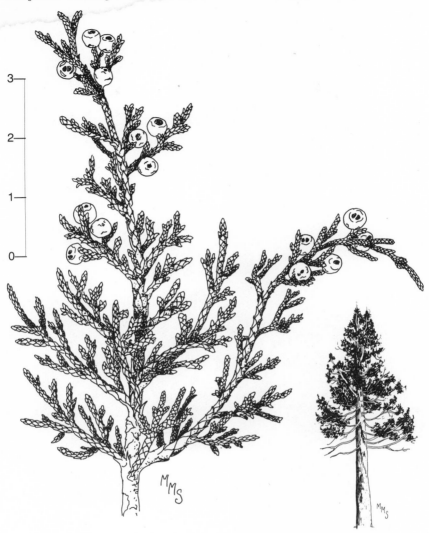

WESTERN JUNIPER　　*Juniperus occidentalis*　　CYPRESS

Height: Over 25 ft.　　　　　　Tree
Habitat: DRY
Trail: LONG LAKE TRAIL 🌲 ON SOUTH-FACING SLOPES

Occidentalis means western. The Western Juniper often grows in rock crevices in high, exposed places, where the tree is sculpted by the wind. Our Junipers are not stressed and therefore lack the contorted shapes characteristic of this species when it grows in cracks in granite. Junipers produce lots of berries, which the Indians dried into cakes. Because Juniper often grows where other plants cannot, Indians have used it for medicine, beads, feasts, and a multitude of other purposes.

227

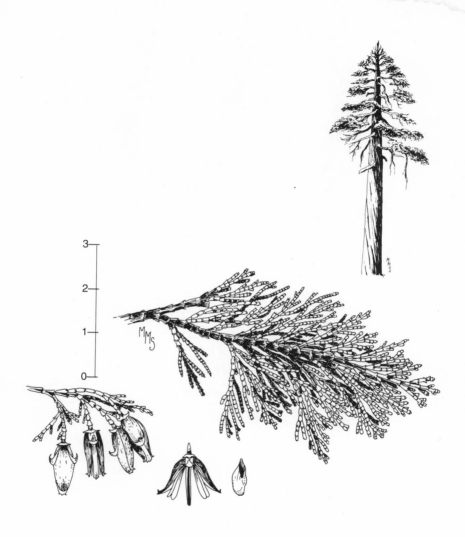

INCENSE CEDAR *Calocedrus decurrens* CYPRESS

Height: 50 to 125 ft. Tree
Habitat: WOODS, CLIMAX SPECIES
Trail: LONG LAKE 🐾 VICINITY OF GRAY EAGLE LODGE

The Greek word *kallos* means beautiful and *decurrent* means running down the stem; this refers to the leaf margin that runs into the stem. The Incense Cedar is the climax species of the mid-elevation forest. Its seedlings can grow and mature in the shade of other trees, and it will outcompete other plants for sunlight.

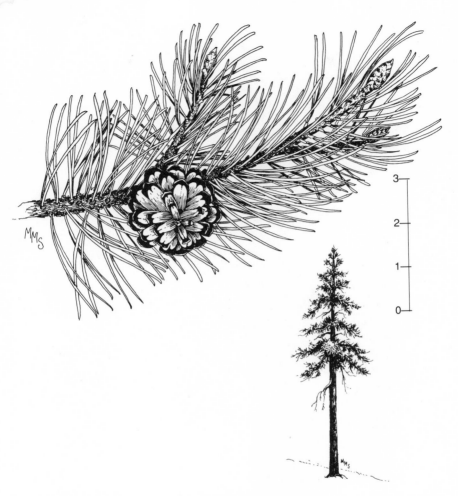

LODGEPOLE PINE   *Pinus murrayana*   PINE
TAMARACK

Height: 50 to 125 ft.   Tree

Habitat: DRY TO MOIST

Trail: GRAY EAGLE LODGE MEADOW

The Lodgepole Pine needles grow in bundles of two, and the small cones are two to three inches in diameter. The bark on mature trees looks like rough alligator hide. This tree is the first pine to colonize a meadow. It often grows on lake banks, and in a meadow you might see a few lone trees that will eventually invade and become a forest. It is interesting to see this forest succession reversing itself in the beaver ponds by Sardine Lake campground.

229

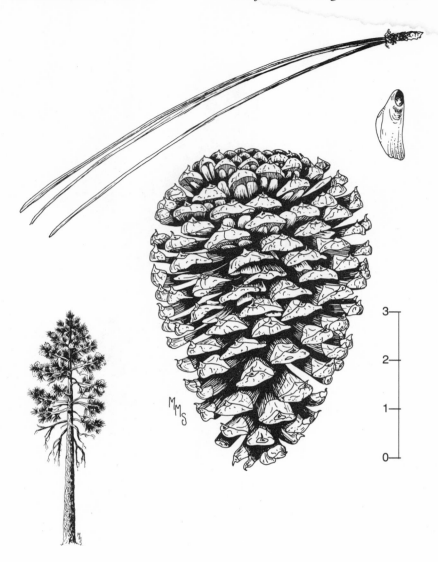

JEFFREY PINE   *Pinus jeffreyi*   PINE

Height: To 170 ft.   Tree
Habitat: DRY
Trail: ROUND LAKE TRAIL 🐾 BEYOND GOLD LAKE LODGE

There are two giant Jeffrey Pines, one dead and one alive, on either side of the Round Lake trail just before you reach the dry meadow garden. Because the pinecone does not prick the fingers, the tree is sometimes called the "gentle Jeffrey." The puzzle-pattern bark has a vanilla odor when it is warmed by the sun. There are some weathered, contorted Jeffrey Pines on the PCT. The nuts and inner bark are edible.

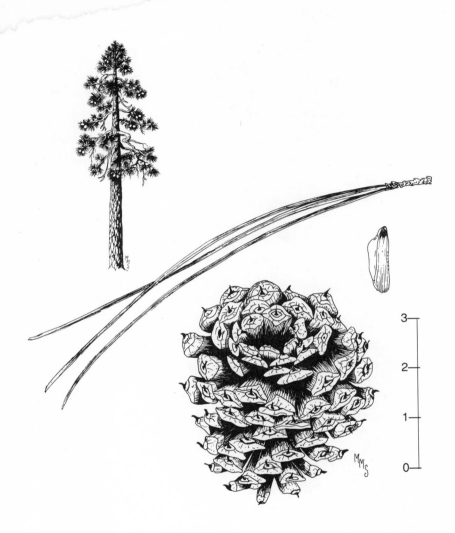

YELLOW PINE 　　*Pinus ponderosa* 　　　PINE
PONDEROSA PINE

Height: To 225 ft. 　　　　　Tree
Habitat: DRY
Trail: GRAY EAGLE LODGE TRAIL TO LILY LAKE
This tree closely resembles the Jeffrey Pine. The easiest way to tell the two
apart is to pick up the pinecone; if the bracts have prickles and make you
yell, you have the Yellow Pine. Look at the illustrations and see why one
cone hurts and the other does not. There are very few Yellow Pines in the
Lakes Basin region, but below Gray Eagle Lodge is a Yellow Pine forest in
the valley along Highway 89.

231

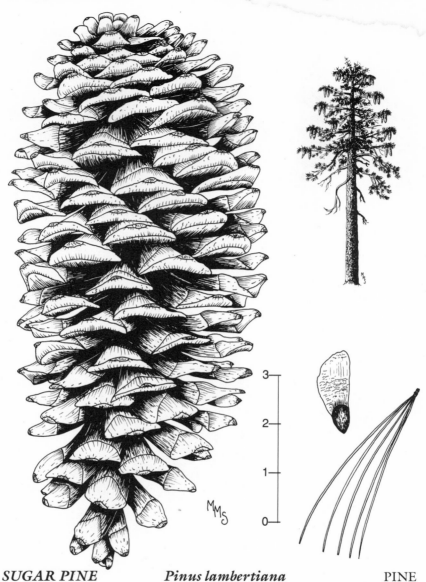

SUGAR PINE   ***Pinus lambertiana***   PINE

Height: To 180 ft.   Tree
Habitat: SLOPES
Trail: LILY LAKE

The Sugar Pine has very long cones, up to 18 inches, that are pendulous on stalks at the end of the branches. These trees are very noticeable along Highway 80 between Colfax and Gold Run at an elevation of about 3,500 feet. There are only a few Sugar Pines in Lakes Basin. This is a five-needle pine and is affected by the White Pine Blister Rust, a fungus that has as a second host the genus *Ribes* or currants and gooseberries.

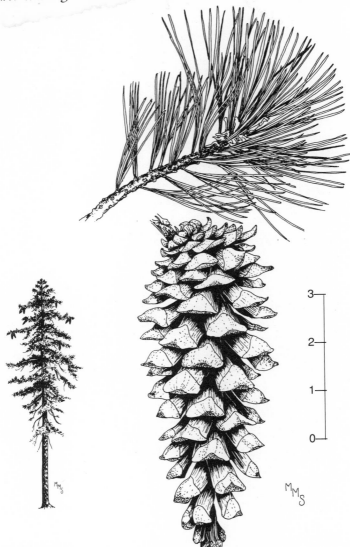

WESTERN WHITE PINE   *Pinus monticola*   PINE
SILVER PINE

Height: 50 to 175 ft.   Tree
Habitat: SLOPES, DRY
Trail: BEAR LAKE TO LONG LAKE 🌿 ON SOUTH-FACING SLOPES

The species name, *monticola*, means living in the mountains. Western White Pine has needles in bundles of five. The bark on older trees has a square pattern. Clusters of "perfect" pinecones hang from the branch tips and look like small Sugar Pine cones. The staminate cones (miniature scale, conelike structure bearing pine pollen) are the favorite food of grouse, whose pellets are bright yellow from the pollen.

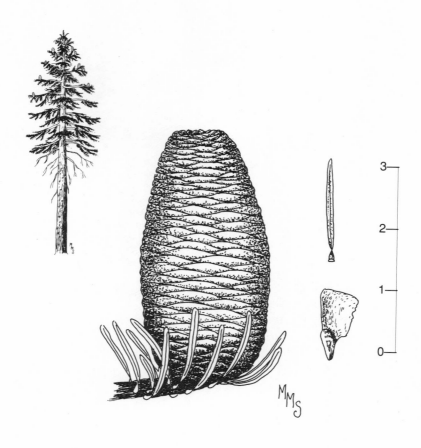

WHITE FIR   *Abies concolor*   PINE

Height: 60 to 150 ft.   Tree
Habitat: SLOPES
Trail: GRAY EAGLE LODGE GATES

Abies is the Latin name for evergreen conifer, while *concolor* means of the same color, referring to the leaf surfaces. White Fir differs from Red Fir (*Abies magnifica*) in that the underbark of Red Fir is burgundy-colored and the underbark of White Fir is yellow. This species of fir can reseed in the shade of other trees and therefore becomes the climax species that can inherit the forest at the 6,000 to 7,000 foot elevation. The Bay Tree (*Umbellularia californica*) is the climax species of low elevation; Incense Cedar (*Calocedrus decurrens*) is the climax species of mid-elevation.

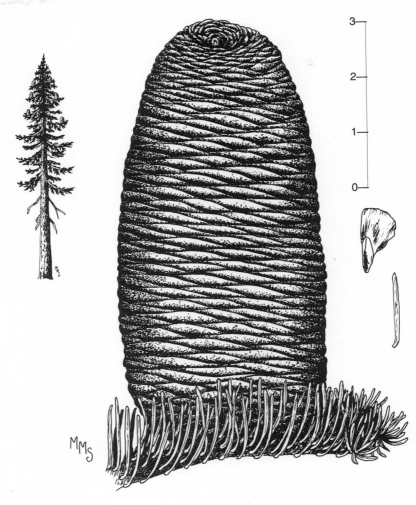

RED FIR   *Abies magnifica*   PINE

Height: To 200 ft.   Tree

Habitat: SLOPES, DRY

Trail: ROUND LAKE 🌿 NEAR GOLD LAKE LODGE

The species name, *magnifica*, means distinguished or magnificent. An easy way to identify the Red Fir is to peel the bark from a mature tree and see the burgundy-colored patch where the bark was removed. Looking up at the crown of the tree, you see a very lacy pattern of branches. Red Fir's other common name is Silvertip Christmas Tree. The White Fir needle has a twist at the base; the Red Fir's does not. The Red Fir forest near Gold Lake Lodge has Staghorn Lichen (*Letharia columbiana*—see illustration on page 16) growing on the trees indicating the level of the snowpack.

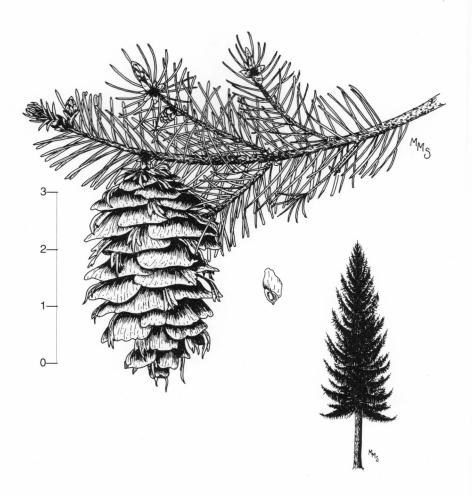

DOUGLAS FIR   *Pseudotsuga menziesii*   PINE
DOUGLAS SPRUCE

Height: To 250 ft.   Tree
Habitat: MOIST
Trail: GRAY EAGLE LODGE TO LILY LAKE

The botanical name is derived from *pseudo*, meaning false, and *tsuga*, meaning hemlock. Notice the little bracts between the scales on the cone. A delicious tea can be made from the needles. Buy a potted Douglas Fir as a Christmas tree and then plant it in your garden either on the coast or in the mountains.

MOUNTAIN HEMLOCK   *Tsuga mertensiana*   PINE

Height: 50 to 90 ft.   Tree

Habitat: SLOPES

Trail: ROUND LAKE TRAIL 🌿 BEFORE CLIMB TO ROUND LAKE MINE

The presence of Mountain Hemlock indicates that you are nearly high enough for alpine plants. The hemlocks occur here as low as 6,540 feet. Some other common names for Mountain Hemlock are Floppy Tops, because of the drooping leader (you can pick them out in the distance by this characteristic), and "Little Blue Star Tree," from the appearance of the new growth.

Plants by Habitat

DRY SCREE

I.D. Hint	Color	Name	Page
4 petals	WHITE	GRAY'S BEDSTRAW *Galium grayanum*	47
round cluster	WHITE	BALL-HEADED GILIA *Ipomopsis congesta*	52
3 petals	WHITE	MARIPOSA LILY *Calochortus leichtlinii*	73
5-9 petals	WHITE, PINK	KELLOGG'S LEWISIA *Lewisia kelloggii*	81
white puffs	WHITE	SHASTA KNOTWEED *Polygonum shastense*	64
composite	WHITE	PINCUSHION FLOWER *Chaenactis douglasii*	*
composite	WHITE-PALE PINK	SIERRA CHAENACTIS *Chaenactis nevadensis*	*
prostrate shrub	YELLOW	BITTERBRUSH *Purshia tridentata*	100
tiny flowers	YELLOW-GREEN	SIBBALDIA *Sibbaldia procumbens*	**
clusters	YELLOW	WHITE-STEM RABBIT BRUSH *Chrysothamnus nauseosus ssp. albicaulis*	136
daisylike	YELLOW	BALSAM ROOT *Balsamorhiza sagittata*	120
no ray flowers	YELLOW	GREEN-LEAVED RAILLARDELLA *Raillardella scaposa*	123
no ray flowers	YELLOW	SILVER RAILLARDELLA *Raillardella argentea*	123
5 petals	SALMON-PINK	LARGE-FLOWERED COLLOMIA *Collomia grandiflora*	149
4 petals	ROSY-PINK	ROCK-FRINGE *Epilobium obcordatum*	145
5 petals	ROSY-PINK	SIERRA PRIMROSE *Primula suffrutescens*	146
puffy cluster	PINK	LOBB'S BUCKWHEAT *Eriogonum lobbii*	160
trailing stems	BLUE	LOBB'S NAMA *Nama lobbii*	195
almost shrublike	BLUE	SHOWY POLEMONIUM *Polemonium pulcherrimum*	193
grasslike	BROWN	WOOD RUSH *Luzula divaricata*	222

ROCKS

I.D. Hint	Color	Name	Page
clusters	WHITE	CREAM BUSH *Holodiscus microphyllus*	38
matlike	WHITE, LAVENDER, or PINK	SPREADING PHLOX *Phlox diffusa*	50
spiral bud	WHITE- PINK	GRANITE GILIA *Leptodactylon pungens ssp.pulchriflorum*	51
clasping leaves	YELLOW	JEWEL FLOWER *Streptanthus tortuosus*	98
puffy cluster	YELLOW	BEAR BUCKWHEAT *Eriogonum ursinum*	108
only disk flowers	YELLOW	PINE ERIGERON *Erigeron inornatus*	*
composite	YELLOW	FREMONT'S GROUNDSEL *Senecio fremontii*	124
opposite leaves	PALE PINK	MOUNTAIN SNOWBERRY *Symphoricarpos vaccinioides*	171
resembles dock	PINK	MOUNTAIN SORREL *Oxyria digyna*	159
wandlike flower stem	PINK	PINK HEUCHERA *Heuchera rubescens var. glandulosa*	142
succulent	PINK	STONECROP *Sedum obtusatum*	176
funnel-like	RED	CALIFORNIA FUCHSIA *Zauschneria californica ssp. latifolia*	144
irregular flower	MAGENTA	PRIDE OF THE MOUNTAIN *Penstemon newberryi*	184
4 petals	PURPLE	BREWER'S ROCK CRESS *Arabis breweri*	188
clusters	LAVENDER	WESTERN EUPATORIUM *Eupatorium occidentale*	207
mat-forming	CONIFER	DWARF JUNIPER *Juniperus communis var. montana*	226
small round berries	CONIFER	WESTERN JUNIPER *Juniperus occidentalis*	227
	FERN	PARSLEY FERN *Cryptogramma acrostichoides*	224
	FERN	CLIFF-BRAKE *Onychium densum*	224
	FERN	BRIDGE'S CLIFF-BRAKE *Pellaea bridgesii*	224

GRAVEL FLATS AND SLOPES

I.D. Hint	Color	Name	Page
stem spines	WHITE with RED sepals	SIERRA GOOSEBERRY *Ribes roezlii*	28
4 petals	WHITE	HOLBOELL'S ROCK CRESS *Arabis holboellii var. retrofracta*	44
4 petals	WHITE	DIFFUSE GAYOPHYTUM *Gayophytum diffusum*	45
red stems	WHITE	DAVIS'S KNOTWEED *Polygonum davisiae*	62
5 petals	WHITE	DWARF CHAMAESARACHA *Chamaesaracha nana*	53
rounded clusters	WHITE	NUDE BUCKWHEAT *Eriogonum latifolium ssp. nudum*	65
5 petals	WHITE	VARI-LEAF PHACELIA *Phacelia heterophylla*	57
tiny clusters	WHITE	CAPITATE SANDWORT *Arenaria congesta*	54
5 petals	WHITE	SANDWORT *Arenaria kingii var. glabrescens*	54
5 petals	WHITE	DOUGLAS'S CATCH-FLY *Silene douglasii*	55
drooping flower head	WHITE	LEMMON'S CATCH-FLY *Silene lemmonii*	55
off white	WHITE DUSTY-PINK	HAIRY PAINTBRUSH *Castilleja pilosa*	87
irregular flower	WHITE	HOT-ROCK PENSTEMON *Penstemon deustus*	86
papery flowers	WHITE PALE PINK	PUSSY TOES *Antennaria rosea*	91
6 tepals	WHITE PALE YELLOW	FAWN LILY *Erythronium purpurascens*	74
6 tepals	YELLOW	GOLDEN BRODIAEA *Brodiaea lutea var. analina*	97
5 petals	YELLOW	STICKY CINQUEFOIL *Potentilla glandulosa*	103
small clusters	YELLOW	DELICATE YELLOW BUCKWHEAT *Eriogonum marifolium*	106
bright puffs	YELLOW	SULPHUR BUCKWHEAT *Eriogonum umbellatum ssp. polyanthum*	107
umbel shape	YELLOW	TUBEROUS SANICLE *Sanicula tuberosa*	111
fernlike leaves	YELLOW	TEREBINTH'S PTERYXIA *Pteryxia terebinthina var. californica*	111

I.D. Hint	Color	Name	Page
pea flower	PALE YELLOW, LAVENDER or WHITE	ANDERSON'S LUPINE *Lupinus andersonii*	115
irregular flower	YELLOW	MOUNTAIN VIOLET *Viola purpurea*	117
irregular flower	YELLOW	SHELTON'S VIOLET *Viola sheltonii*	117
aromatic	YELLOW	MOUNTAIN MUGWORT *Artemisia norvegica var. saxatilis*	134
daisylike flower	YELLOW	TWIN ARNICA *Arnica sororia*	127
daisylike flower	YELLOW	WOOLLY MULE EARS *Wyethia mollis*	121
daisylike flower	YELLOW	CALIFORNIA HELIANTHELLA *Helianthella californica var. nevadensis*	122
dandelion -like	YELLOW	SPEAR-LEAVED AGOSERIS *Agoseris retrorsa*	131
only ray flowers	YELLOW	LONG-LEAVED HAWKBEARD *Crepis acuminata*	132
climbs on plants	YELLOW STEMS	DODDER *Cuscuta suksdorfii ssp. subpedicellata*	137
tiny 4 petal flower	PALE PINK	KELLOGGIA *Kelloggia galioides*	152
5 petals	PINK	PINK WOODLAND STAR *Lithophragma parviflora*	143
bellyflower	PINK	NARROW-LEAVED COLLOMIA *Collomia linearis*	150
bellyflower	PINK	WHISKER-BRUSH *Linanthus ciliatus*	151
puffy cluster	PINK OFF-WHITE	PUSSY PAWS *Calyptridium umbellatum*	161
6 tepals	PINK	DWARF SIERRA ONION *Allium obtusum*	156
onion smell	PINK	SIERRA ONION *Allium campanulatum*	156
6 tepals	PALE MAROON	PURPLE FRITILLARY *Fritillaria atropurpurea*	155
clusters of bells	PINK	DOGBANE *Apocynum androsaemifolium*	168
heavy flower head	MAROON	WILD PEONY *Paeonia brownii*	154
irregular flower	PINK	STEER'S HEAD *Dicentra uniflora*	178
showy, 5 petals	RED	SCARLET GILIA *Ipomopsis aggregata*	148

I.D. Hint	Color	Name	Page
wavy leaves	RED	WAVY-LEAF PAINTBRUSH *Castilleja applegatei*	182
5 petals	LAVENDER	BRIDGE'S GILIA *Gilia leptalea*	192
5 petals	BLUE	BLUE WITCH *Solanum xantii var. montanum*	196
irregular flower	BLUE	GAY PENSTEMON *Penstemon laetus ssp. roezlii*	204
irregular flower	BLUE	SHOWY PENSTEMON *Penstemon speciosus*	205
larkspur	BLUE	BILOBED DELPHINIUM *Delphinium nuttallianum*	198
no disk flowers	LAVENDER	NARROW-LEAVED STEPHANOMERIA *Stephanomeria tenuifolia*	185
shiny leaves	GREEN	ALDERLEAF COFFEEBERRY *Rhamnus alnifolia*	211
	GRASS	SQUIRRELTAIL GRASS *Sitanion hystrix var. californicum*	220
huge cones	CONIFER	SUGAR PINE *Pinus lambertiana*	232
5 needle bundle	CONIFER	WESTERN WHITE PINE *Pinus monticola*	233
long needles	CONIFER	JEFFREY PINE *Pinus jeffreyi*	230
upright needles	CONIFER	RED FIR *Abies magnifica*	235

MONTANE CHAPARRAL

I.D. Hint	Color	Name	Page
pinkish galls	ACORNS	HUCKLEBERRY OAK *Quercus vaccinifolia*	212
dusty leaf back	SPINY FRUIT	SIERRA CHINQUAPIN *Castanopsis sempervirens*	213
	CATKINS	FREMONT'S SILK TASSEL BUSH *Garrya fremontii*	210
clusters	WHITE	BITTER CHERRY *Prunus emarginata*	41
6 tepals	WHITE	WASHINGTON LILY *Lilium washingtonianum*	72
rounded clusters	WHITE	TOBACCO BRUSH *Ceanothus velutinus*	33
spiny	WHITE	SNOW BUSH *Ceanothus cordulatus*	32
mat	BLUE LAVENDER	SQUAW CARPET *Ceanothus prostratus*	197
leathery leaves	PINK	GREENLEAF MANZANITA *Arctostaphylos patula*	165

I.D. Hint	Color	Name	Page
low-growing	PINK	PINE-MAT MANZANITA *Arctostaphylos nevadensis*	164

WOODS

I.D. Hint	Color	Name	Page
4 petals	WHITE	BEDSTRAW *Galium aparine*	46
flat flower clusters	WHITE	BLUE ELDERBERRY *Sambucus caerulea*	25
no spines	WHITE	STICKY CURRANT *Ribes viscosissimum*	29
5 petals	WHITE	THIMBLEBERRY *Rubus parviflorus*	42
5 petals	WHITE	SERVICE-BERRY *Amelanchier pumila*	40
leaf venation	WHITE	WHITE-VEINED SHINLEAF *Pyrola picta*	84
5 petals	WHITE	SIDEBELLS *Pyrola secunda*	84
flower cluster	WHITE	CALIFORNIA VALERIAN *Valeriana capitata ssp.* *californica*	56
6 tepals	WHITE	STAR-LIKE SOLOMON'S SEAL *Smilacina stellata*	79
6 tepals	WHITE	FAT SOLOMON *Smilacina racemosa*	78
large umbel	WHITE	BREWER'S ANGELICA *Angelica breweri*	68
delicate umbel	WHITE	GRAY'S LOVAGE *Ligusticum grayii*	66
strawlike flower	WHITE	PEARLY EVERLASTING *Anaphalis margaritacea*	90
no ray flowers	WHITE	WHITE-FLOWERED HAWKWEED *Hieracium albiflorum*	92
4 petals	YELLOW	WALLFLOWER *Erysimum perenne*	99
licorice smell	YELLOW	WESTERN SWEET-CICELY *Osmorhiza occidentalis*	110
irregular flower	YELLOW	PINE WOODS LOUSEWORT *Pedicularis semibarbata*	112
no ray flowers	YELLOW	RAYLESS ARNICA *Arnica discoidea var. alata*	128
no disk flowers	YELLOW	NODDING MICROSERIS *Microseris nutans*	133
large fleshy leaf	YELLOW	GROUNDSEL *Senecio integerrimus var. exaltatus*	124
late blooming	YELLOW	BREWER'S GOLDEN ASTER *Chrysopsis breweri*	129

I.D. Hint	Color	Name	Page
delicate rose	PINK	PINE ROSE *Rosa pinetorum*	140
opposite leaves	PALE PINK	CREEPING SNOWBERRY *Symphoricarpos acutus*	170
5 petals	PALE PINK	PIPSISSEWA *Chimaphila menziesii*	175
showy	RED	SNOW PLANT *Sarcodes sanguinea*	172
tall flower stalk	PINK	PINEDROPS *Pterospora andromedea*	173
aromatic	PINK	HEDGE NETTLE *Stachys rigida*	179
orchid flowers	RED	SPOTTED CORAL ROOT *Corallorhiza maculata*	177
5 petals	BLUE	MOUNTAIN FORGET-ME-NOT *Hackelia nervosa*	190
5 petals	BLUE	CALIFORNIA WATERLEAF *Hydrophyllum occidentale*	194
irregular flower	BLUE	TORREY'S COLLINSIA *Collinsia torreyi*	206
pea flower	BLUE	SPURRED LUPINE *Lupinus arbustus ssp. silvicola*	200
leaves col-umbinelike	GREEN	MEADOW-RUE *Thalictrum fendleri*	219
small maple leaf	GREEN	MOUNTAIN MAPLE *Acer glabrum var. torreyi*	218
yellow underbark	CONIFER	WHITE FIR *Abies concolor*	234
hanging cones	CONIFER	DOUGLAS FIR *Pseudotsuga menziesii*	236
floppy tops	CONIFER	MOUNTAIN HEMLOCK *Tsuga mertensiana*	237
duck-bill seeds	CONIFER	INCENSE CEDAR *Calocedrus decurrens*	228
small cones	CONIFER	LODGEPOLE PINE *Pinus murrayana*	229
prickly cones	CONIFER	PONDEROSA PINE *Pinus ponderosa*	231

MOIST AREAS

flat flower clusters	WHITE	AMERICAN DOGWOOD *Cornus stolonifera*	26
flower clusters	WHITE	MOUNTAIN ASH *Sorbus californica*	39
lilaclike cluster	WHITE	MOUNTAIN RED ELDERBERRY *Sambucus microbotrys*	24

I.D. Hint	Color	Name	Page
fragrant	WHITE	WESTERN AZALEA *Rhododendron occidentale*	34
azalealike	WHITE	LABRADOR TEA *Ledum glandulosum var. californicum*	37
bell-shaped flowers	WHITE	SIERRA-LAUREL *Leucothoe davisiae*	36
matlike	WHITE	MOUNTAIN WHITE HEATHER *Cassiope mertensiana*	35
5 petals	WHITE	WILD STRAWBERRY *Fragaria platypetala*	43
stream-side	WHITE	BROOK SAXIFRAGE *Saxifraga punctata ssp. arguta*	31
tiny cluster	WHITE	BOG SAXIFRAGE *Saxifraga oregana*	30
tiny 5 petal flower	WHITE	BUD SAXIFRAGE *Saxifraga bryophora*	*
greenish flower	WHITE	BISHOP'S CAP *Mitella breweri*	49
5 petal	WHITE	GRASS OF PARNASSUS *Parnassia palustris var. californica*	48
tall plant	WHITE	ALPINE KNOTWEED *Polygonum phytolaccaefolium*	63
large umbel	WHITE	COW PARSNIP *Heracleum lanatum*	69
clustered umbel	WHITE	RANGER BUTTONS *Sphenosciadium capitellatum*	67
6 tepals	WHITE	WHITE BRODIAEA *Brodiaea hyacinthina*	75
sticky stem	WHITE	TOFIELDIA *Tofieldia glutinosa ssp. occidentalis*	77
6 tepals	WHITE	DEATH CAMAS *Zigadenus venenosus*	76
6-8 petals	WHITE	NEVADA LEWISIA *Lewisia nevadensis*	80
orchid flower	WHITE	SIERRA REIN ORCHID *Habenaria dilatata*	82
orchid flower	WHITE to PALE GREEN	BOG ORCHID *Habenaria sparsiflora*	82
spiraled flowers	WHITE	LADIES' TRESSES *Spiranthes romanzoffiana*	83
tiny viola	WHITE	MACLOSKEY'S VIOLET *Viola macloskeyi*	85
old-age droop	WHITE	LONG-STALKED CLOVER *Trifolium longipes*	88
daisy	WHITE	COULTER'S DAISY *Erigeron coulteri*	89

I.D. Hint	Color	Name	Page
5 petals	YELLOW	WATER-PLANTAIN BUTTERCUP *Ranunculus alismaefolius*	101
5 petals	YELLOW	FAN-LEAF CINQUEFOIL *Potentilla flabellifolia*	102
opposite leaves	YELLOW	SCOULER'S HYPERICUM *Hypericum formosum var. scouleri*	105
lakeside mat	YELLOW	TINKER'S PENNY *Hypericum anagalloides*	104
6 tepals	YELLOW	BOG-ASPHODEL *Narthecium californicum*	96
6 tepals	ORANGE	LEOPARD LILY *Lilium pardalinum*	95
tiny plant irregular flower	YELLOW	MEADOW MONKEY-FLOWER *Mimulus primuloides var. pilosellus*	113
irregular flower	YELLOW	MOUNTAIN MONKEY-FLOWER *Mimulus tilingii*	113
cool-feeling leaf	YELLOW	MUSK FLOWER *Mimulus moschatus*	*
viola	YELLOW	STREAM VIOLET *Viola glabella*	116
pea flower	YELLOW	MEADOW HOSACKIA *Lotus oblongifolius*	114
daisylike flower	YELLOW	TARWEED *Madia bolanderi*	119
daisylike flower	YELLOW	BIGELOW'S SNEEZEWEED *Helenium bigelovii*	118
daisylike flower	YELLOW	LAWLESS ARNICA *Arnica diversifolia*	126
flat flower cluster	ROSY-PINK	MOUNTAIN SPIRAEA *Spiraea densiflora*	138
spike flower cluster	ROSY-PINK	DOUGLAS'S SPIRAEA *Spiraea douglasii*	139
5 petals	ROSY-PINK	SIERRA CURRANT *Ribes nevadense*	141
needlelike leaves	MAGENTA	RED MOUNTAIN HEATHER *Phyllodoce breweri*	162
5 petals	PINK	BOG-LAUREL *Kalmia polifolia var. microphylla*	163
bell-like flower	PALE PINK	DWARF HUCKLEBERRY *Vaccinium arbuscula*	166
bell-like flower	PINK	SIERRA BILBERRY *Vaccinium nivictum*	167
flat stem	PINK	FLAT-STEMMED ONION *Allium platycaule*	157
round flr. cluster	PINK	SWAMP ONION *Allium validum*	157

I.D. Hint	Color	Name	Page
2 or 3 leaves	PINK	THREE-LEAVED LEWISIA *Lewisia triphylla*	158
5 petals	PINK	GINGER-LEAF PYROLA *Pyrola asarifolia var. purpurea*	174
red spurs	RED	COLUMBINE *Aquilegia formosa*	169
irregular flower	PINK	LEWIS'S MONKEY-FLOWER *Mimulus lewisii*	180
showy	RED OR MAGENTA	GIANT RED PAINTBRUSH *Castilleja miniata*	183
4 petals	BLUE	HIKER'S GENTIAN *Gentiana simplex*	187
grassy leaves	BLUE	IDAHO BLUE-EYED GRASS *Sisyrinchium idahoense*	189
hanging bells	BLUE	MOUNTAIN BLUEBELLS *Mertensia ciliata var. stomatechoides*	191
irregular flower	BLUE	MARSH SPEEDWELL *Veronica scutellata*	*
irregular pale flower	BLUE	MONKSHOOD *Aconitum columbianum*	199
tall plant	BLUE	TOWER DELPHINIUM *Delphinium glaucum*	*
pea flower	BLUE	BOG LUPINE *Lupinus latifolius*	201
mini-cones	CATKINS	MOUNTAIN ALDER *Alnus tenuifolia*	217
	CATKINS	QUAKING ASPEN *Populus tremuloides*	215
seedy fluff	CATKINS	COTTONWOOD *Populus trichocarpa*	214
pussywillow flowers	CATKINS	WILLOW *Salix* (several species)	216
	FERN	FIVE-FINGER FERN *Adiantum pedatum var. aleuticum*	225
	FERN	ALPINE LADY FERN *Athyrium alpestre var. americanum*	225
	GRASSLIKE	SEDGE *Carex sp.*	221
	GRASSLIKE	RUSH *Juncus sp.*	221

MEADOWS

tight flower cluster	WHITE	LADIES' THUMB *Polygonum bistortoides*	61
pleated leaves	WHITE	CORN LILY *Veratrum californicum*	71

I.D. Hint	Color	Name	Page
delicate umbel	WHITE	YAMPA *Perideridia bolanderi*	70
delicate umbel	WHITE	PARISH'S YAMPA *Perideridia parishii*	70
flat flower cluster	WHITE	YARROW *Achillea lanulosa*	93
5 petals	YELLOW	GRACEFUL CINQUEFOIL *Potentilla gracilis ssp. nuttallii*	102
dandelion	YELLOW	COMMON DANDELION *Taraxacum officinale*	130
composite	YELLOW	GROUNDSEL *Senecio triangularis*	125
spikey cluster	YELLOW	MEADOW GOLDENROD *Solidago canadensis ssp. elongata*	135
4 petals	ROSY-PINK	FIREWEED *Epilobium angustifolium*	145
spike	PINK	SPIKE CHECKER, MALLOW *Sidalcea oregana ssp. spicata*	153
4 petals	PINK	SHOOTING STAR *Dodecatheon alpinum*	147
heavy flower	MAROON	PEONY *Paeonia brownii*	154
straight trunks	PINK	ELEPHANT HEADS *Pedicularis groenlandica*	181
twisted trunks	PINK	LITTLE ELEPHANT HEADS *Pedicularis attolens*	181
6 tepals	BLUE	CAMASSIA *Camassia quamash ssp. breviflora*	186
whorled clusters	BLUE	WHORLED PENSTEMON *Penstemon rydbergii var. oreocharis*	204
aromatic	BLUE	NETTLELEAF HORSEMINT *Agastache urticifolia*	202
aromatic	LAVENDER	MOUNTAIN PENNYROYAL *Monardella odoratissima*	203
flat daisy head	LAVENDER	WANDERING DAISY *Erigeron peregrinus var. angustifolius*	208
slender stems	LAVENDER	LONG-LEAVED ASTER *Aster adscendens*	209
untidy	BLUE	SCRUFFY MOUNTAIN ASTER *Aster integrifolius*	209
large	FERN	BRACKEN FERN *Pteridium aquilinum var. pubescens*	223

PONDS OR LAKES

I.D. Hint	Color	Name	Page
showy	WHITE	BUCKBEAN *Menyanthes trifoliata*	60
floating long leaves	CREAMY- WHITE	BUR-REED *Sparganium multipedunculatum*	59
flower spikes	GREENISH- WHITE	VARIOUS-LEAVED PONDWEED *Potamogeton gramineus*	58
round flower head	YELLOW	YELLOW POND LILY *Nuphar polysepalum*	94

* not illustrated.
** not seen by the author.

Birds of Lakes Basin

Common Loon
Western Grebe
Pied-billed Grebe
Double-crested Cormorant
Great Blue Heron
Snow Goose
Canada Goose
Mallard
Ring Neck Duck
Bald Eagle
Cooper's Hawk
Red-tailed Hawk
Goshawk
Osprey
Blue Grouse
Mountain Quail
Common Snipe
California Gull
Band-tailed Pigeon
Great Horned Owl
Northern Pygmy Owl
Spotted Owl
Common Nighthawk
Common Poorwill
Anna's Hummingbird*
Belted Kingfisher
Northern Flicker
Yellow-bellied Sapsucker
Black-backed Woodpecker
Downy Woodpecker
Hairy Woodpecker
White-headed Woodpecker
Western Flycatcher*
Western Wood Pewee
Olive-sided Flycatcher
Violet-green Swallow
Clark's Nutcracker
Steller's Jay
Mountain Chickadee
Dipper

Red-breasted Nuthatch
White-breasted Nuthatch
Brown Creeper
Bewick's Wren*
Winter Wren*
Robin
Townsend's Solitaire
Mountain Bluebird*
Western Gnatcatcher†
Golden-crowned Kinglet
Ruby-crowned Kinglet
Warbling Vireo*
Solitary Vireo*
Yellow Warbler
Black Throated Gray Warbler*
Nashville Warbler*
Yellow-rumped Warbler
Wilson's Warbler
Hermit Warbler
MacGillivray's Warbler
Brewer's Blackbird
Brown-headed Blackbird
Western Tanager
Black-headed Grosbeak*
Evening Grosbeak
Pine Siskin*
Green-tailed Towhee
Dark-eyed Junco
Chipping Sparrow
Fox Sparrow
White-crowned Sparrow

Compiled from the *Lakes Basin Species List*, U.S.D.A., Plumas National Forest, Beckwourth RD, Blairsden, CA 96103

*Sighted by Bruce and Jeannette Howard
† Sighted by Toni Fauver

Mammals, Reptiles, Frogs, and Fishes

Yellow-bellied Marmot
Beaver
Chipmunk
Golden-mantled Squirrel
Douglas Squirrel
Botta Pocket Gopher
Black Bear
Raccoon
Marten
Fisher
Long-tailed Weasel
Mink
Wolverine
Mountain Lion
Bobcat
Mule Deer
Black-tailed Deer

Western Toad
Pacific Treefrog
Mountain Yellow-legged Frog

Southern Alligator Lizard
Common Garter Snake
Western Terrestrial Garter Snake
Western Aquatic Garter Snake
Western Blackheaded Snake

Rainbow Trout
Eastern Brook Trout
Lake Trout
Lahontan Redside
Arctic Grayling

A Natural History of the Sierra Nevada by Storer and Usinger has illustrations of most of the species listed above.

Compiled from the *Lakes Basin Species List*, U.S.D.A., Plumas National Forest, Beckwourth RD, Blairsden, CA 96103

Glossary

(Illustrated Glossary inside front cover)

Achene: a dry, hard, one seeded fruit, such as a sunflower seed.

Acuminate: tapered and pinched in to a point.

Alkaloid: slightly alkaline, which may be poisonous.

Alternate leaves: only one leaf from each node; a staggered arrangement.

Annual: a plant that flowers, fruits, and dies in one year.

Anther: the pollen-containing structure at the tip of the filament.

Axil: the angle between a leaf and the stem.

Banner: the upper petal of a pea flower (see Lupine, pp. 115, 200, 201).

Bract: the much-reduced leaf subtending a flower or flower cluster (see Aster, p. 209).

Calyx: the outer whorl, usually green, of a flower.

Campanulate: bell-shaped (see *Apocynum*, p. 168).

Capitate: gathered into a head, rather ball shaped or spherical (see Onion, pp. 156, 157).

Catkin: a scaly spike or dense cluster of minute flowers that lack petals, most often pollen-bearing, as in Willows, Pines, and Alders.

Chaparral: term referring to the group of rigid or thorny shrubs found growing on dry mountain slopes, such as Manzanita, *Ceanothus*, and Huckleberry Oak.

Ciliate: a line of tiny hairs along the margin of a leaf, petal or sepal.

Clasping: a leaf partly surrounding a stem.

Claw: a narrow, elongated base of a petal (see *Arabis*, pp. 44, 188).

Climax community: the final stage of succession of plants, in which the dominant species can reseed itself in spite of deep shade. It takes fire, flood, disease, or mechanical clearing to change this stable community.

Corolla: the whorl of usually colorful petals in a flower, found outside the stamens and within the calyx.

Deciduous: refers to plants that shed their leaves each fall.

Decurrent: describes a leaf edge continuing down the stem to form a line on the stem (see *Helenium*, p. 118).

Dentate: margins of leaves cut into teeth.

Dioecious: refers to staminate and pistilate flowers on different plants (see *Garrya*, p. 210).

Disk-flower: in the sunflower family; a tubular, usually perfect flower, but lacking a raylike extension on the corolla.

Entire: a leaf with smooth edges.

Evergreen: a plant that keeps its leaves all winter, such as manzanita and pines.

Exserted: extending beyond an opening, as the stamens of the *Phacelia* extend beyond the petals.

Fertile stamen: stamen containing an anther and pollen.

Filament: the stalk that holds the pollen sac or anther.

Follicle: a dry, elongate fruit or seed pod, such as Columbine.

Galea: the long upper hoodlike lip of the Mint or Figwort family.

Glabrous: bald, hairless.

Glandular: bearing glands, or having a surface that exudes a sticky liquid.

Habitat: the general environment or location in which a plant grows.

Head: a rounded cluster of sessile flowers such as Pennyroyal.

Herb: a plant without woody stems.

Imbricate: overlapping, like shingles.

Inferior: situated below; often refers to the ovary below the other floral parts (see Fireweed, p. 145).

Inflorescence: a flower cluster.

Involucre: a whorl of bracts subtending a flower cluster.

Irregular: having different-shaped petals or sepals on the same flower (see inside front cover).

Keel: the lower two petals that are fused together on the pea flower.

Key: a method of identifying a plant by choosing characteristics that eventually will fit only a specific plant. Weeden's book (see bibliography) has a good key for mountain plants.

Leaflet: a leaflike division of a compound leaf.

Monoecious: stamens and pistils in separate flowers on the same plant.

Montane: of or growing in the mountains.

Node: the joint of a stem where leaves, branches, or flowers originate.

Ocrea: a membranous structure that surrounds the stem above the petiole base, such as on *Polygonum*.

Opposite leaves: two leaves from each node on opposite sides of the stem.

Ovary: the seed-containing portion of the pistil.

Palmate: having lobes that radiate from a central point such as the Maple leaf.

Panicle: a compound flower cluster; a branched raceme.

Pappus: the whorl or hairs, bristles, or scales at the apex of the achene in some of the Sunflower family.

Parasitic: growing upon and deriving nourishment from another plant.

Pedicel: the stalk or stem of a flower.

Peduncle: the stalk or stem on an inflorescence, such as an umbel.

Perennial: a plant that lives for more than one year; it often has enlarged roots to store nutrients during the winter.

Perfect: having both stamens and pistils in the same flower.

Perianth: a collective term for the calyx and corolla.

Petal: one of the divisions of the corolla, usually colored, located between the stamens and the sepals.

Petiole: the stalk of a leaf.

Pinnate: a compound leaf with the leaflets arranged on each side of the central axis; featherlike.

Pistil: the female organ of the flower, consisting of ovary, stigma, and style.

Raceme: an elongate flower cluster with one main axis and smaller pedicels bearing one flower each as in Lupine.

Ray-flower: a flower in the Sunflower family that bears a straplike extension on one side of the corolla; the ray-flowers are usually along the margin of the head.

Receptacle: in the Sunflower family, the fleshy base of the inflorescence in which the flowers and developing achenes sit.

Revolute: curled-under margins, such as the leaves of *Kalmia*.

Saggitate: arrowhead shape.

Saprophyte: living on dead organic matter and thus lacking chlorophyll.

Scape: a leafless flowering stem arising from basal leaves, as in the primrose.

Sepal: the usually green outer whorl of flower parts.

Sessile: stemless; a leaf without a petiole or a flower without a pedicel. A sessile ovary is one without a stipe.

Sheath: the lower part of the leaf is wrapped around the stem.

Shrub: a branching woody plant, usually without a distinct trunk.

Silique: a two-celled capsule, several times longer than it is wide (see *Erysimum*, p. 99).

Spatulate: shaped like a spatula, with a long, narrow base and rounded at the tip.

Stamen: the pollen-bearing organ of a flower, consisting of a filament, an anther, and pollen.

Staminode: a sterile stamen lacking anther or pollen.

Stigma: the sticky portion of the style that is receptive to pollen.

Stipe: a stalk that raises the ovary above the receptacle; also the petiole of a fern leaf.

Style: the slender portion of the pistil between the ovary and the stigma.

Succession: the progressive replacement of one plant community by another until stability is reached in the climax community. Think of how a lake becomes a meadow and then a forest.

Superior ovary: one free from the calyx, above the other floral parts.

Tepal: in the Lily family, collective term for the sepals and petals composing the corolla when they are identical in color and shape.

Umbel: an inflorescence in which all the pedicels arise from the same point so as to form a flat-topped flower cluster.

Bibliography

Abrams, LeRoy. *Illustrated Flora of the Pacific States.* Stanford: Stanford University Press, Vol.I, 1940; Vol. II, 1944; Vol.III, 1951; Vol. IV, with Roxanne Ferris, 1960.

Arno, Stephen F. *Discovering Sierra Trees.* Yosemite Natural History Assn. and Sequoia Natural History Assn. in cooperation with the National Park Service, 1973.

Bailey, L. H. *How Plants Get Their Names.* New York: Dover Publications, 1963.

Carville, Julie Stauffer. *Lingering in Tahoe's Wild Gardens.* Chicago Park CA: Mountain Gypsy Press, 1989.

Coombes, Allen J. *Dictionary of Plant Names.* Portland OR: Timber Press, 1985.

Durrell, Cordell. *Geologic History of the Feather River Country, California.* Berkeley: University of California Press, 1987.

Heizer, Robert F., and Martin A. Baumhoff. *Rock Art of Nevada and Eastern California.* Berkeley: University of California Press, 1963.

Hood, Mary and Bill. *Yosemite Wildflowers and Their Stories.* Yosemite, CA: Flying Spur Press.

Munz, P. A. *A California Flora and Supplement.* Berkeley: University of California Press, 1959.

Murphy, Edith Van Allen. *Indian Uses of Native Plants.* Fort Bragg, CA: Mendocino County Historical Society, 1959.

Niehaus, T. F. *A Field Guide to Pacific States Wildflowers.* Boston: Houghton Mifflin, 1976.

Parsons, Mary Elizabeth. *The Wildflowers of California.* San Francisco: California School Book Depository, 1930.

Rodin, Robert J. *Ferns of the Sierra.* Yosemite Nature Notes, Vol.39, No.4.

Schaffer, Jeffrey P. *The Tahoe Sierra.* Berkeley, CA: Wilderness Press, 1975.

Smith, Gladys L. *A Flora of Tahoe Basin and Neighboring Areas and Supplement.* San Francisco: University of San Francisco Press, 1973, 1983.

Sudworth, George B. *Forest Trees of the Pacific Slope.* USDA, Forest Service, 1908.

Sweet, M. *Common Edible and Useful Plants of the West.* Healdsburg CA: California Naturegraph Company, 1962.

USDA, Forest Service, Region 5, Calif. "A Determination of Eligibility for Elwell Lakes Lodge, Gold Lake Lodge, Gray Eagle Lodge and Lakes Center Lodge in Lakes Basin Recreation Area," 1988.

Weeden, Norman. *Sierra Nevada Flora,* 3rd ed. Berkeley: Wilderness Press, 1986.

Wilson, Lynn and Jim. *Wildflowers of Yosemite*. Yosemite, CA: Sunrise Publications, 1987.

Useful Guidebooks from the Bibliography

Durrell, Cordell. *Geologic History of the Feather River Country*. A technical book for geologists. Elwell Lakes Lodge sells it.

Munz, P. A. *A California Flora and Supplement*. The recognized authority on California plants. Few illustrations.

Niehaus, T. F. *A Field Guide to Pacific States Wildflowers*. Many colored pictures; a good supplement to this book.

Schaffer, Jeffrey P. *The Tahoe Sierra*. Detailed descriptions of all of the trails in the Highway 49 area, with an emphasis on geology.

Weeden, Norman. *Sierra Nevada Flora*. Interesting facts about plant edibility. A good book to use to learn the key plants. An excellent supplement to this book.

Native Plant Societies

There are several active California Native Plant Society chapters not far from Lakes Basin. The main office in Sacramento can tell you who to contact to find out about meetings and field trips. There is a Chico chapter and a Grass Valley chapter.

California Native Plant Society:
1722 J Street, Sacramento, CA 95814
(916) 447-2677   http://www.cnps.org

The Northern Nevada Native Plant Society in Reno generally visits Lakes Basin once a year.

Northern Nevada Native Plant Society:
P.O. Box 8965, Reno, NV 89507-8965
(775) 329-1645 (Arnold Tiehm)   atiehm@juno.com

Plant List by Family

Common names are followed by page numbers for this book. Scientific names are followed by page numbers in *The Jepson Manual* (1993)

ACERACEAE
Acer glabrum var. *torreyi* 126

MAPLE FAMILY
Mountain Maple 218

APIACEAE (Umbelliferae)
Angelica breweri 140
Heracleum lanatum 148
Ligusticum grayi 150
Osmorhiza chilensis 158
Osmorhiza occidentalis 158
Perideridia bolanderi 162
Perideridia parishii 162
Pteryxia terebinthina var. *californica* =
    Cymopterus terebinthinus var. *californicus* 145
Sanicula graveolens 163
Sanicula tuberosa 164
Sphenosciadium capitellatum 165

CARROT-PARSLEY FAMILY
Brewer's Angelica 68
Cow Parsnip 69
Gray's Lovage 66
Mountain Sweet Cicely 110
Western Sweet Cicely 110
Bolander's Yampa 70
Parish's Yampa 70
Terebinth's Pteryxia 111

Sierra Snake-root §
Tuberous Sanicle 111
Swamp White-Heads/Ranger's
    Buttons 67

APOCYNACEAE
Apocynum androsaemifolium 168

DOGBANE FAMILY
Dogbane 168

ARISTOLOCHIACEAE
Asarum lemmonii 170

PIPEVINE FAMILY
Wild Ginger §

ASTERACEAE (Compositae)
Achillea lanulosa = *Achillea millefolium* 189
Adenocaulon bicolor 189
Agoseris retrorsa 192
Anaphalls margaritacea 194
Antennaria corymbosa 197
Antennaria rosea 197
Arnica discoidea 201
Arnica diversifolia 201
Arnica sororia 202
Artemisia arbuscula ssp. *thermopola* 203
Artemisia norvegica var. *saxatilis* 204
Aster adscendens = *Aster ascendens* 206
Aster integrifolius 208
Balsamorhiza deltoidea 212
Balsamorhiza sagittata 213
Chaenactis douglasii 224
Chaenactis nevadensis 223
Chrysopsis breweri = *Aster breweri* 206
Chrysothamnus nauseosus ssp. *albicaulis* 280
Crepis acuminata 244
Crepis intermedia 244
Erigeron coulteri 258

SUNFLOWER FAMILY
Yarrow or Milfoll 93
Pathfinder or Trail Plant §
Spear-leaved Agoseris 131
Pearly Everlasting 90
Pussytoes or Everlasting 91
Rosy Everlasting or Pussytoes 91
Rayless Arnica 128
Lawless Arnica 126
Twin Arnica 127
Low Sagebrush §
Sagewort or Mountain Mugwort 134
Long-leaved Aster 209
Scruffy Mountain Aster 209
Northwest Balsam Root 120
Arrow-leaved Balsam Root 120
Hoary Chaenactis or Dusty Maiden *
Nevada Pincushion 258
Brewer's Golden Aster 129
Gray Rabbitbrush 136
Long-leaved Hawksbeard 132
Intermediate Hawksbeard 258
Coulter's Daisy 89

Erigeron inornatus 260 — Rayless Erigeron *
Erigeron peregrinus var. *angustifolius* =
   Erigeron peregrinus var. *callianthemus* 260 — Wandering Daisy 208
Eupatorium occidentale =
   Ageratina occidentalis 190 — Western Eupatorium 207
Helenium bigelovii 277 — Bigelow's Sneezeweed 118
Helianthella californica var. *nevadensis* 277 — California Helianthella 122
Hieracium albiflorum 287 — White-Flowered Hawkweed 92
Madia bolanderi 312 — Bolander's Madia or Tarweed 119
Madia gracilis 312 — Slender Tarweed §
Microseris nutans 318 — Nodding Microseris 133
Raillardella argentea 332 — Silvery (or Silky) Raillardella 123
Raillardella scaposa 332 — Green-Leaved Raillardella 123
Rudbeckia occidentalis 334 — Western Coneflower
Senecio Integerrimus var. *exaltatus* 340 — Groundsel 124
Senecio fremontli 338 — Fremont's Groundsel 124
Senecio triangularis 342 — Old Man's Beard or Groundsel 125
Solidago canadensis ssp. *elongata* 343 — Meadow Goldenrod 135
Stephanomeria tenuifolia 348 — Narrow-leaved Stephanomeria 185
Taraxacum officinale 350 — Common Dandelion 130
Tragopogon dubius 354 — Yellow Salsify §
Wyethia mollis 359 — Woolly Mule Ears 121

BETULACEAE — BIRCH FAMILY
Alnus tenuifolia =
   Alnus incana ssp. *tenuifolia* 364 — Mountain Alder 217

BORAGINACEAE — BORAGE FAIMILY
Hackelia nervosa 190 — Stickseed or Mountain
   Forget-Me-Not 380

Mertensiana ciliata 382 — Lungwort, Streamside or Mt.
   Bluebells 191

BRASSICACEAE (Cruciferae) — MUSTARD FAMILY
Arabis breweri 399 — Brewer's Rock Cress 188
Arabis holboellii var. *retrofracta* 400 — Holboell's Rock Cress 44
Arabis platysperma 402 — Flat-Pod (or Pioneer) Rock Cress §
Erysimum perenne = Wallflower 99
   Erysimum capitatum ssp. *perenne* 421
Streptanthus tortuosus 444 — Mountain Jewel Flower 98

CAPRIFOLIACEAE — HONEYSUCKLE FAMILY
Lonicera conjugialis 472 — Wedded, Purple-flowered
   Honeysuckle 109

Lonicera involucrata 472 — Twinberry Honeysuckle 109
Sambucus caerulea =
   Sambucus mexicana 474 — Blue Elderberry 25
Sambucus microbotrys =
   Sambucus racemosa var. *microbotrys* 474 — Mountain Red Elderberry 24
Symphoricarpos acutus =
   Symphoricarpos mollis 415 — Creeping Snowberry 170
Symphoricarpos vaccinioides =
   Symphoricarpos rotundifolius 475 — Mountain Snowberry 171

Lupinus andersonii 627 — Anderson's Lupine 200
Lupinus arbustus 627 — Spurred Lupine, Crest Lupine 200
Lupinus latifolius 632 — Broad-leaved or Bog Lupine 201
Trifolium longipes 652 — Long-stalked Clover 88
Trifolium repens 653 — White Clover *

FAGACEAE — OAK FAMILY
Castanopsis sempervirens = Chrysolepis sempervirens 658 — Sierra Chinquapin 213
Quercus vaccinifolia 662 — Huckleberry Oak 212

GARRYACEAE — SILK TASSEL FAMILY
Garrya fremontii 666 — Fremont's Silk Tassel Brush 210

GENTIANACEAE — GENTIAN FAMILY
Gentiana simplex = Gentianopsis simplex 669 — Hiker's or Fringed Gentian 187

GROSSULARIACEAE — GOOSEBERRY FAMILY
Ribes cereum 678 — Squaw or Wax Currant 27
Ribes nevadensis 679 — Sierra Currant 141
Ribes roezlii 679 — Sierra Gooseberry 28
Ribes viscosissimum 680 — Sticky Currant 29

HYDROPHYLIACEAE — WATERLEAF FAMILY
Hydrophyllum occidentalis 687 — California Waterleaf 194
Nama lobbii 688 — Lobb's Nama 195
Nemophila parviflora var. austinae 691 — Small-flowered Nemophila §
Phacelia heterophylla ssp. virgata 700 — Varied-leaved Phacelia 57
Phacelia mutabilis 702 — Variable Phacelia §

HYPERICACEAE — ST. JOHN'S WORT FAMILY
Hypericum anagalloides 709 — Tinker's Penny or Bog St. John's Wort 104
Hypericum formosum var. scouleri 709 — Scouler's Hypericum or Western St. John's Wort 105
Hypericum perforatum 709 — Klamath Weed/Common St. John's Wort 105

IRIDACEAE — IRIS FAMILY
Sisyrinchium idahoense 1156 — Idaho Blue-eyed Grass 189

JUNCACEAE — RUSH FAMILY
Luzula divaricata 1166 — Wood-Rush 222

LAMIACEAE (Labiatae) — MINT FAMILY
Agastache urticifolia 713 — Nettleleaf Horsemint, Hyssop 202
Monardella odoratissima 721 — Mountain Pennyroyal 203
Stachys rigida = Stachys ajugoides var. rigida 731 — Hedge Nettle 179

LENTIBULARIACEAE — BLADDERWORT FAMILY
Utricularia vulgaris 735 — Common Bladderwort *

LILIACEAE — LILY FAMILY
Allium campanulatum 1178 — Sierra Onion 156
Allium obtusum 1176 — Red or Dwarf Sierra Onion 156

Habenaria unalascensis =
Piperia unalascensis 1216
Listera convallarioides 1215
Spiranthes romanzoffiana 1218

Short-spurred Rein Orchid §

Broad-leaved Tway-Blade 217
Hooded Ladies Tresses 83

PAEONIACEAE
Paeonia brownii 810

PEONY FAMILY
Peony 154

PAPAVERACEAE
Dicentra uniflora 812

POPPY FAMILY
Steer's Head 178

PINACEAE
Abies concolor 116
Abies magnifica 116
Pinus murrayana =
Pinus contorta ssp. murrayana 118
Pinus jeffreyi 118
Pinus lambertiana 120
Pinus monticola 120
Pinus ponderosa 120
Pseudotsuga menziesii 121
Tsuga mertensiana 1121

PINE FAMILY
White Fir 234
Red Fir 235
Lodgepole Pine 229

Jeffery Pine 230
Sugar Pine 232
Western White Pine 233
Ponderosa Pine 231
Douglas Fir 236
Mountain Hemlock 237

POACEAE (Graminae)
Phleum alpinum 1282
Sitanion hystrix = Elymus elymoides 1254
Stipa occidentatis =
Achnatherum occidentalis 1226

GRASS FAMILY
Alpine Timothy 221
Squirrel-tail Grass 220
Western Needlegrass §

POLEMONIACEAE
Collomia grandiflora 825

Collomia linearis 826
Gilia leptalea =
Gilia sinistra ssp. sinistra 835
Ipomopsis aggregata 838
Ipomopsis congesta 838

Leptodactylon pungens 840
Linanthus ciliatus 842
Navarretia divaricata 847

Phlox diffusa 850
Phlox gracilis 850
Polemonium pulcherrimum 852

PHLOX FAMILY
Large-flowered or Apricot
Collomia 149
Narrow-leaved Collomia 150
Bridge's Gilia 192

Scarlet Gilia or Sky Rocket Gilia 148
Many-flowered Gilia or Ball-headed
Gilia 52
Granite Gilia 51
Whisker-Brush 151
Short-stemmed (or Mountain)
Navarretia §
Spreading Phlox 50
Slender (or Pink Annual) Phlox §
Showy Polemonium 193

POLYGONACEAE
Eriogonum marifolium 874
Eriogonum latifolium ssp. nudum =
Eriogonum nudum 876
Erigonum lobbii 874
Eriogonum umbellatum ssp.
polyanthum 882
Eriogonum ursinum 882
Oxyria digyna 884

KNOTWEED FAMILY
Marum-leaved Buckwheat 106
Nude Buckwheat 65

Lobb's Buckwheat 160
Sulphur Buckwheat 107

Bear Buckwheat 108
Mountain Sorrel 159

Rhamnus purshiana 942 Cascara or Coffeeberry 211

ROSACEAE ROSE FAMILY
Amelanchier pumila = Serviceberry 40
   Amelanchier alnifolia var. *pumila 946*
Fragaria platypetala = Wild or Broad-petaled Strawberry 43
   Fragaria virginiana 952
Geum macrophyllum 953 Large-leaved (or Bigleaf) Avens *
Holodiscus microphyllus 953 Cream Bush or Dwarf Ocean-Spray
   38

Horkelia fusca ssp. *parviflora 956* Pinewoods Horkelia *
Potentilla flabellifolia 968 Fan-leaf Cinquefoil 102
Potentilla glandulosa 967 Sticky Cinquefoil 103
Potentilla gracilis ssp. *nuttalliii =* Slender or Graceful Cinquefoil 102
   Potentilla gracilis var. *fastigata 968*
Prunus emarginata 970 Bittercherry 41
Purshia tridentata 972 Antelope Brush or Bitterbrush 100
Rosa pinetorum 973 Pine Rose 140
Rubus parviflorus 974 Thimbleberry 42
Sibbaldia procumbens 975 Sibbaldia 261
Sorbus californica 976 Mountain Ash 39
Spiraea densiflora 976 Mountain Spiraea 138
Spiraea douglasii 976 Western Spiraea 139

RUBIACEAE MADDER FAMILY
Galium aparine 982 Bedstraw, Cleavers 46
Galium grayanum 984 Gray's Bedstraw 47
Kelloggia gailoides 986 Kelloggia 152

SALICACEAE WILLOW FAMILY
Populus tremuloides 990 Quaking Aspen 215
Populus trichocarpa = Black Cottonwood 214
   Populus balsamifera ssp. *trichocarpa 990*
Salix eastwoodiae 996 Sierra or Eastwood's Willow *
Salix ligulifolia 997 Ligulate Willow 216
Salix lemmonii 997 Lemmon's Willow *
Salix mackenziana = Salix prolixa 998 Mackenzie's Willow 216

SAXIFRAGACEAE SAXIFRAGE FAMILY
Heuchera rubescens var. *glandulosa 1005* Pink Heuchera or Alumroot 142
Lithophragma parviflora = Pink Woodland Star or Prairie Star or
   Lithophragma parviflorum 1006   Small-flowered Fringe Cup 143
Mitella breweri 1008 Bishop's Cap or Feathery
   Mitrewort 49
Parnassia palustris var. *californica =* Grass-of-Parnassus 48
   Parnassia californica 1008
Saxifraga aprica 1009 Sierra Saxifrage 30
Saxifraga bryophora 1009 Bud Saxifrage *
Saxifraga punctata var. *arguta =* Brook Saxifrage 31
   Saxifraga odontoloma 1010
Saxifraga oregana 1010 Bog Saxifrage 30

SCROPHULARIACEAE FIGWORT FAMILY
Castilleja applegatei 1018 Applegate's Paintbrush 182

Castilleja miniata 1022	Giant Red Paintbrush 183
Castilleja pilosa 1022	Hairy Paintbrush 87
Collinsia parviflora 1027	Blue-eyed Mary 206
Collinsia torreyi 1027	Torrey's Collinsia 206
Mimulus breweri 1042	Brewer's Monkey-flower *
Mimulus lewisii 1043	Lewis' (or Pink) Monkey-flower 180
Mimulus moschatus 1044	Musk Monkey-flower 113
Mimulus primuloides 1044	Primrose Monkey-flower 113
Mimulus tilingii 1046	Mountain Monkey-flower 113
Orthocarpus hispidus =	Hairy Owl's Clover §
Castilleja tenuis 1024	
Pedicularis attolens 1050	Little Elephant Heads 181
Pedicularis groenlandica 1050	Elephant Heads 181
Pedicularis semibarbata 1050	Pine Woods Lousewort 112
Penstemon deustus 1055	Hot-rock Penstemon 86
Penstemon gracilentus 1056	Slender Penstemon §
Penstemon laetus ssp.	Gay Penstemon 204
roezlii Penstemon roezlii 1060	
Penstemon newberryi 1058	Newberry's Penstemon or Pride of the Mountain 184
Penstemon rydbergii var. *oreocharis 1060*	Whorled Penstemon 204
Penstemon speciosus 1060	Showy Penstemon 205
Veronica scutellata 1067	Marsh Speedwell *
Veronica serpyllifolia ssp. *humifusa 1067*	Thyme-leaved Speedwell §

SOLANACEAE	NIGHTSHADE FAMILY
Chamaesaracha nana 1070	Dwarf Chamaesaracha 53
Solanum xantii 1077	Deadly Nightshade or Blue Witch 196

TYPHACEA	CATTAIL FAMILY
Sparganium multipedunculatum =	Simple-stemmed Bur-reed 59
Sparganium emersum ssp. *emersum 1309*	

VALERIANACEAE	VALERIAN FAMILY
Valeriana capitata var. *californica* =	California Valerian 56
Valeriana californica 1085	

VIOLACEAE	VIOLET FAMILY
Viola bakeri 1090	Baker's Violet §
Viola glabella 1091	Stream Violet 116
Viola macloskeyi 1091	Macloskey's Violet 85
Viola purpurea 1092	Purple-tinged or Mountain Violet 117
Viola sheltonii 1092	Shelton's Violet 117

* No illustration, just the name to help key plants.

§ Thank you to Wendell Wood of the Oregon Natural Resources Council for plants I had overlooked or not seen, and for including *Jepson Flora* page numbers and *Lakes Basin* page numbers.

Name Changes

The *Jepson Manual* (1993) changed many botanical names—some because chromosome counts have indicated that those plants had been classified incorrectly, and others because the first published name for a plant must be honored, and some older published names have been discovered in recent years. Thank you to Gary Monroe of the Northern Nevada Native Plant Society for assistance with this list.

OLD BOTANICAL NAMES	NEW BOTANICAL NAMES	Pages
Achillea lanulosa	*Achillea millefolium*	93
Adiantum pedatum var. *aleuticum*	*Adiantum aleuticum*	225
Alnus tenulfolia	*Alnus incana* ssp. *tenulfolia*	217
Amelanchier pumila	*Amelanchier alnifolia* var. *pumila*	40
Aster adscendens	*Aster ascenders*	209
Athyrium alpestre var. *americanum*	*Athyrium americanum*	225
Brodiaea hyacinthina	*Triteleia hyacinthina*	75
Brodiaea lutea var. *analina*	*Triteleia ixiodes* var. *analina*	97
Castanopsis sempervirens	*Chrysolepis sempervirens*	213
Chrysopsis breweri	*Aster breweri*	129
Cornus stolonifera	*Cornus sericea*	26
Cuscuta suksdorfli ssp. *subpedicellata*	*Cuscuta californica* var. *breviflora*	137
Epilobium angustifolium	*Epilobium angustifolium* ssp. *circumvagum*	145
Erigeron perigrinus var. *angustifolius*	*Erigeron perigrinus* var. *callianthemus*	208
Eriogonum latifolium ssp. *nudum*	*Eriogonum nudum* var. *nudum*	65
Erysimum perenne	*Erysimum capitatum* ssp. *perenne*	99
Eupatorium occidentale	*Agertina occidentalis*	207
Fragaria platypetala	*Fragaria virginiana*	43
Gentiana simplex	*Gentianopsis simplex*	187
Gilia leptalea	*Gilia sinispra* ssp. *sinispra*	192
Habenaria dilatata	*Platanthera leucostachys*	82
Habenaria sparsiflora	*Platanthera sparsiflora*	82
Habenaria unalascensis	*Piperia unalascensis*	§
Nuphar polysepalum	*Nuphar luteum* ssp. *polysepalum*	94
Onchium densum	*Aspidotis dense*	224
Parnassia palustris var. *californica*	*Parnassia californica*	48
Penstemon laetus ssp. *roezlli*	*Penstemon roezlli*	204
Pinus murrayana	*Pinus contorta* ssp. *murrayana*	229
Populus trichocarpa	*Populus balsamifera* ssp. *trichocarpa*	214
Potentilla gracilis ssp. *nuttallli*	*Potentilla gracilis* var. *fastigata*	102
Pteryxia terebinthina var. *californica*	*Cymopterus terebinthinus* var. *californicus*	111
Pyrola asarifolia var. *purpurea*	*Pyrola asarifolia* ssp. *asarifolia*	174
Pyrola secunda	*Orthilla secunda*	84
Rhamnus alnifolia	*Rhamnus purshiana*	211
Salix mackenziana	*Salix prolixa*	216
Sambucus cerulea	*Sambucus mexicana*	25
Sambucus microbotrys	*Sambucus racemosa* var. *microbotrys*	24
Saxifraga punctata ssp. *arguta*	*Saxifraga odontoloma*	31
Sitanion hystrix var. *californicum*	*Elymus elymoides* ssp. *elymoides*	220

* No illustration, just the name to help key plants.

§ From Wendell Wood's list of plants I had overlooked or not seen.

New Names in Alphabetical Order

Index

* Seen by author, but not illustrated.

† Recorded in Herbarium, but not illustrated or seen by author.

§ Seen by Wendell Wood of the Oregon Natural Resources Council, but not illustrated or seen by the author.